R4.70.

REBEL PITY:
The Life of Eddie Roux

REBEL PITY
The Life of Eddie Roux

Eddie & Win Roux

His speech is a burning fire,
   With his lips he travaileth;
In his heart is a blind desire,
   In his eyes foreknowledge of death;
He weaves and is clothed with derision,
   Sows and he shall not reap;
His life is a watch or a vision
   Between a sleep and a sleep.
                    A. C. SWINBURNE

Rex Collings
London
1970

First published in 1970 by
Rex Collings Ltd, 42/44 Hanway Street, London W.1.

© 1970 Winifred Roux

SBN 9017 2007 0

Printed and bound in the Republic of Ireland
by Hely Thom Limited Dublin

Preface   by Win Roux

                                                    Page
PART I DREAM AND VISION   by Eddie Roux

Chapter I   The Shop on the Corner   (1903–21)   1
        II   Lock Out   (1922–3)   19
        III Y.C.L. and Bugs in my Bed (1923–5)   30
        IV   Hooligans   (1925–6)   42
        V   Cambridge and Moscow   (1926–9)   49
        VI   African Comrades   (1929)   66
        VII The Happy Year   (1930)   74
        VIII End of Cape Town Days   (1930–31)   84
        IX   First Expulsions   (1931)   95
        X   Germiston Campaign   (1932)   109
        XI   Party Discipline   (1933–4)   127
        XII More Expulsions   (1935–6)   141

PART II THE VISION LOST   by Win Roux

        XIII   Fruit, Fish and Family   (1937–46)   151
        XIV   Three Books were Written   (1937–49)   166
        XV   The Academic World   (1946–54)   180
        XVI   Persecution of the Left   (1950–63)   197
        XVII   Rationalism   (1953–64)   218
        XVIII Of Cabbages and Things   (1953–65)   232
        XIX   Clothed with Derision   (1962–66)   251
        XX   Rationalist Tribute   (1963–66)   268
        XXI   The Next Page   (1966–69)   274

Appendix I Books by Edward Roux   280
            1. General and Scientific
            2. In Basic English
            3. In Easy English
         II Scientific Papers by E.R. Roux

Index   283

PREFACE

When Roux died he had already written at least in note form the early chapters of this book. In the later chapters, though I have tried to write carefully, there may be omissions and errors: for these I am responsible.

My excuse for writing is that Eddie Roux's life was consistent, compassionate and brave. It is a story that should be told and since there seemed to be no one else who would write it I thought that I must try.

To all who disliked or despised Eddie Roux, I say that they did not know him; to the great number of his friends and admirers I say that I wish I could have told the story better. Bertrand Russell wrote that Roux was a 'worthy addition to the long list of victims of bigotry from Socrates to the present day'. His life deserves to be remembered. He should be of those whose name liveth for evermore.

JOHANNESBURG AUGUST 1969   WINIFRED M. ROUX

CHAPTER I

The Shop on the Corner

IT all began with my father so perhaps I should first tell what I know of him. Philip Roux was born at Dordrecht in the eastern Cape Province on the 11 November 1875. His early boyhood was spent at Aliwal North, a village on the Orange River not far from the Basutoland border. His parents were typical Boer farmers, of Huguenot ancestry as the name suggests. In the family tree which goes back for six generations are none but Huguenot names. From France in 1688 came Paul Roux from Orange, first schoolmaster of Groot Drakenstein, also Gabriel le Roux from Blois, Pierre Lombard, Jacques Pinard, Jacques Thérond, Jean Prieur du Plessis, François du Toit, Pierre Rousseau and others. From Germany came Christiaan Rabie and Frans Joosten and there are names from Holland and one from Denmark.

The Roux family were Calvinist, not wealthy, industrious and frugal in habit by preference as well as by necessity. They ruled their children strictly and of these they had a quiverful. Philip was a younger son.

The speech of ordinary family life was Afrikaans which was then emerging as a young language, a variant of Nederlands. High Dutch, the language of the Bible and of all formality, was used ceremonially in sermons and for writing letters. But in the schools of the Cape education was entirely in English though Nederlands was also taught. At school in Aliwal North, under schoolmaster Snell, the Roux children acquired a sound knowledge of English and this young Philip was later to find of great value.

Leaving school at about fourteen he went to work as an assistant in a local general store in Aliwal North. He had a lively and enquiring mind and soon found his daily work tedious and unrewarding. He suggested to his parents that he would like to become an apothecary. Accordingly and with what effort on their part I can only guess, at the age of fifteen he was apprenticed to a chemist and druggist at Fort Beaufort, some two hundred miles to the south. His new employer, McKenzie, was a Scotsman and not only the household but the whole environment in which the boy now found himself was predominantly English-speaking. In these surroundings my father became rapidly anglicized and in these his impressionable years it came about that he soon discarded not only the language but also almost all the ideas and ideologies of his forebears.

In studying for his pharmacy examinations he read books on chemistry and botany. He became interested in geology and then evolution. Soon he began to read publications of the Rationalist Press Association which were to be found in the McKenzie household: writings by Bradlaugh, Darwin, Huxley, Haeckel, and through such reading and the conversation of McKenzie he was attracted towards free thought and atheism. In later years he would relate how on one occasion he was profoundly shocked to see rain falling on the sea, falling uselessly where it was not needed. In church he had been taught that all manifestations of nature were for the service of man. This incident proved decisive: he became an atheist and, inevitably, a militant one. In this and many other respects he was a precursor of the modern angry young man, irritable, resentful and intolerant of all the old ideas.

By nature an extremist, my father never did things by halves. When he turned from the faith of his fathers he revolted also against what seemed to him their narrow nationalism and he became intolerant of all family attitudes. He became in fact an ardent supporter of the British Government. In 1897, at the age of twenty-two, he joined the Kaffrarian Rifles and served in the Bechuanaland campaign. The local Native chiefs had rebelled against the British. They suffered defeat and their lands were confiscated. Philip returned to civil life and found work in a pharmacy in Ladysmith in Natal. He was there when the Anglo-Boer War began and the town was besieged by Boer forces.

His British sympathies were by then a scandal among members of the family. It chanced that a maternal uncle, Oom Hendrik Theron, was a commandant in the commandos which surrounded the town. In the casual manner of the siege some incident of local parley enabled Oom Hendrik to send a message throught he lines. 'Tell my nephew, Philip Roux, that we shall make biltong of him when we take the town.' Young Philip with his taste for opposition was delighted. In the event Ladysmith was not taken. Oom Hendrik cherished no rancour. When the war ended and he found his farm devastated and himself down and out he and his wife came to live for a time with the traitor nephew.

As soon as Ladysmith was relieved my father joined up and saw the rest of the war through as a corporal in Kitchener's Horse. He would boast afterwards that he had fought against a round dozen of brothers and uncles and goodness knows how many cousins, and this I found rather shocking when he told me of it. However, he enjoyed shocking people, even children, and I heard the story many times. Towards the end of the war he went down with an attack of enteric fever and was a patient in the military hospital at Norvals Pont where he met nursing sister Edith May Wilson. She had come out from England with the Army Nursing Service Reserve. They were married in 1902, the year in which peace was signed.

The war was over but the country was confused and troubled, the farms largely destroyed, many farmers seeking work, stores closed down and abandoned. My father now found it difficult to get work as a pharmacist so he ran a canteen, a skof-shop he called it, on a mine near Pietersburg in the Northern Transvaal. It was there that Oom Hendrik Theron and Aunt Betty came to stay and there that I was born in 1903.

My father soon wearied of the skof-shop. In 1904 he went to Johannesburg and managed to find employment with a firm of wholesale chemists. A better job took him to Pretoria but at the beginning of 1907 he was back in Johannesburg and starting his own pharmacy. He began by renting a shop in Bezuidenhout Valley, a suburb on the eastern fringe of the rapidly expanding mining town. The pharmacy yielded a steady modest income and here Dad settled down to rear a family. By 1912 there were five more children: my brother Claud born in 1904, my sisters Edna and Enid, lastly twin boys, Philip and Arthur. Four boys and two girls, not a large family by Boer standards.

Paying rent irked my father and as soon as he could manage it he bought a corner stand on Kitchener Avenue and there built to his own design a shop and dispensary with a house attached. This was in the shape of an L, the shop on the street corner and the house set back facing the main road. By local standards at the time both shop and house were impressive. We had a splendid large sitting room, a good comfortable kitchen, a bathroom, three bedrooms. One of these was for the boys and here were four narrow beds in line. We were trained to do all these things for ourselves, especially to make our own beds and keep the room clean. Also we helped in the kitchen, cleaned all the family shoes, washed dishes, peeled potatoes, scrubbed the linoleum-covered floors, ran on errands.

The kitchen where my mother was usually busy was the centre of our family life. I realize now that in spite of our childish help my mother must have had in those years a very hard life. Family discipline was strict and we all obeyed orders without question. She not only ruled the family and ordered all things well but often when there happened to be a rush of custom she had to leave whatever she was doing and go to help my father in the shop. Here her gentle quiet manner proved invaluable in off-setting my father's characteristic somewhat impatient speech. He was intolerant of stupidity and was quick to show annoyance and even contempt. However, for many years his was the only pharmacy in the neighbourhood and despite his intolerance and helped by my mother's good manners the business prospered. The site had been well-chosen. The noisy trolley trams ran along Kitchener Avenue and there was a fare stage at our corner. One of my earliest memories is of the squeal and grinding sound that told of a passing tram.

In the sitting room behind the shop my father entertained his cronies in the evenings with endless argument and dissertation. Often the company would move to the more homely kitchen and there sit for hours disputing over cups of tea and a plate of homemade cookies. Where we children did our homework I cannot well remember. Sometimes I wrote essays or struggled with algebra kneeling on the floor by my bed or sitting on the bed with book on my knees. Learning assignments I largely ignored. I do not recall that Claud was any more industrious. The girls in their turn were luckier. There were only two of them and they had a dressing table and also a small table of their own. Otherwise we might be permitted to work in sitting room or kitchen whichever my father had left free. But homework was not important in my life.

As in the chemist's shop so in the home, my mother was the source of all calm reasonableness. It was due to her that our family life was harmonious, unmarred by quarrels. I can remember only one really acrimonious dispute and that arose between me and Claud, my constant companion in play. I forget what it was about but Claud and a friend locked me in a shed to teach me manners. In the shed I went berserk, beat and pounded on the door and exploded into a right royal rage. I yelled and screamed but no one came to let me out. After a while I became exhausted and silent and thought things over. I was terrified as I realised how wildly I had behaved and I made the resolve that never, under no matter what provocation, would I lose control again. Later, trying the door once more, I found that I was free. I think this incident was a valuable lesson to me.

My earliest recollections of my father are of an extremely patriotic Britisher-by-adoption. He had joined the Volunteer Medical Corps. On Sunday mornings he donned a khaki uniform—I remember his struggles with the puttees—and rode off on his bicycle to practice on the Booysens range. He brought home quantities of empty cartridge cases in his pockets and these Claud and I used as toy soldiers. We set them up in battalions and then knocked them flying with marbles or a tennis ball. These we appreciated more than the bottles from the pharmacy which we had endlessly to wash and wash in a tub in the back garden, using washing soda in warm water and a little home-made soap. We shook soapy water in the bottles, used a stick to poke out any encrusted dregs, shook again, rinsed in clean water until they shone perfectly clean, then stood them up to dry. My father was a hard taskmaster. And all the while our hands, sore from the washing soda and exposure to the dry air of the highveld, would become chapped and bleed. My mother would sometimes give us some home-made ointment to help the skin to heal. Claud and I have no more hateful memory of childhood than this of bottle-washing.

One day in 1910 my father called me into the shop. He regarded me solemnly and said: 'Eddie, your king is dead.' I realized that an important event had taken place. I had been named Edward partly in honour of the ruling sovereign and partly after a grandfather, Eduard Roux.

But the jingo period of Philip Roux's life was soon to end. In 1911 two Australian brothers, the Furseys, opened a cobbler's shop in Eighth Avenue not far from the pharmacy. They combined socialist propaganda with their boot-repairing and soon became firm friends of the chemist. In a few months my father entered on the second great rebellion of his life: he became a socialist.

Thus began for me at the age of nine or ten a most interesting and as it was to prove fateful experience. Dad was ever a great arguer. In the room behind the shop his socialist and other friends would gather and the most exciting arguments and discussions would ensue. I was permitted to come in and listen until my bedtime and later if I could manage to remain so quiet as to be unnoticed. I was in certain ways a precocious brat. I began in childish fashion to take part in some of the talk. Dad sometimes encouraged me in this. I remember at least one occasion when he called me away from my play in the street to answer some political question. He had been arguing with some anti-socialist who had made some, as Dad considered, ridiculous remark. 'Why, even my son knows better than that,' he said. 'Let's hear what he says.' The question was put to me and I duly gave the correct socialist answer.

All this was of course very bad for me and wrong of Dad. I became an insufferable little know-all. My playmates teased me and dubbed me 'Encyclopaedia'. Also, through knowing too much, I got into difficulties with their parents. I remember the incident of Rodger Keyworth, who lived across the road and at one time argued with me about the existence of God. Finally, to floor me, he said: 'Well, if you don't believe in God, tell me who made you.' I knew the answer to that one though it was not strictly under the heading of socialism. At once I gave Rodger some elementary sex-instruction. He replied not a word but looked at me in blank horror and then ran off to tell his mother. She came that evening to the house to complain to my parents of my disgusting conversation. I do not know what she said exactly nor how my father answered her. No doubt he defended me. I was in bed. But next day Dad told me not to argue with silly little boys whose parents wished them to be ignorant. 'Some people,' he said darkly, 'are afraid of knowledge.' He rebuked me in a way but as he did so there was a twinkle in his eye. I think that he was rather pleased by the incident.

Among the socialists who came to visit Dad was Jock Campbell, a Clydeside Irishman, a self-educated working man, though Jock had long since ceased to work at his trade and now lived for and on the movement. Though I never heard him address a public meeting I believe that he was a brilliant orator. What I admired in his conversation was his erudition and his terse logic. I listened enthralled while he expounded the philosophy of socialism. He took a special interest in me and I learned a lot from him.

The particular brand of socialism my father and his friends professed was that of the Socialist Labour Party. It was definitely Marxist in flavour and its leading theoretician was the American Daniel de Leon. Its chief centres of activity seemed to be Chicago and Glasgow and from both sources came streams of journals and pamphlets. As soon as I could read easily I began to investigate the pamphlets. Some were too hard for me but de Leon's writings I found simple and stimulating. They were all popular addresses which had been delivered to working men. 'What means this strike?' was one of my favourites.

Strikes were no merely academic subject in Johannesburg at that time for a serious strike of the white miners occurred in July of 1913. The strikers came into violent conflict with the authorities. Demonstrating outside the Rand Club they were shot down by British Dragoons and retaliated by burning down Park Station and the office of *The Star*, also by breaking all the plate glass windows of Chudleigh's store in Eloff Street. Chudleigh was at that time mayor of Johannesburg and had taken sides against the strikers. After the strike had ended in a victory for the men, my father took me to town and I saw the bullet marks and the broken glass. I remember that one bullet had made a hole in the plaster of the new town hall then under construction. Sightseers, curious to know how deep the bullet had penetrated, had used sticks to probe the hole which was becoming increasingly wide and deep.

There were other strikes during this period and labour

meetings were frequent and exciting. I remember Dad coming home one night plastered with rotten eggs. He had been one of a bodyguard defending a labour speaker. The excitement continued into 1914. The miners struck again, supported this time by railwaymen and other workers. The Government, led by Botha and Smuts, kidnapped a dozen of the strike leaders and deported them to Britain. Most of these men were my father's friends. Some had been visitors at our house. Tom Mann, the British Labour leader, came to the Rand to conduct a campaign for the Labour Party. Smuts and Botha were most unpopular in Johannesburg. To me there seemed no doubt at all that socialism would soon be established.

Meanwhile at school I was beginning to instruct my teachers. I remember how, in 1913, when Mexico was in the news, our teacher Miss Nicholls was explaining the word 'pun'. She asked us why did Vera Cruz and the answer was 'Because Huerta'. She then asked whether anyone knew where Vera Cruz was and who was Huerta. My hand shot up. I proceeded to tell teacher and class how the Mexican peasants were being exploited by land-owners, how they were in revolt and Huerta was their leader. Poor Miss Nicholls who was intelligent enough but probably knew next to nothing of the class struggle in Mexico had no come-back to all this. She was already aware of my socialist leanings.

It happened that earlier that year the Provincial Council elections took place. My father was an active member of the Bezuidenhout Valley branch of the South African Labour Party. (The S.A.L.P. was of course not the same thing as the Socialist Labour Party. The latter was represented only by a small group of extremists who worked within the S.A.L.P.) On election day Claud and I went to school wearing red ties. Miss Nicholls noticed my tie and came to stand near my desk. I was a favourite of hers. She touched the tie and asked: 'Are those your colours, Eddie?' I proudly affirmed that they were. Later Mother heard through indirect channels that one of our teachers had been heard to remark, 'Those nice Roux children —what a pity their father is a socialist!'

However, socialism was only one of many things in my early environment that had the effect of making me the odd man out, the perennial rebel and iconoclast. Another thing was that my father insisted on our being excused from attendance at scripture lessons. In this he was standing on his legal rights for the Education Ordinance had a Conscience Clause making scripture optional. The clause had been, I think, inserted for the benefit of Jews and Catholics some of whom objected to what they considered the Protestant flavour of the lessons. Now, oddly enough, both Claud and I had been baptized into the Roman Catholic Church. Nurse Wilson at the time of her marriage to Philip Roux was a Catholic by conversion. Philip, then in his indignant atheist period, regarded the stipulation that all children of the marriage should be brought up in the Catholic faith as a condition so wholly immoral that he had no scruple in promising with tongue in cheek what he had no intention to perform. So it was left to my mother. As the early years of marriage went by with the coming of children, the various moves and her continual task of stretching the housekeeping money to cover family needs, she came to think less about religious mysteries and church attendance. Moreover she listened many times to the eloquent anti-God outpourings of the angry young man she had married. So it came about that when Edna was born there was no more thought of Catholic baptism. And so it was as atheists and not as Catholics that Claud and I contracted out of scripture lessons. This was with my full approval but Claud did not care much either way. During scripture lessons I did not leave the class but sat at the back of the room and was supposed to study or to begin my homework. I was not fond of homework and usually preferred to listen to the lesson, sometimes so far forgetting myself as to put up my hand and answer a question which seemed to stump the class. This caused, as I heard later, considerable amusement when it was reported in the staff common room.

During my early days at school, in standard four, I was subjected to propaganda which, under slightly different circumstances, might have had a profound effect on me. Our Dutch teacher was a Miss Joubert, a young Afrikaner with strong patriotic feelings. In the course of teaching us the language of Holland she told us a good deal of the history of the Boers, their struggles, their aspirations and their sufferings. She had herself as a child during the Anglo-Boer War been with her mother and sisters herded into a concentration camp. In this camp many of the victims had perished. Had I been living in an Afrikaans-speaking environment among my father's people who had also suffered these things, I might well have become a Afrikaner nationalist. As it was my playmates at school and in the street were all English-speaking, my father seldom used a word of Afrikaans and never to his children. He despised the language, called it the Taal, and said it was a peasant patois and of no importance. My English mother never learned more than half a dozen words of the language and these she pronounced wrongly. Only later when I went to the university did I begin to study Afrikaans and to this day near the end of my days though I read and understand it fairly well I write it stiffly and speak it haltingly and no doubt with an English accent.

In addition to her Afrikaner patriotism Miss Joubert cultivated a great admiration for all things French. She was proud of her Huguenot ancestry and made me conscious that I too was descended from those exiles for spiritual liberty who came to South Africa in 1688 and had since then contributed so much to the development of this country. Stimulated by Miss Joubert I added Henry of Navarre and Napoleon to my list of heroes where they shared this distinction with Karl Marx, Lenin, Engels, Charles Darwin, Huxley, Daniel de Leon and Jack London—a strange assortment. Napoleon did not long survive and as to Jack London I came presently to have mixed feelings.

In 1915 I left Jeppe Preparatory School and went on to Jeppe High School. Here there were no scripture lessons to rouse my father's intransigence but something equally challenging to the socialist conscience in the form of the cadet corps. During my first two years at high school I was, along with all my classmates except a few physically unfit, a member of the Cadets. Once a week we put on uniforms and drilled on the football ground with ancient Martini-Henry rifles. I was taught to shoot at a target with a miniature rifle. Occasionally we were taken out for field exercise and on the veld engaged in sham battles which were most exciting. Actually I enjoyed Cadets but could not help feeling some qualms of conscience about it all. The first world war was on and my father and I were fanatical pacifists. We regarded the slaughter that was happening in Europe as a ghastly business, a quarrel between two groups of capitalists which no true socialist could possibly support on either side. Both my father and I were at first under the impression that cadet drill was compulsory. But in 1917 he found out from Sidney Bunting, of whom I shall tell more later, that there was a conscience clause in the Defence Act. Dad asked me whether I would like to leave the Cadets and I at once agreed that I would. Claud, barely a year younger, was not really consulted as to his views. He was dragged in as well though he was by no means so opinionated about these matters as I was. We became non-cadets.

The non-cadets were a motley crew. They consisted in part of cripples and other boys who for one reason or another were not physically fit, also of some who disliking physical exertion had managed to persuade their parents that cadet drill was bad for their health. For these boys it could be argued that drill was usually conducted under a blazing sun and proved often a test of endurance. Anyway during drill we non-cadets were assembled in a classroom in charge of a sub-prefect. For some years we were left almost entirely to our own devices. The sub-prefect would see to it that there was no rowdyism and we were at liberty to read, study or just loaf in idleness as we preferred.

But in 1919 a new headmaster came to the school. During the war a number of masters had gone to the front and some of them had died. Payne, our headmaster, died of fever in East Africa. Manduel, the second master, went to France as an artillery officer and the French awarded him the Croix de Guerre for conspicuous gallantry under fire. On his return he was appointed head of the school and among other things he began to take an interest in the non-cadets with whom he had little sympathy.

It is possible that at the time an unusually large number of slackers and malingerers had joined the group and Manduel seemed to suspect as much. He proceeded to make non-cadet existence as unpleasant as possible. We were set to various tasks such as writing paraphrases of long and tedious passages in English. We were not actually made to write lines but we all had the feeling that in effect we were being punished for being non-cadets. Manduel would descend on the classroom periodically and without warning to see that his orders were being carried out.

Now in 1921, my matriculation year and thus my last in the non-cadet assembly, Claud and I were joined there by two other conscientious objectors, both from the pre-matriculation form. Benny Sachs had definite socialist leanings. Herman Bosman's motives were not founded on any political or religious conviction. He was a kind of mad genius and already a brilliant writer and talker. At school he had scandalized the staff by various outrageous doings. He had organized a sort of lottery in which the participants paid in the tram coupons which were issued free to scholars by the Johannesburg Municipality. Bosman collected hundreds of coupons. When the draw was held it ended in a riot and coupons were scattered all over the school. He had played some ingenious pranks in the chemistry lab. When ordered to report to the head for a caning he had attempted to commit suicide by slashing his throat with a knife. He disliked regimentation and especially the Cadets which he thought silly. He had a contempt for the schoolboy non-commissioned officers, chosen always as were the school prefects because they were good at sport and often in spite of being the biggest fools in class. He would play the fool on the parade ground and in consequence was often bullied and sometimes beaten up. On one occasion a visiting lieutenant-colonel came to review the Jeppe cadets. He made a stirring oration and did not fail to mention that in every private's knapsack lay a field-marshal's baton. Bosman, then still a cadet, listened with rapt attention. At the end the speaker asked if anyone would like to ask any question. Bosman at once stepped forward and asked, loud and clear, 'Please, sir, what is the next thing higher than a lieutenant-colonel?' Absolutely fearless, a supreme individualist, a thoroughly queer fellow and odd man out, he was later to become one of South Africa's most famous writers, the author of *Mafeking Road*.

The persecution of the non-cadets slackened a little during this year, the year in which we were joined by Sachs and Bosman. We were no longer required to write paraphrases but were allowed to read poetry. We no longer had a sub-prefect in charge of us since at that time all prefects were physically fit and were involved with the Cadets. On one occasion during drill period I was reading a newspaper when someone entered the room. I did not look up but went on reading. A stroke from a cane sent the paper flying from my hands. Beside me stood the uniformed figure of Captain Manduel, the Head. He was in a towering rage and told us that he would not tolerate this sort of thing. We were there to work and he would see to it that work we did. The discipline of the non-cadets would be tightened.

It was shortly after this that I went to Manduel and made him a proposition. I suggested that those non-cadets who were not physically incapacitated should be allowed to meet in the school gymnasium during cadet drill. There they could do suitable physical exercises, Swedish drill and the like. This would provide a healthier atmosphere, our feeling that we were being persecuted would disappear and his own problem of what to do with the non-cadets would be solved. Manduel at once agreed. He placed me in charge of the gym class and I undertook to keep it in order.

Before going to Manduel I had consulted with my fellow non-cadets and they had welcomed my idea. On the whole the gym class was a success. Of course Sachs and Bosman were my chief problem. The Swedish drill I organized provided them with opportunities for burlesque but on the whole they did not behave too badly. After half an hour or so of routine exercises I allowed them to play on the jumping horse and the parallel bars and then the group was perfectly happy.

As a result of this incident Manduel and I became firm friends. I dared even to lend him a book by Jack London. When I left school I tried to get work in the South African Institute for Medical Research but there was a long waiting list and no prospect of immediate employment. Presently Claud brought home a message from Manduel. Would I come to see him? There was a chance of a scholarship. I had no idea then that there could be any possibility of my going on to university. My father who still had five children in the Jeppe schools could not afford to keep me in idleness for another three years and pay university fees. Also, though I had done well in science I had achieved only a second class matriculation. With Manduel's recommendation I obtained a Johannesburg Municipal Bursary worth £30 a year, enough to pay my university fees. Dad agreed to continue to provide me with board and lodging and clothes.

Before closing this account of my school days I should say

something more about my political development during this period. In spite of my concern with the social revolution I was in most ways a normal boy. I played cricket and football both at school and with my friends in the Valley, swam in the spruit, ran on paper chases and went for long bicycle rides, flew kites, collected stamps, joined a local gang and took part in fights with other gangs. I liked to play cowboys and Indians but always insisted on being an Indian: here my political tendencies were revealed in that the Redskin was obviously the bottom dog.

Our gang had its headquarters at the corner of Carnarvon Road and here we assembled and made plans. One day one of the older members, Ronnie Thorne, suggested we form a football club. This we called the Carnarvon United Football Club. There were similar small clubs in the neighbourhood and against these we played matches. Then I suggested that we should run our own newspaper. I had been acquainted with form magazines in school. I was made editor and for a year or two produced a monthly, laboriously written out by hand with carbon duplicates. I even attempted cartoons. This was my first experience of real journalism as we considered it.

But I never ceased to be interested in political events. In 1917 came the great Bolshevik Revolution. To me this proved conclusively that Jock Campbell, my Dad and all the socialist writers I had read had been perfectly right. I made a map of the world showing in red all the countries that had established soviets—Russia that noble expanse of territory, Hungary, Bavaria, north-west Germany. I put red dots where revolutionary outbreaks had occurred—Winnipeg, Clydeside, and later even Johannesburg itself. Our local soviet was a committee of trade unionists set up during a tramway strike in 1919. In order 'not to inconvenience the public' they decided to run the trams while a dispute with the municipality was in progress. This soviet endured about a week.

It was on a day during this Tramway Strike at a time when the trams were not running that Claud and I and some friends went walking into town to see if anything exciting was afoot. We found an open-air meeting of white strikers in progress outside the power station gates. Here an audience largely of tramwaymen was being harangued by members of the Building Workers Union. The Town Council had come to terms with the tramwaymen who had agreed to call their strike off. The building workers however were on strike and had been out for three weeks with no sign of capitulation on the part of the contractors. Their leaders now urged the tramwaymen not to return to work but to continue with a sympathetic strike to help the building workers. As we listened and felt the lack of response it was clear to me that there was not enough feeling of workers' solidarity to make this likely. But as we were coming away from this meeting we passed through Von Brandis Square and here we saw large numbers of police and the ground littered with torn papers. We found out that a large gathering of Africans had assembled there a little while before to protest against the Native Pass Laws. Speakers had urged the crowd to tear up their passes, those bits of paper that every African must carry on his person at all times, and this they were doing when the police arrived and roughly dispersed the meeting. Picking up fragments and piecing them together we saw that these were indeed passes.

This incident seems to have had little effect on my political outlook at the time though later I was to recall it vividly. I knew of course that every male African must carry a pass. I had often seen police stopping black men in the street and demanding to see their passes. I had seen my father writing out a pass for his Native messenger, Branson, who lived in a small room in our back garden. But I had never till then imagined that the blacks might resent and hate the Pass Laws. My father and his socialist friends were glib with their talk of the workers. But by workers they meant the white workers and did not at all consider that in South Africa the majority of the workers were black. Later this attitude of my father's was to make a deep rift between us.

I realize now that I was slow to become aware of the situation of the Natives. I had been surrounded by evidence yet had not taken notice of the signs. One happening that should have taught me was the arrest of S. P. Bunting. Bunting, an occasional visitor to the talkshop behind the chemist's shop, was arrested at the time of the Bucket Strike in 1918. In those days there was no water-borne sewerage in the city. Night soil was collected in large buckets which were loaded on to mule-drawn carts and removed to pits at some distance. This unsavoury work was of course performed by Natives in the small hours of the night. The night soil workers at this time downed buckets and demanded sixpence a day more pay. To break the strike the authorities brought in Native police to act as scabs. But there were not nearly enough of these so that only hospitals, schools, hotels and such centres were served. Private households were left unrelieved. The Golden City stank. How my father coped with this emergency I cannot now remember. This is an odd gap in memory for I was fifteen at the time and must have noticed what was going on. But memory is selective: the stench of the Bucket Strike is gone, the sight of the torn passes on Von Brandis Square remains.

At school I found a few kindred spirits, in particular Frank Ross Bresler, Floris van der Stoep and Ronald McKibben. We lent books to each other and held interminable discussions. During my last years at school my interest in sport declined. With Ross Bresler I shared an interest in the local veld and especially in the peat soil of Bez valley which in parts was hot and smoking from undersurface fire. Bresler, using the pen name Silva, began to write articles on soil conservation. These appeared in the Farmers Supplement of the *Sunday Times*. Bresler had at that time little knowledge of the subject but he was a great reader and fluent writer. The articles attracted attention and farmers wrote to the paper asking detailed questions in connection with their soil conservation problems. These questions were referred to Bresler who often had difficulty in answering them. No one realized that the articles were written by a boy of seventeen. With the others I shared interests that were largely political. During the morning break while others kicked balls about, Bresler, van der Stoep and I walked to and fro along the far boundary of the playground and engaged in serious conversation.

Politics often came up in class. Our Latin master, Childe, was a tory of the old school, a graduate of Oxford. Almost invariably he devoted the first five minutes of every lesson to a general discussion of affairs. Usually the subject was sport: the latest football match against King Edward School, our prospects for the Inter-High athletics contest, the house matches, Catteral's bowling. Often the subject was political and the bolshies in the class came under fire. I considered that Childe behaved unfairly. He would tease and goad but when you began to answer him he would say, 'No more of this. You are supposed to be learning Latin. Now the ablative absolute . .' Sometimes when we were construing he would say to one of us, 'Your turn, bolshie'. We got our own back by refusing to stand up until he had called us by our names.

But it was in the school debating society that one had the chance of a really satisfactory political argument. This met on certain Saturday evenings and was patronized mainly by boarders. I should explain that though Jeppe was a day school there were some boarders. These came from a distance and on the whole they were from families rather better off than those of the local day boys. They were almost exclusively gentiles, while among the day boys there was a fair proportion of Jews. The boarders in so far as they had any political views were naturally conservatives, supporters of the South African Party of Smuts and Botha. The day boys and particularly the Jews were more susceptible to radical ideas. Alignments in debates often took the form of the boarders versus the rest.

The first debate in which I was one of the chosen speakers occurred in 1920. The motion was 'that strikes under present economic conditions are justifiable'. Among the opposers was one Hertsel Schlosberg, a Jewish boy who had recently become a boarder. I had known Schlosberg well as a day boy and had regarded him as one of us. Unfortunately he had developed a talent for cricket and had become an excellent slow bowler. This combined with the fact that he had already proved himself an outstanding footballer had led to his being offered a boarding bursary. A few places became available in the boarding house each year and these were nearly always offered to day boys who had distinguished themselves in sport. When Schlosberg became a boarder his views underwent a complete change. I was now startled and shocked to find him an opponent of the motion. The chairman of the debate was Johnny Leslie, a day boy, a Labourite in politics. He ruled the occasion with careful justice. When the motion was put it was defeated by 41 votes to 16. No sooner was the count announced than Schlosberg was on his feet. 'I move, Mr Chairman,' he said, 'that this house rise and sing "God save the King".' Amid cries of approval the whole meeting came to its feet. I at once began to walk out of the room. There was silence while I passed down the aisle and out of the door. Downstairs I waited listening but it was a minute or two before I heard the strains of the national anthem. I learned afterwards that Leslie had refused to allow the meeting to sing until he had formally closed the debate. He then left the chair. I admired him for that. I did not admire Schlosberg. 'Just for a handful of silver he left us.'

And now I must leave this memory world of childhood and school, of debates and of furious argument in the kitchen of the house in Bez Valley. Claud had still one more year at school, Edna and Enid were at the Jeppe Girls High School, the twins at the Jeppe Preparatory School. There were still five Roux children to climb over the koppie to school and back every day. The Rouxs were still a united family.

In March of 1922 I went to the University of the Witwatersrand to study botany and zoology. My interest in biology had grown from my concern with politics. I had once been told by someone—who? Not Jock Campbell, not Bunting; here is another odd memory gap—that there were four books which every serious socialist must read. These were Karl Marx's *Das Kapital*, Morgan's *Ancient Society*, Winwood Reade's *Martyrdom of Man* and Darwin's *Origin of Species*. I tried them all. Karl Marx's weighty tome I did not at that time achieve though I returned to it later. I did not at the age of fifteen find Darwin's masterpiece easy reading. It took me about three months, when possible neglecting homework which I regarded always as a tiresome interruption of the serious business of getting to know about life. I found the *Descent of Man* easier and more exciting. I turned then to other writers on evolution, Ernst Haeckel, T. H. Huxley and Herbert Spencer. Preoccupation with these works did not help my Latin and algebra which remained mediocre but did mean that when I went to the university I had no doubt as to what I wanted to study. I shall never forget the thrill I had when I first used a microscope.

CHAPTER II
Lock Out

I HAVE said that the Rouxs were still a united family, but just a year later, in April 1923, at the beginning of my second year at the university, I came home one night to find that my father had locked me out. I was unhappy about this but not taken by surprise. The reason was that my father disapproved of my political activities. It came about in this way.

In 1921 a young man, Maurice P., came to a meeting of the International Socialist League. The League had come into being in 1915 as a result of a breakaway from the Labour Party. The new organization had been started by a radical group which disapproved of the Labour Party's pro-war policy. Among other activities the I.S.L. ran a socialist Sunday school and Maurice was one of the young people who attended this school. For some reason I had never joined though I knew about it. I think that I thought it too 'sissy'.

At this particular meeting one of the older comrades said to Maurice, 'Why don't you young fellows start a Young Communist League?' The I.S.L. was at that time about to change its name to the Communist Party of South Africa and to affiliate to the Communist International with headquarters in Moscow. Already in many other countries youth leagues had been formed as appendages of the Communist Party. Maurice took up the suggestion with enthusiasm, collected names of boys and girls whose parents were then or had been members of the I.S.L., and called us to a meeting in the Trades Hall one Sunday morning.

I well remember that morning. The door of the Communist Party office was locked, so we held our meeting on the roof of the Trades Hall, in the bright highveld sunshine with the young city of Johannesburg all about us and the mine dumps shining in the distance. Below us Kerk Street was wrapped in Sunday peace. There were about a dozen boys and two or three girls.

We were all inexperienced in organization. None of us had ever been in a youth league before. We realized that this was no Sunday school. Adult party members might give us advice if we asked them but we must run the League ourselves. What were we going to do? Suggestions were slow in coming. We decided that we would meet weekly and have lectures and debates. We might start a study group.

The group carried on in this somewhat desultory manner for some time without achieving very much. Then came the great miners' strike and Rand Revolt of 1922. We were quite unprepared for such a situation. We at once forgot about the youth group and went our various ways to attend strike meetings and support demonstrations. These we found more to our taste than studying the writings of Marx and Lenin. The strike began in January and culminated in an armed revolt in March. This was followed by a period of martial law which lasted for some months.

During that strike I learned much about the South African Labour movement, not book knowledge but in actual experience. I became aware of the complexity of South African affairs and of a peculiar type of social blindness from which I myself had suffered all my life without being aware of it. Now for the first time I opened my eyes and saw the South African Native, the black man, the African as we call him today. Of course I had known about Natives. They outnumber the whites in our country by about four to one. One cannot help seeing them. There was the succession of Native men who had worked in my father's shop, the shop 'boys' who cleaned the shop, washed bottles and delivered parcels, also the various maids who had occasionally assisted Mother in the house, washing, sweeping, scrubbing floors and dusting or minding the twins. The fact that I can remember none of them by name is evidence not only of the short time most of them stayed with us but more still of my indifference to them. They were just the 'boy' or the 'girl' as the case might be. In the mines and factories and stores and offices and in other white households there were thousands of such workers. The streets were full of them particularly on Sundays when they gathered here and there in noisy groups. They talked with each other in loud and musical voices in languages of which neither I nor my parents nor my playmates understood more than a word or two.

It was not until my last year in school that it had occurred to me that these black people, these voteless masses, were in any way concerned with the socialism which I professed or that they had any role to play in the great social revolution which in those days seemed to be imminent. The 'workers' who were destined to inherit the new world were naturally the white carpenters and bricklayers, the tramworkers and miners who were organized in their trade unions and who voted for the Labour Party. I would no more have thought of discussing politics with a Native youth than of inviting him home to play with me or to a meal or asking him to join the Carnarvon Football Club. The African was on a different plane, hardly human, part of the scene as were dogs and trees and, more remotely, cows. I had no special feelings about him, not interest nor hate nor love. He just did not come into the social picture. So completely had I accepted the traditional attitudes of the time. Of course in the school debating society meetings, and especially in my final year, I had made occasional reference to 'the oppressed Bantu workers' but such references had been academic and devoid of emotional content. Only once, when I was sixteen, had I come near to awareness of the black man and that was the occasion when I saw Von Brandis Square littered with torn passes. But I had not deeply pondered this incident and it was soon forgotten.

Only now in the Great Strike of 1922 did I begin to think about the black man, even if at first in only a rather negative way. The twenty-five thousand or so white miners had gone on strike because the Chamber of Mines proposed to dismiss some two thousand of them and to alter the ratio of white to black labour which had previously been about one to ten. The whites were in fact overseers; the blacks handled the drills, shovelled the broken ore and filled the coco-pans.

The slogan of this strike was 'For a white South Africa'. The quarter of a million of black miners took no active part in it. They merely stopped work because there were no whites to direct them, no engineers to operate the skips. Almost all strikes, on the mines and elsewhere, had been like this. The skilled white artisan was in a strategic position. When he ceased work industry ground to a stop and the employer had to come to terms with him.

To me there was nothing wrong in the strike itself and in its aims. The workers were fighting the bosses. So much was clear. It was the slogan which now began to seem to me a little off-key. It semed odder still to some of the other socialists or communists who had of course thought much more about these matters than I had. Particularly to Sidney Bunting who was a founder leader of the new Communist Party and one of the most regular contributors to its paper, *The International*. I read his commentaries on the strike with interest. The Communist Party was wholehearted in support of the white miners. If it had a troubled conscience over any features of the struggle that conscience was in Bunting, not in the Party as a whole. Bunting seemed to regret that the Natives, the great majority of the workers, were not being drawn into the strike which would then have been really worthy of Communist support. The official line of the Party was that hostility to the black man was a sort of red herring brought in by the bosses to confuse the issue and it must not be allowed to interfere with the strike. 'The Chamber of Mines is the enemy. Leave the blacks alone.' That seemed to me then to be not only practical but also a satisfactory solution of the problem and for the time being I left it at that. Things were happening so swiftly as the strike moved on to its dramatic climax that there was no time to think deeply on theoretical problems.

The strikers organized themselves into commandos and marched through the streets. In Johannesburg we had the Fordsburg Commando and the Jeppe Commando. The latter had its headquarters near my home and with my friends I took a particular interest in all its doings. The Government was rapidly mobilizing the Defence Force and had established a camp at Ellis Park. It was rumoured that the Jeppe Commando was preparing an attack on the soldiers in this camp. Van der Stoep and I decided to do a bit of reconnoitring on our own and one afternoon we went off to the park to see what the position was. We had unknowingly chosen the very time scheduled for the attack. We were some fifty yards from the park when bullets began to fly. We took shelter in a house and waited, convinced that this at last must be the beginning of the revolution. The battle was over in a few minutes. It appeared that a small group of miners, armed with half a dozen rifles and a few revolvers had attacked the camp. The military, taken by surprise, suffered a few casualties but soon rallied and drove off the attack.

In the next few days fighting became general. The police stations at Fordsburg and Newlands were captured and the police in them disarmed. On the East Rand Benoni was said to be in the hands of the strikers. But in a few days the revolt was suppressed. The strikers' stronghold at Fordsburg was bombarded by guns and planes and then stormed by infantry. Spendiff and Fisher, the two leading figures in the revolt, killed themselves just before the troops came in. Their motive for this suicide cannot ever be known. It must have been a sudden decision for they had apparently no time to leave any message. The general belief was that they had died for the cause so that blame for the rebellion could be placed on them and the survivors should not be held guilty. However, thousands of strikers were arrested and imprisoned. A period of martial law followed. The government set up special tribunals to try the strikers some of whom they charged with public violence others with murder.

It was during this period that the Young Communist League came to life again. Events had taught us that there was work to do. A Strike Prisoners Release Committee had been formed. Young people were wanted to distribute leaflets. Meetings had to be organized, propaganda carried on. Men had to be saved from the gallows. Four had already been executed. Three of these, Long, Hull and Lewis, went to their death on the scaffold singing the Red Flag. Some fifty thousand demonstrated at their funeral, walking in closed ranks in a procession four miles long, a sight which must have convinced the government of their own deep unpopularity. Nevertheless the trials went on.

In addition to holding street corner meetings, in Jeppe, in Fordsburg and in Benoni, we Young Communists started a chalking and sticker campaign. We plastered the town with stickers and pasted them on railway coaches so that their message was carried to the four corners of South Africa. On walls and pavements we chalked our slogan 'Release the Strike Prisoners', and when the words were rubbed out we chalked them again. At the time there were fewer than twenty of us in the Y.C.L. but we must have created the impression that a vast underground organization was at work. No doubt we had exaggerated notions of the value of our activities but, when the government withdrew the murder charges against certain strikers and finally granted an amnesty to all strike prisoners, we felt that we had contributed to this result.

The Young Communist League had by this time become a well-knit and efficient little organization, and we were beginning to get into the public eye. We had affiliated to the Young Communist International which at that time had its headquarters in Berlin. Following directives from the Y.C.I. we now started an anti-militarist agitation. The young workers of South Africa were called upon to refuse to join the Defence Force which had been used so hideously to shoot down their brothers and fathers during the recent strike and which would no doubt become the tool of the capitalists in the next world war. Since military training began in the schools, it was clear that we had to carry our message to the cadets. There were various ways of distributing leaflets to the schoolboys. The simplest was to go to the school gates in the morning and hand them out. This was the procedure we followed in most cases. But it was much more exciting to go to a school at dead of night with pots of paste and to plaster leaflets on all the doors and windows. Jeppe High was one of the first schools to be treated in this way. I led the pasting party because I knew the lie of the land.

We also attacked the Johannesburg Teachers' Training College. Herman Bosman, now a student at the college, joined our pasting party, though he was not a member of the Y.C.L. It appeared that he had a strong dislike for McGregor, the principal of the college, and thought in this way to pay off some old scores. McGregor, he explained, treated the students as children and not as young men and women. There were five of us in the pasting party, rather too many for efficiency, and I suggested that Bosman should drop out. But he insisted on coming. We scaled the high gates successfully though one of our number, now a prominent lawyer in Johannesburg, was temporarily stuck on the top. After we had pasted all the windows, I was prepared to go home. But Bosman said, 'Why not do the inside as well?' We broke a window pane, waited till we were sure that no one had been alarmed by the noise, opened the catch and climbed in. We made a thoroughly good job of the inside of the college, both upstairs and down. Bosman wrote on one blackboard 'Be thorough'. That was the motto of the college and the text of most of McGregor's sermons.

The next day the students found their college excitingly unusual in appearance. McGregor refused to allow the leaflets to be removed until he had summoned the police. Detectives came and took finger prints. Bosman casually strolled up and chatted with them. 'Who do you think did it?' he asked. They did not think it was the young communists but some students out for a rag. How nearly right they were! There were no further developments.

Our anti-militarist campaign had an excellent press. Not the Normal College affair, for that was hushed up, but the open distribution of leaflets to schoolboys. Reporters got copies of the tracts and these were quoted in newspaper articles. It was seriously suggested that the communists were trying to corrupt the youth of South Africa.

It was at this stage that my father and I began to fall out. The cause of the trouble between us seemed on the surface to be political. Actually, I realize now, it was a personal clash between two extremely obstinate people. In fact what now came about had some resemblance to the break that my father as a young man had made with all the ways of his family.

My father had introduced me to socialism and at first had been my chief teacher. In the early days of his own socialism he had been very active. In 1914 he became honorary secretary of the War on War League. He joined the International Socialist League when it was founded in 1915. In 1918 he declared himself a Bolshevik, a supporter of Lenin and Trotsky. But his active role in the I.S.L. steadily declined. By 1921, at the age of forty-six, he had become what I called an armchair socialist. He had decided that the workers in Britain, America and South Africa were too foolish to create a revolution on their own initiative. It was the capitalists themselves who would destroy the whole capitalist system by 'running it over the precipice'. Then the workers would be forced to accept socialism. It was therefore in the meantime quite unnecessary and useless to have a socialist or communist party.

While my father was thus developing convenient theories to

justify his own inactivity, I was becoming more and more tied up with the Left organization and I propounded arguments to prove that the Communist Party was the organizing centre of the revolution. I quoted de Leon and Lenin against my father. I wrote an article for *The International*, the organ of the Party, in which I developed my views. This must have annoyed him considerably.

Apart from these general considerations there was one particular aspect of communist policy on which my father and I disagreed, and during the turmoil of the strike this came to a head. At this time there were three main schools of thought. The orthodox trade union leadership which nominally controlled the strikers was essentially reformist. In the event they were soon superseded by a Council of Action formed by certain intransigents who had been expelled from the Mine Workers Union for conducting illegal strikes. This active group, led by Spendiff, Fisher, Shaw and Wordingham, was supported by the leaders of the newly formed Communist Party, W.H. Andrews, Bunting and others. This group was not hostile to the Natives and on more than one occasion intervened to stop attacks on Natives which were apt to develop at meetings. 'Let the blacks alone! There is the enemy!' cried Fisher as he pointed to the cordon of soldiers about the telephone exchange. The third group consisted of the miners' commandos, Afrikaner nationalists, whose leaders were openly nigrophobe and who developed the strike slogan 'For a White South Africa'.

Bunting, writing his impassioned leaflets and articles in *The International*, supported the second group but went much further. He perceived that solidarity of the workers must include the black man. He warned the white miners that their cause was in danger if they did not have the Natives on their side. Bunting himself was not invited to speak at any of the meetings perhaps because the leaders would not have relished his message. He was beginning to be known as a *kafir boetie* chiefly because as an attorney he often appeared in the courts defending Africans who had been arrested. On one occasion he was seized outside the court, frog-marched and roughly handled by a mob of white hooligans.

During this period, when I was beginning to sort out my own ideas, I came more and more under the influence of Bunting and came to share his belief in carrying the message of communism to the black workers. But my father, in spite of his socialism, had remained very much the typical white South African in his attitude to the Natives. At no time had he ever thought of them as playing any part in the movement and indeed he did not consider them capable of grasping ideas at that level. 'After the revolution', he would say, 'they will be segregated in their own territories where they will grow food under expert guidance.' He had no great regard for Bunting as a theoretician. He recalled how when the 1914 war broke out Bunting had not known where he stood and how he, Philip Roux, had been one of those who had persuaded Bunting to join the anti-war group of socialists. As for Bunting's campaign for socialist propaganda among Africans, my father's comment was: 'Having failed to get the support of the white workers, they now go and preach to the Natives.'

It will be clear that Philip Roux and his son were now finding many things to disagree about. As I look back over the years I realize that the great offence was my interest in Africans, but at the time it seemed to be the doings of the Young Communist League that brought matters to a head. On every occasion when a report appeared in the newspapers describing our activities my father would storm and rage. He shouted that we ought to stop that sort of nonsense and that I must leave the Y.C.L. These outbursts usually happened over the supper table which was the natural family meeting place. Immoderate in anger my father filled the kitchen with fury and fear. Claud was away on a citrus farm in Eastern Transvaal, Edna sat pale and silent as my father and I shouted at one another, the twins, heads down, bolted their food in misery, my mother, tight-lipped, served the ruined meal. Afterwards Edna said to me, 'Why do you argue with Dad? You know it's no use.' And this was true but I would not give up the Y.C.L. The disputes continued and grew more violent. It happened that the Y.C.L. met every Tuesday night in the Trades Hall and my regular absence from home on Tuesday evenings was evidence that I was disobeying my parent's command. He told me that if I attended one more meeting I would find the door locked against me when I came home.

And so it proved. My father was as good as his word. Locked

out of home one Tuesday night in 1923 I shrugged my shoulders and went off to my friend Ross Bresler to ask him to put me up for the night. This he did with not much question. But I did not want to trouble him again the following night for his parents would require an explanation. So the next night I spent under a tree in Milner Park. I did not sleep much. For the rest of that week I slept in the Communist Party office in the Trades Hall. Old Comrade Oates, one time miner, now Party typist, office-boy and general factotum, left the door unlocked for me but bound me to secrecy over this as Comrade Bill Andrews, Party secretary, would surely disapprove. The offices in the Trades Hall were not meant to be used as lodgings. All this was very foolish, even melodramatic. In my own eyes I was a fine fellow. What I ought to have done was to go to some comrade in the movement and ask him to put me up. But in spite of having been in the movement proper for more than a year, I knew few of the older members intimately. Perhaps also I was shy and not a little proud. I was not a sissy. I could take it. I could sleep under trees. My clothes grew more crumpled and dirty. I needed a bath.

On the following Sunday evening the Party held its usual open-air meeting on the City Hall steps, a meeting which I always attended. My mother and Edna came to meet me there. Mother said: 'You must come home. I have spoken to Dad'. So I returned home.

A few days later I got a message from Willy Blumberg. I was to come and see him. He said, 'Why didn't you come to me? I have a spare bed. I will put you up. Come and stay with me.' I thanked him and explained that I was now back at home.

An uneasy truce followed. My parents had planned to go on three months' holiday to England to visit the Wilson relations, but now Mother was afraid that I might get into trouble during their absence. To set her mind at rest I now agreed to give up my political activities during their absence. For those three months I kept the pact. I resigned from the Y.C.L. committee, went no longer to the Trades Hall on Tuesday evenings, took no part in political work. Only one thing I did not give up: attendance at the Sunday evening meetings on the City Hall steps. And at home Aunt Pietjie came from Aliwal North to keep house for us. For a time I was head of the family and managed things as best I could. One day I encountered Johnny G. in the street. Eagerly I questioned him about the doings of the Y.C.L. Yes, it was carrying on. I promised him that I should soon return to help.

When my parents came back from Europe I at once resumed membership of the Y.C.L. Political activity had become with me a master passion. I could not stay away. Dad said nothing to me. But one day I came home late to find the house in darkness and a note lying on my pillow. This was from Mother. It read something like this: 'I am afraid, Eddie, that this can not go on. You seem determined to set yourself against your father's wishes. I cannot bear all this shouting and quarrelling. You will have to go. I have put your shirts ready and I have darned your socks. It hurts me to write this. Mother.'

I packed a bag with my clothes and books, said goodbye to my mother and to Edna and went off to Willy Blumberg. 'Willy,' I said, 'it has happened and I have come to stay with you.'

Willy beamed a welcome. 'Come in. We'll make your bed,' he said. For that first night this was on cushions on the floor. I slept uneasily.

CHAPTER III

Y.C.L.—and Bugs in my Bed

FOR the next year or two life was strenuous but never dull. Willy Blumberg was a little blond Jew, loud-voiced and excitable. He had come out from Lithuania about a dozen years before I met him and had been befriended by the Germiston socialist, the dentist Colin Wade, who had taught him his trade.

Willy's daily habits were eccentric. He rose at midday, had his lunch then went off to Germiston and the East Rand where most of his clients were. During the afternoon he worked at fittings and taking mouth impressions and returned to his room in the evening. He would begin work at about eight and usually continued into the small hours of the morning. I watched fascinated as he stuck porcelain teeth on to pink wax mounted on the plaster-of-Paris models of his clients' mouths.

Willy had two rooms in an ancient three-storey brick and iron building at the corner of Jeppe and von Brandis Streets. I got a stretcher and shared the bedroom. There were bugs everywhere. They got into my stretcher, my books and my clothes. If you left a jacket hanging on the wall for a day or two, colonies would be established in the seams and under the lapels. I never really got used to these insects and the sour sad smell.

My financial position was not very satisfactory though it might have been worse. My municipal bursary just covered my fees at the university. In addition I earned a total of forty pounds a year by demonstrating to first-year students in the botany and zoology departments. I was lucky to get this work: second-year students were seldom chosen as demonstrators. The money was paid in two instalments. To receive twenty pounds every six months was something to look forward to. I had to spend part of it on books. For most of the time I had no money in my pocket. To remedy this I got part-time work with a comrade who ran a butcher's shop. My job was to deliver parcels of meat. To do this I had to rise early and cycle furiously on my errands until it was time for lectures. The business was not flourishing and my pay was postponed. In the end it went bankrupt and I never did get paid.

Food was always available in Willy's workshop: Jewish rye bread which I ate hungrily though I disliked the caraway seeds, butter, and sometimes a few bananas. Bread and bananas made an unbalanced diet. Always prone to spots and pimples, I soon developed a succession of boils. Later my diet was better organized. Comrades in the movement realized that I was not eating properly and a number of families invited me to come regularly for meals. Except for one Italian family, the Bosazzas, these were all Jews. I remain ever grateful to the warm-hearted Yiddisher mommas who fed me so lavishly during those years when I was always hungry. Four I remember in particular. Mrs Rabb, Mrs Sabel and Mrs Ginsberg have long since passed away. Mrs Rubin still recalls how she cured my boils with tomatoes, sour milk and cheese. Each night in the week I had dinner in a different house and my hosts did not mind my rushing off to meetings immediately after the meal. Sometimes I stayed and talked or studied. I became proficient in concentrating on a book while a political argument raged about my ears. If man is what he eats then certainly I became a Jew during that period. Some of my friends still call me Gonka.

Politics and biology took up nearly all my time. During the day I had lectures and labs at the university. In the evening there was usually a meeting. Group meetings, committee meetings, public meetings—there were dozens of them every month. After the meetings we often went to a café and listened to music. My particular friends were Willy Kalk and Benny Sachs. Benny I have already mentioned. He had come from Lithuania when still very young and lived in the Jewish quarter of Ferreirastown. Willy was the son of a German immigrant. His father had been a social democrat in the Germany of the Kaiser. Willy was one of the few real proletarians in the Y.C.L., a furniture maker by trade and an excellent craftsman. Unlike Benny and me he had a regular income. It was always Willy who paid when we went to a café.

Then coming back to my bug-ridden stretcher at about midnight I would find Willy Blumberg busy with his teeth. I felt I owed it to him to stay up and talk or listen for an hour or so. He was a great talker and liked company. He was an anarchist rather than a communist, a man who had read widely though I thought sometimes that he had read more than he had digested. We agreed about very little except for poetry where our tastes coincided. I often read to him while he worked. He had an extensive library, partly inherited from Colin Wade but continually added to by himself. Wisely he did not keep the books at his lodging where they would certainly have been ruined. They were looked after by the Germiston public library. However Willy always had some books in his rooms and we had great pleasure from them.

1923 was a year of depression and unemployment. I got to know Harry Haynes, one of the active members of the Unemployed Committee. Harry had long been a leading exponent of Marxist socialism in South Africa, another of those self-educated and class-conscious workingmen of whom Jock Campbell was, for me the prototype. He had been a miner and had played a leading part in the great strikes of 1913 and 1914. As a result he had been blacklisted and had tramped the Reef for months looking for work. He was a wonderful speaker, a good actor and a singer of popular songs. He told interesting stories of his past, some of which I suspected had improved with the telling. However the following story I believe to be true.

During 1914 he had been unemployed for months and he and his family were starving. One night on his way home he picked up a tickey, that is a threepenny bit. Finding a tickey is considered lucky. There was literally no food in the house. Harry sent his young son to the Chinese grocer on the corner to buy mealie-meal with the tickey. When the boy came back Harry took the paper bag, emptied out most of its contents on to a plate and went to the shopkeeper. He pretended to be in a great rage. 'Is this all you give for a tickey?' He showed the bag only quarter full. The Chinese was profuse in his apologies. To placate this irate customer he filled the bag to the brim. Harry and his family ate their fill of mealie-meal that morning and in the afternoon Harry at last found a job.

I have known other brilliant public speakers but have never met one who had so great a gift of rousing an audience to heights of emotion while he himself remained completely unmoved. Haynes would have made a wonderful actor. I remember how the unemployed held a meeting at the Tivoli Theatre. 'Watch me hit them up,' he said to me just before the meeting. He had the crowd alternately laughing and crying. Undoubtedly he was a great asset to the movement.

Notices of meetings of the workless were posted outside the Trades Hall. An unemployed signwriter painted them beautifully and they were composed by Harry. One day the poster, after detailing the programme for the next meeting, stated at the bottom: 'Bomb Practice at the Usual Time and Place.' That was one of Harry's jokes.

He was always full of enthusiasm or in the depths of despair. I wanted him to speak at a Y.C.L. meeting. I asked him 'What are you doing tomorrow, Harry?' He was in gloomy mood. 'Tomorrow? Why tomorrow I may be myself with yesterday's sev'n thousand years.' Not only did he know Omar Khayyam by heart—some of us could equal him in that—but he had memorized the Communist Manifesto of Marx and Engels and he could reel off verbatim pages from other socialist writers, especially from Labriola, an Italian Marxist with romantic leanings. I recall one particularly striking passage which Harry would often quote.

> Whether those people of the future, of whom socialists often entertain such exalted ideas, will still produce any religion or not, I can neither affirm nor deny. And I leave it to them to arrange their own lives, which will not be too easy I hope, in order that they may not become imbeciles in paradisian beatitude. But this much I see clearly. Christianity, which up to now has been the religion of the most advanced nations, will not leave room for any other religion after it. He who will not be a Christian henceforth must be without religion. *Primus in orbe Deum fecit timor.* Fear was the first in this world to make gods. The statement is very old but it is valuable and therefore I perpetuate it.

At that time one did not see that communism itself might become, might already have become, a religion.

Harry Haynes was one of the Chain Gang. That is he and

two fellow workers, Woudberg and McCarthy, were sent to Cape Town to demonstrate in the House of Assembly. There they chained themselves to the railings in the public gallery and before a blacksmith could be summoned to remove them they delivered speeches to a startled parliament.

Harry later became editor of the independent Labour paper *Forward*. Today he works for his ancient enemy the Chamber of Mines and edits their monthly journal with great competence.

However, it was the Y.C.L. which claimed most of my attention at this time. We started a monthly paper, *The Young Communist*, produced on an ancient duplicating machine. I did most of the writing and Sarah S., our secretary, typed the stencils. Branches of the youth organization were started at Benoni, on the East Rand and at Germiston. The last consisted entirely of Afrikaans-speaking members, all of them workers. It did not survive more than six months or so.

To improve our theoretical knowledge we of the Johannesburg branch started a class on Marxian economics. Bravely we tackled the first volume of Marx's *Capital*. Chapter by chapter we waded through it. I prepared summaries of the various sections and read out to the class what I thought were spicy bits. We began with twenty members and ended with six. Willy Kalk and I were among the survivors. It was as a result of this study that I developed my first heresy. More were to come. I found that I could not accept Marx's theory of value. I thought it the product of a magnificent piece of deductive reasoning from certain assumptions. But I could not see that the assumptions were necessarily true and the resulting theory of value seemed to be at variance with obvious economic facts. However this discovery did not shake my faith in Marxism as a whole. I felt that the theory of value was not necessary to the argument. When in later years my heresies broke out in other and more practical forms Willy Kalk would point out that the root of the trouble had been revealed in the Y.C.L. study class.

There was one matter in which Willy and I were agreed, even in opposition to the rest of the League. This was the so-called Native question. Bunting had influenced me towards awareness of the black workers, but it was Willy who helped me to my first contact with Native workers. He had got into touch with some African riksha men. There were many of these in

Johannesburg in those days. Human beasts of burden, they transported passengers and luggage and had their stands near the main station. The vehicles did not belong to them but were rented from the European riksha company. It was said that most of them died young.

Willy's chief contact lived in New Doornfontein, a slum near the railway and to the east of the city. Willy and I went there one evening. The riksha man lived in a typical Doornfontein yard, an open space with a ring of tumble-down shacks made of bits of corrugated iron and pieces of cardboard. It was a winter night and the man was squatting near his brazier. Willy and I squatted with him and Willy began to talk about industrial organization and how the riksha pullers should unite to improve their conditions. But the man was a rough Zulu and spoke little English. We found it hard to communicate with him. I don't remember that anything came of that meeting.

Willy was interested primarily in the workers but I was more concerned with what I called 'the Native youth'. I called often at the office of the *Abantu-Batho*, the organ of the African National Congress. There I met two educated Africans, Dunjwa and Letanka. With them I could converse with ease. They were pleased to meet a young white man who was interested in the cause of African emancipation. I think it was they who introduced me to two more young Africans, Stanley Silwana and Thomas Mbeki. The former was a schoolteacher, the latter a labourer but already an aspiring politician. I invited them to attend a Y.C.L. meeting. It was thrilling to see for the first time two black faces among the many white ones.

My two black friends however were not so much interested in the Young Communist League as in the new and rapidly growing African organization, the I.C.U. The Industrial and Commercial Workers Union had been founded some five years earlier in Cape Town. Under the leadership of a Nyasaland Native, Clements Kadalie, it was spreading rapidly northwards. It had already established a branch in Bloemfontein and it was there that Mbeki had joined. With Silwana he was now trying to start a branch in Johannesburg. I offered to help and soon I found myself addressing a mass meeting of Africans in the Inchcape Hall. I told them that I was a Communist, that the Communist Party believed in the union of all workers irrespective of race or colour, that we were working for the overthrow of the rule of the exploiters and the establishment of soviets when the workers would take over the mines and factories and govern themselves through their own elected representatives. I went on to tell them of the great Russian revolution which had happened and which would in due course be followed by a world revolution in which South Africa would play its part. Then would follow a world of comradeship between black and white in which all would work together for the benefit of all. The revolution, I implied, would come soon, was just round the corner. All that was needed was for the workers of the world to unite. So perhaps my head was in the stars: but as I spoke I believed every word I uttered. I spoke in English and my remarks were translated a sentence at a time by two interpreters, one of whom spoke either Zulu or Xhosa, the other either Sotho or Tswana. I should explain that, though many Bantu languages are spoken in South Africa, they fall into two main groups, Zulu and Xhosa are very similar and so are Sotho and Tswana.

This was the first of many similar meetings at which I spoke. Speakers from the Communist Party came occasionally but for me it became a regular routine. The African audiences seemed to welcome white speakers at their meetings. It was at that time most unusual to hear any white man holding forth against the pass laws and demanding equality of treatment for the blacks. In general we, the lordly white masters, bore the indignities inflicted on the black men with indifference or with fortitude. My own speeches became infected more and more as I went on and came to know more of these friendly and warm-hearted black people with a kind of revolutionary nigrophilism. I thought and cared less about Russia, the workers of the world and all communist theories, and ever more about the national aspirations of the oppressed blacks of Africa. These tendencies were to grow with time but for many years I remained a devoted communist.

In 1924 an important political event occurred in South Africa. The Smuts government had become extremely unpopular in consequence of its handling of the 1922 strike. The strike itself had been a united effort on the part of English (predominantly Labour) and Afrikaner (predominantly Nationalist) workers. The Nationalist-Labour electoral pact was the logical outcome of this. A number of by-elections went against the government and these precipitated the general election of 1924. The first of these by-elections was at Turffontein, a Johannesburg constituency. Major Hall, the sitting S.A.P. (Smuts party) member had resigned in protest against certain government financial measures of which he did not approve. He contested the seat again but refrained from holding meetings or issuing leaflets. He said he would leave it to the voters to decide. Nourse, the Government candidate, carried on the usual election campaign. To the Communist Party, unasked, it now seemed good to campaign for Hall. Under one of their numerous pseudonyms (I think they were the United Front Committee) they issued a violent anti-Smuts leaflet composed by me, heckled at all Nourse's meetings and in general so roused the electorate that Hall was returned with a substantial majority.

In the general election which followed, the Labour-Nationalist Pact romped home. In the new parliament under the Pact Government Labour held the balance of power. They were given two, later three, seats in the cabinet, and at their behest the Mines and Works (Colour Bar) Act was passed in 1926. This laid it down as a principle that skilled work in the mines and in certain other industries was to be for whites only. Other anti-Native legislation was to follow. Many of us felt that we had helped to throw out a reactionary government only to put something much worse in its place. And in this we were not alone. The I.C.U. had persuaded many of its followers in the Cape, where some Africans were still able to qualify as voters, to support the Pact.

It was inevitable that the Native question should cause a crisis in the Y.C.L. Willy Kalk and I had thought that we were making some progress in converting our fellow members to our point of view. We now met with a serious reverse at the hands of Solly Sachs. Solly had joined the Y.C.L. in 1922 but had been working away from Johannesburg and had had little opportunity to attend our meetings. Meetings and arguments were as the breath of life to him so that when, early in 1924, he returned to Johannesburg, he at once began to play a dominating role in League affairs. Forceful as well as intelligent, a competent speaker who bludgeoned his hearers into agreement by sheer repetition of his views, he was older and more experienced than most of us and he did not believe in half measures. To the suggestion that we should now set about organizing the Native youth and bringing them into the Y.C.L. he countered with the proposal that the blacks should be enrolled in a separate organization. At a conference of the Y.C.L., held early in 1924, Sachs with a masterly speech carried the day. Willy and I now found ourselves in a minority of three, ourselves and one other member.

However, in any small organization such as ours, those who work steadily and persuasively usually get their own way in the end. Sachs, that meteoric visitant, now shot off on a trip to Europe and left the field to us. Our secretary, Sarah, retired from the League. I wrote a lengthy report to our headquarters in Berlin and we duly received from the Executive Committee of the Y.C.I. a friendly but uncompromising letter of advice supporting the policy of bringing the Natives into the League. A Cape Town branch was established at about this time and, after some internal debate, took the same line.

In the meantime the Communist Party was itself being torn by differences of opinion on the Native issue. In 1923 Willy Kalk and I had joined the C.P. We found the party divided into two factions: one, led by Bunting, favoured an active pro-Native policy; the other, led by Bill Andrews, desired to place the chief emphasis on the organized white workers. At a national conference of the C.P., held in December, 1924, the Bunting faction, supported by the delegates of the Cape Town branch of the Party and by the Y.C.L. delegates, secured a narrow majority. But this was followed shortly afterwards by the resignation of Bill Andrews from the secretaryship. He accepted the post of secretary to the Trade Union Co-ordinating Committee, later known as the South African Trade Union Congress, but retained his membership of the C.P.

With its new policy the Communist Party was now definitely committed to recruiting Africans as a major part of its activities. Many of its old members now fell away and financial support from fellow travelers became more difficult to obtain. Kalk and I were brought into the depleted executive. In a short time I found myself honorary secretary of the C.P.S.A.

The task of making the C.P. predominantly African in character and composition was found in practice to be no easy one. Years of hard work lay ahead before this object could be achieved. It was difficult to recruit any Africans into the Party. Africans were often, and with reason, suspicious of the white man. The few that came to our branch meetings felt strange and uncomfortable and often did not fully understand or not at all understand what was going on. It was far easier for me to work through the I.C.U., and the I.C.U. was still growing rapidly in Johannesburg.

Their leader Kadalie had not previously visited the Rand but the growing strength of the local I.C.U. branch here and the obvious importance of Johannesburg as the industrial centre of South Africa brought him to Johannesburg early in 1925.

I had long heard of Kadalie and had looked forward to meeting him. Our meeting, when it did occur, was casual, unplanned. I had gone one evening to visit Mbeki. Outside the dormitory where he lived he introduced me to a tall, handsome and unusually dark-skinned African. 'This is Comrade Kadalie,' he said. We had a long talk. I happened to be carrying a copy of Swinburne's *Songs before Sunrise*. I opened it at *Messidor*. Kadalie took the book into his hands and in his gentle high-pitched voice read some of the verses.

> Put in the sickles and reap,
>   For the morning of harvest is red,
>   And the long large ranks of the corn,
>   Coloured and clothed with the morn,
>   Stand full in the fields and deep
>   For them that faint to be fed.
>   Let all that hunger and weep
>   Come hither, and who would have bread
>   Put in the sickles and reap . . .

> The dumb, dread people that sat
>   All night without screen for the night,
>   All day without food for the day,
>   They shall give not their harvest away,
>   They shall eat of its fruit and wax fat,
>   They shall see the desire of their sight
>   Though the ways of the seasons be steep,
>   They shall climb with face to the light,
>   Put in the sickles and reap.

Kadalie, the tough politician, the leader, the orator who swayed the multitude, was essentially a poet. Not that he ever wrote a line of poetry but his life was lived with epic grandeur. As he read Swinburne that night he glowed and was kindled. We became friends and the tragic future was unknown to us, undreamed.

It was soon after this meeting that the I.C.U. headquarters were transferred from Cape Town to Johannesburg. Premises were hired in Market Street and the building was called the Workers Hall. Regular crowded meetings were held there or on the vacant ground opposite. There were dances to raise funds. It was at one of these dances that I danced for the first time with an African girl, a Miss Nayiya, one of Kadalie's favourites. It was a demonstration of one's belief in the social equality of black and white. I was a poor dancer, untrained, and she moved with all the natural grace of her people and bore my clumsiness without protest. I found her charming.

Now at the end of 1924 I wrote my final examinations for the B.Sc. degree. In spite of the time lavished on politics I managed to achieve first class passes in both botany and zoology. Perhaps this was because most of the diversions which usually distract students did not affect me. I was not in the least interested in sport and did not go to student dances. In any case I had no money and no clothes suitable to such occasions but I did not feel this as a deprivation. The Debating Society and the Biological Society did take up some of my time and in both of these I held office. In December 1924, my botany professor, Charles Moss, offered me a junior post in his department. This was a senior demonstratorship worth £150 a year. This wealth enabled me to continue with special studies in botany leading to the B.Sc. Honours degree.

Thus for the first time in my life I had an income sufficient for my needs. I now left Willy Blumberg's workshop and rented a room in Braamfontein, not far from the university, and bought myself some new ready-made clothes. I had not been embarrassed by my shabbiness but I took much pleasure in my new suit and shirts.

Towards the end of that year it happened that I was able to pay an unexpected and unplanned visit to my home in Bezuidenhout Valley. It was shortly before the final examinations in

December 1924 that I went one evening to Joubert Park to spend an hour or two with a book on fossil botany. I was sitting on a bench reading under a convenient lamp when I looked up and saw a tall man with a walking stick striding along one of the paths. It was my father on his way, as I guessed, to a meeting of the Pharmaceutical Society. He had not noticed me. I hastily shut my book and took the next tram to Bez Valley. The rest of the family was at home and we spent a pleasant evening together. I had not seen my mother, sisters and brothers for over two years, nor had we exchanged letters. We had much to talk about. My sister Edna said that she had known it was I by the click of the gate and the sound of my steps on the path. She was now eighteen and radiantly beautiful, in her final year at school. Claud had left school and gone off to a citrus estate in eastern Transvaal. Edna was worried about my rather shabby clothes. I said this was not important. All I wanted was to catch up on family news. Enid had still two more years in school. Phil had left on his own initiative and gone to be apprenticed as a garage mechanic. Arthur was still struggling with Latin and Afrikaans. My mother, calm as ever, took all this easily, made tea and produced some of her home-made cookies. All was as it used to be. I stayed about two hours, kept a careful watch on the time and left before Dad was due home.

CHAPTER IV

Hooligans

Now in South Africa a tradition has arisen that political disagreement shall be expressed in violence, the idea being apparently that if you don't like the other fellow's politics you beat him up to teach him better. Thus by a neat short cut you avoid all tedium of argument, prove yourself in the right and have the direct satisfaction of inflicting physical damage on your opponent. One instance of such violence in vicious form achieved world-wide notoriety. This was the case of Henry P. Lamont, who became known thereafter as the tar-and-feathers man. Lamont was at the time, in the post-war years, professor of French in the Transvaal University College, later University of Pretoria. He had served and suffered on the western front in Europe and now wrote a book telling of his war experiences and also something of his subsequent life in South Africa. The book *War, Wine and Women* was published by Cassell's and became a best-seller. However, in it Lamont permitted one character to criticize predikants and rural Boers as he had known them. This gave gross offence to certain persons. They planned their own rough justice. They lay in wait for Lamont, seized him, stripped him and coated him with hot tar in which they stuck feathers. They left him near dead. He did not die but after a long spell in hospital he resigned his post and also left the country, adding to his note book the comment that some South Africans cannot take criticism. Indeed it would seem that the ability to tolerate an unfavourable judgment on one's personality, opinions or behaviour, is an extremely adult quality. It is not possessed by the immature. South Africa is still a young country. The tradition of resolving disagreement by violence should not be surprising. However that may be I now go on to record certain incidents which took place in Johannesburg in the years 1925 and 1926.

True to its avowed interracial policy, the Communist Party

in Johannesburg was not confining its attention to the black workers. Propaganda among the whites was conducted chiefly at the regular Sunday evening meetings held on the City Hall steps. The youth section of the Party held similar meetings on Saturday evenings in Jeppestown. These meetings frequently provided a little excitement and sometimes physical danger as well. The disturbances usually arose over our insistence that the slogan Workers of the World Unite must include the black workers. My friend Julius recently reminded me of a typical incident at one of these Jeppestown meetings. According to Julius it went somewhat as follows:

Roux, on soapbox, addressing the meeting: 'We believe in equal rights for black and white.'

A heckler, interrupting: 'Would you let your sister marry a kafir?'

Roux: 'Certainly I would.'

Uproar. Fists fly. The meeting breaks up in a free fight. Afterwards Roux is reproached by his comrades for leading them into trouble.

Julius is probably exaggerating the unequivocal nature of my reply. It is more likely that I said: 'Well, it would depend on what my sister wanted.'

This question with its deep meaning, would you concede to the black man absolute equality in all personal relations, was a hardy perennial at our meetings. Issy Diamond, the brilliant soapbox performer who diverted the Sunday evening crowds, had no fear of hecklers. In fact he relished interjections for the opportunities they gave him to make people laugh. To deal with this recurring question he had his own special technique. He would reply: 'I would, if I had the needle to the Native,' or sometimes 'Ah, you don't know my sister!' And danger dissolved in laughter.

But in these years the trouble went further than sporadic heckling. The communists, ever an unpopular minority, were now considered fair game. It began with the visit of the Prince of Wales in 1925 when we annoyed some of our audience by referring to that popular young man as a lackey of imperialism and by calling for a boycott of the celebrations. We had at the time a number of rough-house meetings but after the Prince had gone we had expected that the rowdyism would cease.

However, it did not but disconcertingly became a regular feature of our meetings.

What had happened was that a group of young toughs had found in communist baiting an amusing Sunday evening sport and intended to keep it up. They seemed to be aided and abetted by the police who stood by and looked benevolently on their attacks. Presently we found it necessary to organize a bodyguard of Party supporters to defend the platform every Sunday evening. The hooligans, as we called them, then began to follow and attack individual communists after the meetings ended. Benny Sachs was once set upon by a number of young men in the street and in broad daylight, and was lucky to escape a beating. We formed the habit of going off in groups after the Sunday meetings but even this did not save us from attack.

More than once we found it policy to board a tram in order to escape. An economic struggle would ensue: who would first run out of tramfares, we or the hooligans? Usually it was our tormenters who wearied first. I remember one occasion when some of them got off while others remained. We found that we were now outnumbered only by about two to one. Willy Kalk was with us. He was not a big fellow but he was in good condition and could hit hard. We got off the tram. So did the opposition but they kept at a respectful distance. We realized they were not really keen on fighting unless the odds were heavily in their favour.

Once I found myself on a tram with a single comrade and a crowd of hooligans. I had become careless and had wandered away from the neighbourhood of the platform during the meeting. I had been selling the Party newspaper among the crowd. I suddenly noticed that I was cut off from the bodyguard by a hostile section of the audience and saw that they were closing in on me. I turned and ran and just managed to board a tram as it moved off. A dozen or so of my pursuers piled on. With me was a young building worker, a sympathizer with the movement, who had seen me run and had run with me. We now sat together on the lower deck and the hooligans were upstairs. The tram went its way to Kensington. When it came to the Jeppe subway some of them got off and spoke to a young policeman on point duty. What they said to him I don't know but he came on to the tram apparently with the intention of arresting me, though on what charge it would be difficult to imagine. My companion argued with the policeman telling him that I was the victim and that the mob was trying to assault me. The tram-driver was impatient to be on his way; so the policeman arrested the two of us and took us to the Jeppe police station. The triumphant mob accompanied us. Our names and addresses were taken and a charge was laid, not against me but against the young building worker who was accused of 'obstructing a police officer in the execution of his duty'.

So it happened that I came home rather late that night to my lodging with Willy Blumberg in Braamfontein. The house was in a very steep street and one usually walked up to it from the lower or town end. On this occasion I chanced to approach from the top of the street. To my complete surprise there, seated on the pavement, were half a dozen or more of the same hooligans. They were so intently gazing down the street that I was close upon them before they noticed me. Instead of turning back uphill I broke into a run and continued on my way down the hill. I dodged one or two and was soon clear of them. They did not catch up with me. I slept that night at the house of comrade Julius. I wondered at first how the hooligans had found out where I lived, until I realized that of course they had overheard me giving my address at the Jeppe police station.

The trial of the young building worker, whose name unfortunately I have forgotten, ended in the discomfiture of police and hooligans. A number of these had come to give evidence but they were not called. Bunting had engaged for the defence an attorney named Benson, an eccentric fellow often at loggerheads with the magistrates but a clever lawyer for all that. After the young policeman had given his evidence Benson asked for the discharge of the accused on the ground that the officer was not acting in the course of his duty when he set out to make an arrest, since he had not seen either of us commit an offence. The request was granted.

The trouble with the hooligans, which seemed to have become a feature of our meetings, was finally ended by the action of the Party executive. We found out that some of the youths were inmates of the Cottesloe hostel. This was an institution for young criminals released from the reformatory who were supposed to be in process of rehabilitation to ordinary civilian life. We asked for and were granted an interview with the Minister for Justice, Tielman Roos, in Pretoria. Roos proved unexpectedly sympathetic. He listened to our story and said that he would give instructions to the police to see that order was maintained at our meetings. Now Tielman Roos was a leader in the Nationalist Party which was why we had not expected much help from him. It appeared however that he remembered the anti-War stand made by Bunting and others in 1914–18. He said that he admired the socialists for their courage in those days when the Nationalists too had been a persecuted minority.

So we returned to Johannesburg highly pleased with our interview. For a number of Sundays there was peace at our meetings. It was obvious that the police had been reprimanded for their former behaviour and they now protected us against assaults. However heckling continued and rowdyism slowly began once more to increase. It had almost regained its original pitch when one night Tom Matthews of the Amalgamated Engineering Union appeared on our platform. This was some 'united front' occasion—I cannot remember exactly which—when various sections of the labour movement made common cause. Tom, who was a leading trade unionist, was appalled at the rowdyism. Happening to meet Tielman Roos a few days later on official business he mentioned the matter. Roos was much annoyed that the police had disregarded his instructions. He must have spoken again, this time personally and most strongly to the police officials in Johannesburg. So zealous in protecting us did the police now become that thereafter any member of the audience who merely asked a question immediately found a policeman at his elbow. This was rather more protection than we wanted for we were not averse to being questioned; questions often added some spice to what might otherwise have been dull meetings. However, the particular set of hooligans whose meaningless interruptions had troubled us for so long now found their fun was over so that they finally gave up coming and we heard no more of them.

I have made mention of our campaign at the time of the visit of the Prince of Wales. This led to my first acquaintance with the inside of a police cell. The Y.C.L. had indulged in one of its leaflet campaigns. The leaflet contained the usual sort of communist propaganda, 'thousands wasted on parasite while workers starve' and so on. We plastered the town very thoroughly one Saturday night and must have annoyed the authorities. On the following evening Benny Sachs and I were on our way home. We had not been doing any pasting but had gone after the usual City Hall meeting to the Corner Lounge to talk and listen to the music. However, we both had a few of the leaflets in our pockets. At the end of Rissik Street our way lay over a footbridge which crossed the railway line. We were about halfway up the steps on the near side of the bridge when we heard someone call our names. Looking back we beheld one Pannigennis, a tall athletic Greek of mephistophelian appearance whom we knew well as a detective who was often present at our meetings. With him was a policeman. He shouted to us to stop. We did not stop but ran on while the two charged after us. The policeman caught Benny. Pannigennis grabbed me and I tried to get away from his clutch. In this I might have succeeded but I was hampered by my overcoat to which he clung desperately, blowing his whistle the while. I had pulled him as far as the other side of the bridge when reinforcements of police arrived and I ceased to resist.

They took us to Marshall Square and after searching us put us in the cells. In one of my pockets they found a bunch of the offending leaflets. None were found on Benny. He told me afterwards that in the course of the struggle he had contrived to drop his packet over the bridge on to the railway line. Benny was put into a cell by himself. I had a couple of drunks for company. To Benny they said in the morning, 'The Dutch boy has confessed but we don't trust him. Tell us your version.' To me the story was that the Jew boy had confessed, etc. Neither of us gave them anything. When we were brought before Major Trigger, the head of the C.I.D., he said: 'I am not going to charge you under the municipal by-laws with pasting-up leaflets. You are going to get into much more serious trouble than that. I am going to charge you with sedition.' He ordered us back to the cells. A few hours later we were released.

Trigger no doubt thought that he had given us a good fright. Actually the police would have had a poor case had they taken us to court. Pannigennis had not caught us in the act of pasting leaflets and indeed the leaflet itself, in Bunting's careful legal opinion, was innocuous.

This incident occurred during a university vacation. I had not been to the botany laboratory for some days. Professor Moss, hearing a rumour that I was in prison, telephoned Marshall Square and offered to bail me out. Fortunately his help was not needed.

About a year or so later I was in need of a passport to go overseas and my application required the signature of a Justice of the Peace. I knew that Trigger was a J.P. so I went to him. He signed with the greatest affability.

My need of a passport arose from the fact that I had been awarded an 1851 Exhibition Scholarship and was going to England to study. I had completed the B.Sc. Honours course in 1925 and had been appointed junior lecturer in botany in 1926. The scholarship was for two years with a possible extension for a third year. On the advice of Professor Moss I was going to Downing College at Cambridge University to do research work in plant physiology under Dr F.F. Blackman. I left in September 1926. A crowd of communists came to the station to see me off and to sing the Red Flag. Bunting, on behalf of the Party, presented me with a wrist watch, to keep me up to scratch, he said. I had a parting present too from the students' biological society and five golden sovereigns from Dad who had decided to forgive and forget.

Bunting had not been enthusiastic about my going to Oxford or Cambridge. He considered that the life at either of these ancient universities was pleasant but insidious, as he knew from experience. He urged me rather to go to London University. I was inclined to agree with him, not that I feared that I might lose my revolutionary purpose but that I thought that in a non-residential university I should enjoy more freedom. But Professor Moss, who wanted me to work under Blackman, carried the day. So to Cambridge I went and did not regret the choice.

CHAPTER V

Cambridge and Moscow

MY three years at Cambridge have left me with the most pleasant memories of that English university and town. I was there not as an undergraduate but as a research student. The head of Downing College, Seward, was Professor of Botany in the University and a number of other leading botanists were there also. My work was at the Botany School and my supervisor was Dr F. F. Blackman, a pioneer in plant physiology in Britain. I developed a great admiration for Blackman.

What pleased me most about Cambridge was the independence of the students which was in sharp contrast to conditions in the University of the Witwatersrand. There were no student representative councils, no compulsory payment of sports dues. Students were gated at midnight, fined if they came in after 10 p.m., compelled to wear gowns in the streets after dark. But on the other hand the university exercised no control over student affairs. The debating society had its own Union, owned and managed by a student committee. Similarly the sports clubs were run by the students themselves and had their own buildings and grounds.

Cambridge provided a wealth of intellectual fare. I soon found my way into the Labour Club and there met about half-a-dozen fellow communists. They introduced me to Maurice Dobb, a fellow of Clare College and university lecturer in economics. The only avowed communist on the university staff, Dobb was regarded with pride. In his rooms our Left group, a fraction within the Labour Club, met frequently to enjoy the most stimulating discussions.

I also joined the Heretics, a rationalist society which had been considered daringly revolutionary when it was established about 1911, but which by 1927 had become most respectable, just an ordinary Cambridge society to which prominent people were invited to give lectures. Here I heard, among others,

Leonard Woolf, the writer, Adler the psychologist, W. Turner and T.S. Eliot, also Driberg, the anthropologist.

I made a number of good friends in the Labour Club, both men and women. It was the done thing at Cambridge in those years never to get excited about anything. The enthusiast, the fanatic, was gently ridiculed. This spirit of underplaying our enthusiasms existed also in the Labour Club. We did not sing the Red Flag but parodies of that famous song, such as the ribald version that begins:

The people's flag is palest pink—
It's not so red as you might think!

Our chairman, Donald Barber, was adept in composing and singing doggerel to various popular tunes, most of these aimed at caricaturing the doings of the ultra Left. I recall:

Put the thing through quickly,
Wage the class war slickly,
Hang the rich on lampost high
But don't hang me!
Stick to Marx my hearties,
Damn the Labour parties,
Keep the hell-fires burning bright
For the bourgeoisie.

It was perhaps due to this prevailing atmosphere of gentle mockery or possibly in some way my own fault that I never managed to become really interested in the British working class. The proletarians I encountered at Cambridge were meek and snobbish, corrupted as I thought by generations of fawning on the rich undergraduates. Unfortunately I never visited South Wales or had the chance of rubbing shoulders with the workers of the industrial north. Had I done this I might have developed more sympathy with the members of the British working class. As it was I considered them in many ways similar to the white aristocracy of labour in South Africa. While the white workers of my own country battened on the Natives, those of Britain, whether they realized it or not, owed their high standard of living to the exploitation of the colonial masses, the Indians,

Arabs, Chinese and Africans, who were exploited by British Imperialism.

Also I heard a story somewhat to the discredit of the movement. I was told how a workers' delegation to Moscow had visited a clinic and there heard a lecture given by a woman commissar on problems relating to abortion and birth control in the Soviet Union. The French, German, Scandinavian, Italian and other delegates had listened attentively and asked sensible questions. But the British delegates, in contrast, had blushed, sniggered or guffawed for all the world like a lot of prurient schoolboys.

In fairness to the left wing of the British proletariat I must quote another story concerning political naivety exhibited in Moscow. I did not hear this until much later. It is related by Ignazio Silone in *The God that Failed*, which appeared in 1950. He writes:

> They were discussing once, in a special commission of the Executive, the ultimatum issued by the central committee of the British trade unions, ordering its branches not to support the Communist-led minority movement, on pain of expulsion. After the representative of the British Communist Party had explained the serious disadvantage of both solutions, because one meant the liquidation of the minority movement and the other the exit of the minority from the trade unions, the Russian delegate, Piatnisky, put forward a suggestion which seemed as obvious to him as Columbus' egg: 'The branches should declare that they submit to the discipline demands and then, in practice, should do exactly the contrary.' The English Communist interrupted: 'But that would be a lie.' Loud laughter greeted this ingenuous objection, frank, cordial, interminable laughter, the like of which the gloomy offices of the Communist International had perhaps never heard before.

Back to my own experiences. Just before I left Cambridge I was honoured by a party given by the Left Group, the members of which were at that time chiefly working-class youths who had come to Cambridge on trade union scholarships. I had anticipated that we would get slightly tipsy, sing some of our ribald parodies and indulge in reminiscences concerning the lighter side of the labour movement. Instead what happened was that my hosts settled down in all sobriety to an evening of smutty stories. It was not at all my idea of a worthwhile party.

During vacations I made frequent cycling trips to London and when there always attended the meetings of the colonial committee of the Communist Party of Great Britain. There I met some well-informed and serious revolutionaries, among them Ralph Fox, who was later to die in Spain, Emile and Elinor Burns, who ran the Labour Research Bureau, also Clements Dutt, brother of Palme Dutt the communist writer. Clements was a tall, sallow Eurasian, devoted to his brilliant brother and to the movement. Their mother was Norwegian, their father Indian. I learnt much from these people and from the meetings of the colonial committee. We discussed the revolutionary movements in Cyprus, Palestine, Egypt, India, as well as the movements in Africa. I was able to contribute some first-hand information on the situation in South Africa.

The Cambridge Labour Club was affiliated to the University Labour Federation which held annual conferences in different centres. At these conferences one met socialist students from other universities as well as Labour M.P.s and trade union l aders. At a conference in Manchester I met Lord Olivier, whose book *The Anatomy of African Misery* had just been published by Leonard and Virginia Woolf at the Hogarth Press. I had long talks with him about South Africa and afterwards we exchanged a number of letters. I tried to show him that the policy he advocated for South African labour coincided closely with that of the Communist Party of South Africa; that the minority report of the Economic and Wage Commission of 1925, from which he quoted more than once approvingly in his book, owed much to the Communist Bill Andrews who was one of the signatories; that various liberal resolutions passed by the S.A. Trades Union Congress had been drafted by its Communist members.

I have always considered Olivier's book to be the most valuable critical analysis of the South African situation. He quotes the Economic Commission report as saying:

> . . . the contact of native and European has lasted too long and their economic co-operation is too intimate and well-

established for the native to be excluded from European areas and European industries. The provision of adequate native reserves has been delayed too long for it to be possible now to provide reserves within which it would be possible for the present native population of the Union to live without dependence on outside employment: and it was for too long the policy of the Union to drive the native by taxation and other devices to work for Europeans for it to be possible now to exclude him from the field of employment he is occupying.

The crazy quilt of Botha's Native Land Act of 1913 could no longer be considered possible. Hertzog's Native Land Bill was now attempting to achieve a degree of segregation. It was in a passage of Olivier's book that I found the title for my own book: *Time Longer Than Rope*.

Among the students who came from London to attend the U.L.F. conferences was Freda Utley who subsequently wrote *The Dream We Lost*. At that time she was a member of the I.L.P. Later she married a Russian diplomat, joined the Communist Party and went to live in the Soviet Union.

Of my communist fellow students at Cambridge the one I remember most vividly was Barney Woolf, a cockney Jew from the East End of London, a research worker in biochemistry. At every U.L.F. conference Woolf produced a small play, written and rehearsed during the conference, with the delegates as players. I remember one that was a take-off on Viscount Ennismore, a prominent member of the Cambridge Labour Club. The part of Nevermore in the play was acted by Piper, one of our Left group. He had evidently made a study of the lord's mannerisms for he gave a brilliant portrayal.

Ennismore, who subsequently renounced his title and became plain Mr Hare, was an extremely serious fellow with little sense of humour. On one occasion he and I were paired off to go canvassing for the Labour Party in the Cambridge borough elections. In our assigned section was a row of semi-detached cottages belonging to an institution for the aged and occupied by numerous aged spinsters. These dear old things knew nothing of politics, many of them were deaf and we had great difficulty in explaining why we had called on them. I became terribly bored and said: 'We're wasting our time here. Let's go on to these workingmen on our list. That will be more profitable.' But Ennismore, stickler for the letter of his instructions, would not budge and for the rest of that evening we went on trying to make contact with the ancient ladies.

I heard subsequently that Ennismore later joined a society the members of which pledged themselves to live on their share of the national income and to give the rest to good works. I believe the maximum allowed to members was found by dividing the national income by the number of the adult population with a proper allowance for children. The balance of each member's income was then handed over to the society which decided how it should be spent. Ennismore was in all things a man who practised what he preached.

One Sunday in my first summer at Cambridge we members of the Labour Club got on our bicycles and rode to Thaxted in Essex, a distance of some twenty miles. We went to visit Conrad Noel, the 'bolshevik parson'. In my early youth I had always taken it for granted that socialism, at any rate the more extreme variety, and atheism went hand in hand. To meet a leftist who was also a Christian was a new experience. But Conrad Noel was an Anglo-Catholic priest. The women who worshipped in his church all wore veils instead of hats. Music was provided by violins. A procession with banners marched round the inside of the church and incense was much in evidence. However the sermon preached by Conrad Noel resembled nothing so much as an ordinary socialist propagandist speech. I do not recall much reference to religion. He was dealing with economic problems. The service concluded with the singing of Blake's 'Jerusalem', which I was told that many Christian socialists wished to substitute for 'God save the King' as Britain's national anthem. After the service was over we all joined with the villagers in dancing Sir Roger de Coverley on the vicarage lawn. I was much puzzled by all this.

Seventeen years later I was on a visit to the Transkei, South Africa's largest Native reserve. I went to Engcobo where my African contact, the local postmaster, said: 'You must meet Father R.' R. was the head of the local Anglican mission. He invited me into his home, a large hut the walls of which were covered with books. He had a socialist library of hundreds of volumes. We discussed politics and I found that he belonged to the extreme Left with strong leanings to Trotskyism. Presently a bell rang. R., who was dressed as I was, in khaki shirt and shorts, sprang up, hastily donned a peculiar black garment, a cassock I understood, and placed an even more peculiar hat on hish ead. 'Excuse me,' he said, 'I must go and conduct a service. Back soon.' He departed at a brisk trot. In less than half-an-hour he returned, flung the black garb into a corner and resumed the conversation. That sort of thing still makes me gasp.

In the course of my stay in England I met examples of the various social classes so clearly to be observed in that country. My own relations there, my mother's people, the Wilson family, were very definitely middle class and included Dr Malcolm Wilson, then lecturer in Plant Pathology at Edinburgh University, also an electrical engineer, a bank official and four civil servants. My seven uncles and their wives were all most kind to me, made me welcome in their homes and showed me round various parts of the country. Politically they ranged from Uncle Ben who worked for the Admiralty and was a high Tory, to Uncle Fred who had left-liberal or even labour views.

My sole experience of the stately homes of England was on a short and not at all happy week-end that I spent with a county family. Nellie Paterson, a fellow student from Johannesburg, then at Newnham College, sent my name to Lady Frances Rider. Lady Frances had, during the 1914–18 war, taken an interest in the welfare of colonial officers in Britain. To rescue them from aimless wandering about the streets during periods of leave, she had arranged for them to be invited to stay at various upper-class homes where they would meet the best people and be nicely entertained. After the war she had continued this social activity, transferring her interest to students from the dominions who were temporarily resident in Britain. However, I do not think that Indians or any other non-Europeans were included.

Through the action of the Lady Frances committee I duly received an invitation from a certain Mrs C. to spend a short holiday in the country at Chepstow in Monmouthshire. The C. estate was situated in wooded hilly country not far from the ruins of Tintern Abbey. I gathered that Mr C. 'did a little farming' but lived chiefly on the rents derived from his property. He was a Conservative member of the local county council but his chief occupation seemed to be hunting. In season he hunted the fox in Monmouthshire, alternating this with months spent in Scotland hunting the stag. The large hall in his house was decorated with foxes' masks and deer's antlers.

Now I had gone on this visit with every careful intention of avoiding political discussion with my hosts. But fate was against me. When I came down to breakfast after my first night in the house I found Mrs C. excitedly waving a copy of the *Morning Post*. She was overjoyed because Chiang Kai Shek in China had suddenly turned against his communist allies. This was the first news I had heard of the Canton massacre and, though I carefully said nothing, my face must have shown my dismay. Presently Mrs C. asked me: 'Are you a socialist?' Thus challenged I could only answer: 'Yes.' From that moment my hostess hardly spoke to me.

Mr C., on the other hand, was not at all put out. He remained most affable and took me to see his fox-hounds of which he was very proud. He had been trying for years, he told me, to breed a strain of white fox-hounds. The ordinary hound has large black and brown patches on a white background. If the hounds were entirely white, he explained, they would be more readily seen against the dark background of hedges and trees and the huntsmen would more easily follow the chase. C. had succeeded to a large extent: the hounds he had bred were not yet pure white but they had lost the clear black and brown patches which were now represented by pale grey markings. We discussed breeding problems at some length and, though I knew little about the breeding of dogs, I gave him a general account of the Mendelian theory of inheritance which I thought should be useful to him as his methods had hitherto been purely empirical.

In the afternoon I went with the family to the service in their private chapel. There was a special pew for the master and his party. The congregation consisted mainly of the labourers and tenants on the estate. An ancient parson conducted the service. I learnt that his stipend was paid by Mr C. During the sermon the old man got rather tied up in a theological argument he was trying to develop. I was surprised when C. turned and winked at me.

Though I should have liked to see more of the fox-hounds and the surrounding country I felt that with Mrs C. continuing to cut me dead it would be injudicious to stay on. So the next morning I thanked my hosts and rode back to Cambridge.

Now in spite of all the interesting things I was seeing and doing in England, my interest in South African affairs remained unabated. I exchanged frequent letters with Bunting who kept me informed of the state of the C.P.S.A. I read the *Times* regularly and also the *Round Table*, both of which published many well-informed articles about my own country.

It was a great shock to me to learn, shortly after my arrival in England, that the communists had been expelled from the I.C.U. The damaging resolution had been passed at the I.C.U. annual conference held in Port Elizabeth in December 1926 and clearly it had had Kadalie's support. Some half-dozen leading I.C.U. officials who had come under communist influence were expelled. My friend Thomas Mbeki was one of these. However, he subsequently left the C.P. and was reinstated in the I.C.U.

It seemed that Kadalie was now finding the communists more of an embarrassment than a help. In the early days of the I.C.U. white supporters were few and every one was an asset. The communists had been welcome then. But by the end of 1926 the I.C.U. had become a force in the land and Kadalie was a national figure. Many whites who were not communists were now prepared to give him advice and assistance. Their advice often included the suggestion that the association of communists with the I.C.U. was damaging and actually hindering the growth of the organization. If the communists were dropped then affiliation with the International Federation of Trade Unions or even with the British Trade Union Congress would be possible. Moreover the communists in the I.C.U. had been annoying Kadalie. They were critical of the loose mismanagement of I.C.U. funds and ceased not, in and out of season, to demand popular control of the cash that came pouring in. Also they criticized the policy of the I.C.U. which was becoming ever less militant. They pointed out, for instance, that for many years the I.C.U. had not initiated a single strike and had not taken any action against the hated passes and other oppressions. In fact Kadalie was finding the communists awkward companions.

It was, of course, a simple matter to get rid of them. The cry of 'white interference' was raised. The motion for expulsion was put by Maduna of the Free State and seconded by Champion of Natal. It was carried by a narrow majority and the expelled communists walked out singing the Red Flag.

Thereafter, in 1927, Kadalie went on a triumphal tour of Europe. I met him at a summer school conducted by the Independent Labour Party, where he gave a lecture on the African trade union movement. He seemed pleased to see me and we parted amicably, though I criticized him severely for his action in expelling the communists.

It was at about this time that I met Norman Leys, an English doctor who had lived for a considerable time in East Africa and had written a critical book on Kenya. I visited him at his home at Brailsford near Derby, and continued to correspond with him at intervals until his death a few years ago. Leys was a pioneer in the cause of African emancipation, a true but critical friend of the black man. His books did much to acquaint educated Englishmen with the true state of affairs in the dark continent. He was no revolutionary but wrote with accuracy and sincerity of conditions in Kenya. He saw that the Africans were now inextricably involved with the white man's way of life. There was no solution in attempting to force the black man back into a tribalism which had ceased to be meaningful. What Leys strove for was less unwisdom in the policy of the rulers. A thing that greatly exercised him was what he saw as the essential pusillanimity of colour bar legislation. It seems that people, suffering from what he called the curse of privilege, could not see that if they indeed had the natural inherent superiority which they claimed to have, then they need not so fear the competition of the black man as to feel it necessary to deny him educational opportunity. He considered that the key move in the change of policy he urged must be the giving to the votes of educated Africans the same value as to votes of Europeans, which indeed is the essence of democracy. Africans, unlike Indians, had no ancient civilization of their own to oppose to European civilization: all they wanted was to be allowed to learn the white man's ways. If this were not recognized by the white rulers then a dark future of violence might follow. In *A Last Chance in Kenya** he was later to write:

**A Last Chance in Kenya*, published by Leonard and Virginia Woolf at the Hogarth Press. 1931.

There are men who say that no just cause is ever helped by violence. The terrible truth is that no nation or race or caste has ever won its liberty without either the use or the threat of violence.

Already when I knew Leys he was fearing the violence that later shocked the world in the cruel murders of Mau-Mau.

Before ending this somewhat disjointed account of my memories of my years in England, I must make some mention of my visit to Moscow in the summer of 1928. I went there as a delegate of the Communist Party of South Africa to attend the Sixth Congress of the Communist International. My seniors in the delegation were Sidney Bunting and his wife Rebecca whom I joined in London on their way to the Soviet Union. I had been included as the third delegate chiefly because I happened to be in England.

For the Buntings and for me this Congress was to prove a heart-breaking experience. When we met in London we were filled with the highest hopes and anticipations, confident that we had a good report to make of work done in South Africa, certain that we had earned commendation. The Party had by now made considerable progress in going Native and by this time, after the middle of 1928, was predominantly African in composition. It had built up purely African branches in a number of areas, had won to its ranks certain gifted young Africans who were developing as leaders, and had already helped to establish a number of African trade unions, not vague all-in organizations like Kadalie's I.C.U. now in sad collapse, but regular industrial unions such as the Laundry Workers' Union, the Clothing Workers' Union and the Bakers' Union. Real progress had been made. We felt that we had no reason to feel any shame over the Party's achievements. And so, like the innocents we were, we journeyed happily towards our doom.

We paused for a few days in Berlin where the Reds had fought on barricades on May Day just a few weeks earlier. The German C.P. was still powerful, still growing in strength, and was then fighting the Social Democrats for leadership of the working class. But there was another party in the field which had not been there on Bunting's previous visit to Germany in

1922. Hitler and his Nazis were becoming a power in the land. We did not see any brown-shirts or red-front fighters and we were unlucky in that there were no big meetings during the few days we were there, but posters we saw everywhere, chiefly Nazi and Communist.

Idly and happily we wandered in the streets, eating cherries, the red-fleshed cherries with their sharp-sweet flavour, from a paper bag, at a cost of a few pfennig a kilogram. As we strolled, carefully collecting the cherry-pips in the bag, I recalled how we had walked the streets eating buns while we were canvassing for C.P.Glass in a provincial council election campaign—it must have been in 1924. Glass had not been elected. Bunting was the most delightful though not the easiest of travel companions. In small things as in great he had to look judicially on all sides of any question before carefully making up his mind. I recall how we stood on a street corner one morning discussing whether we should go to Potsdam or the Tiergarten. Bunting stood considering all aspects of the problem. In the end he decided for the Tiergarten and so we rushed off only to see our bus disappearing round a corner.

No pause in Warsaw. On we sped to Moscow with the light of fanaticism in our eyes. On our arrival we at once encountered hostility and contempt. Along with delegates from all over the world we were welcomed with the pomp of bands and banners and brave speeches. But all the blare and glare could not conceal from us the real lack of comradeship. We had expected to report progress but could not find anyone willing to listen to us for even five minutes. One, Comrade Bennett, alias Petrovsky, alias a whole string of other names, told us that the whole question of the Communist Party of South Africa would be decided by the Anglo-American Secretariat which included Africa in its field and of which he was secretary. The first words Comrade Bennett-Petrovsky spoke to us, by way of greeting, were: 'We are going to attack you!' This was discouraging. Worse was to follow.

The Executive Committee of the Communist International which had hitherto taken little interest in the South African section had at this stage begun to issue definite directives to the C.P.S.A. It had drafted a resolution on South Africa and had put forward as the main slogan for the Party, 'an independent

Native republic as a stage towards a workers' and peasants' government.' This resolution was to be discussed at the Moscow Congress. But discussion, it emerged, did not mean that anything we had to say would be listened to.

Bunting and indeed with him the majority of the South African Party were opposed to the slogan, which they realized would make it impossible for them to continue work among the white workers. I shared this view, agreeing with the Buntings that on purely tactical grounds the slogan was inopportune. The Party had already openly declared its belief that the African majority must inevitably exercise its powers as such. At the same time we had no wish to antagonize the white workers as a whole in particular the white trade unionists. As orthodox Marxists, we believed that these were potential allies of the black workers in their struggle for freedom. 'Workers of the world unite!' was our slogan at meetings. And in all honesty I cannot conceive of a better or grander one. When charged in the courts or by hostile critics with being racialists we were always able to show that we believed in the 'united front of the workers irrespective of colour.'

However, during the so-called discussion in Moscow I suggested an alternative slogan: 'An independent workers' and peasants' South African Republic with equal rights for all toilers irrespective of colour, as a basis for a Native majority government.' This, of course, was rejected without discussion of any possible merit it might have had. In fact it had none. Actually as myself a journalist and soap-box orator I felt that all these versions were in fact small but clumsy essays on policy rather than slogans. I could not imagine the new slogan on a poster or a banner, or in headlines to an article.

Sidney and Rebecca and I now put forward arguments on these lines, the importance of our white trade unionist allies, but we found that our arguments were simply not listened to and we were told in effect that whatever we said it would not affect the outcome: the draft resolution would be passed and we in South Africa would have to make the best of it. We knew, of course, that the Woltons had sent in a written minority report.

But the real misery of the Congress was the uncomradely atmosphere, the contemptuous indifference with which we were treated and against which we were helpless. Rebecca Bunting, in particular, was shocked and dismayed, for she had attended the Fourth Congress in 1922 and then there had been a spirit of hope and comradeship with much exchange of news of conditions in the various countries. We now had the unpleasant experience of being cold-shouldered by some of the Negro delegates from the United States who had been told that we were typical South African white chauvinists. Their leader, Ford, would not even speak to us. I thought this particularly unfair to Bunting, for he, more than any other leader in South Africa, had fought in season and out, for the rights of the blacks and for their inclusion, first in the International Socialist League and then in the Communist Party. It was perhaps this cruel accusation of white chauvinism, so utterly misplaced, that made all three of us so deeply unhappy, so vulnerable to the atmosphere of hostility about us. When Bunting was making his final speech in the sub-committee which was to decide the fate of the resolution on South Africa, two of the American delegates, Lovestone and Pepper, retired from the table to carry on a conversation in a corner of the room. Bennett-Petrovsky, the chairman, sat listening languidly and with a completely bored expression: clearly it did not matter a jot what Bunting said, the result would be the same. I protested that the two should return to the table and pay attention to what was being said, but though my protest was upheld and the two returned somewhat resentfully to the meeting, I was aware that it had been a useless gesture.

My impressions of the Comintern functionaries were on the whole not favourable. They seemed to be a hard-bitten gang of bureaucrats, committed to following the Comintern line regardless of where it might lead. There was an atmosphere of intrigue and wire-pulling, of factions and cliques, each currying favour with the leadership, each with its petty axe to grind, which was in sharp and most dismal contrast with Bunting's selfless enthusiasm and patent honesty. These functionaries did not resemble in any way those people of the future of whom we socialists often entertain such exalted ideas nor were they at all like the eager enthusiasts whom Rebecca had met at the Fourth Congress in 1922.

Of leading figures in the Russian revolution a number were

conspicuously absent. It seemed injudicious to mention them. Trotsky, Zinoviev and Kamenev had disappeared from the scene. Trotsky was then in Siberia. Of his Russian supporters none, so far as we could judge, was present at the Congress. Two American delegates, with whom I shared a room at the hotel, confided to me their Trotskyist sympathies but only when they were slightly drunk. Otherwise they kept quiet. A typed copy of Trotsky's thesis on the situation in China was circulated among some of the delegates, apparently with official knowledge. It was a damaging attack on Stalin's policy in China. Of this Clements Dutt said to me in all seriousness: 'Trotsky's analysis is of course correct, but I'm sorry to say that Trotsky is no longer a communist.' The implication was clear: a communist must follow the line and failure to conform, even objection on the soundest theoretical grounds, put one outside the fold. The policy was now, 'My Comintern, right or wrong!'

Stalin I saw twice. On each occasion he showed himself for a minute or two at the back of the stage and then disappeared. The figurehead of the Congress was the doomed Bukharin. It was he who made the opening speech and took the chair at every important session. We heard later that his fate had already been decided. He had clashed with Stalin on fundamental questions and the Political Bureau had decided against him. His removal had, however, been postponed for tactical reasons until the Sixth Congress should be over.

Though preoccupied with the Congress and deeply troubled about the resolution on South Africa, we managed to see a good deal of Moscow and a little of the surrounding country. Russia was then at the end of NEP, Lenin's New Economic Policy, the period of open trading and compromise with capitalist forms, and was about to embark on its first Five Year Plan. Moscow was a city of contrasts. We duly admired the well-planned factories and the towering blocks of workers flats, but even in these observed also some inefficiency and inconvenience by western standards. We saw Red Army soldiers as they marched singing along the Tverskaya, on their way, we were told, to their weekly bath. The streets were thronged with the drably-clothed communistic workers while beggars importuned us on every corner and pickpockets were active everywhere. The Park of Culture and Rest was impressive but bugs infested the fine hotel where we were lodged; there were no plugs in baths and washbasins; the sanitation stank. A good Woolworth store seemed to be what was needed. We visited a well-patronized black market and saw much evidence of squalid overcrowding in the new flats as well as in old houses.

I wrote my impressions in a series of articles for *The South African Worker* but made no mention of bugs or bath plugs. I waxed enthusiastic about the Soviet films we had seen, particularly Eisenstein's *Potemkin* and Pudovkin's rendering of Gorki's *Mother*.

After the Congress delegates were offered their choice of various free tours. I very much wanted to join the one to Soviet Asia, to see for myself how the backward peoples of Turkestan were developing under the new regime. I felt that here might be some lessons for us in South Africa. Unfortunately I had to return immediately to Cambridge to negotiate the extension of my scholarship for a third year, this having been granted in the first place for two years only.

I met the Buntings later in London on their way back. They were despondent about the Black Republic resolution but determined to go back to South Africa prepared to make the best of it. Bunting had, he told me, asked Bennett-Petrovsky in view of the slogan to compose an election manifesto for use for a Party candidate in the Cape. Petrovsky had not found it convenient to do this.

There was never any question of Bunting's absolute loyalty to the instructions of the Comintern even when he did not agree. For my part, also in loyalty, I now tried to persuade myself that our failure to understand must be due to some lack of theoretical knowledge. I had written a letter on these lines to the C.P.S.A. and had sent a copy to Bunting. He disagreed completely. He could not share my view as to any failure of comprehension on our part. He considered that there was no great question of theory behind the slogan and no lack of theory in our common-sense objections to it.

Of this unhappy slogan Bunting later wrote to me from Johannesburg calling it 'the hundred-word slogan.' In its final form, decreed by Moscow, it ran 'A South African Native Republic as a stage towards a Workers' and Peasants' Government with full protection and equal rights for all national minorities.' This seemed to spell doom for our relations with the white trade unionists. However, for me the immediate future was another year at Cambridge.

The Party in South Africa had by this time a considerable following among the African workers while the I.C.U. was now facing disintegration and collapse. The new 'Red' unions, founded by the Party, were proving a source of fresh inspiration and strength. Benny Weinbren, who was president of the new Non-European Trade Union Federation, wrote to me towards the end of my time at Cambridge, suggesting, that I should take over the secretaryship of the new body. After giving thought to the matter I replied accepting the offer. It would mean abandoning botany and an academic career, but I made the decision with no great feelings of regret, nor did I feel compunction over the use I had made of my scholarship years. I had learned much from my work with Blackman and, though I did not realize it then, this knowledge was to be my stand-by in what later became the driving power of my life.

CHAPTER VI

African Comrades in 1929

THE Communist Party organization in Johannesburg to which I returned in July of 1929, was astonishingly different from the one I had left behind three years earlier. I had known of the changes, chiefly from Bunting's letters, but to see them was something else. And I reflected with some satisfaction that though I had not been there to witness the transition, yet I had played some part in helping to bring it about.

In place of its old headquarters in the Trades Hall among the white aristocrats of labour, the Party now had offices at 41A Fox Street, in the heart of the Ferreirastown slum, at that time inhabited largely by Africans and other Non-Europeans. Here the Party paper, the *South African Worker,* was printed on an ancient cropper with dilapidated type, but no longer exclusively in English. More than half the paper was now devoted to articles in the vernacular, in Zulu, Xhosa, Sotho and Tswana. The Party office was a centre of bustling activity for the various new African trade unions used it as their headquarters. There was also a night school with more than a hundred pupils. At first many of the newcomers were confused as to the nature of Party membership. Asked to produce evidence that they were members of the Party, they would produce a trade union card or a night school pass. This was shocking to the Comintern purists in our midst but as time went on things began to sort themselves out. The new trade unions were organized in a Non-European Trade Union Federation, with the help of Bill Andrews who took the chair at the inaugural meeting. Benny Weinbren was Chairman of the Federation and Thibedi was chief organizer. Thibedi had been with the Party from the days of the I.S.L. For many years he had been the only black man in the movement. Now he displayed talents for organization which made him invaluable as general factotum. He had a natural genius for getting people together as required for special meetings, whether workers in some particular industry, location residents, a group of women, unemployed workers or whatever was wanted at the moment. It was Thibedi who had organized and run the original Party night school, started in 1925. This was held on certain evenings in a Native church building rented for the purpose in Ferreirastown. There by candlelight, certain enthusiastic white comrades tried to teach semi-literate Africans to read involved passages of Bukharin's *ABC of Communism*. It was all very amateur but we felt we were contributing to the beginning of something new and grand.

The white comrades who had brought about these great changes in the Party were in the first place the Buntings. Also Douglas Wolton and his wife Molly Zelikowitz, who had come up from Cape Town some two years earlier, had proved valuable assets. Douglas was now editor of the *South African Worker*. And in charge of the new night school was Charles Baker, a retired teacher, a pensioner. Baker was a fiery little man, an ex-Roman Catholic and now a violent atheist. His chief business in life was to denounce religion as 'the opium of the people' and to castigate all missionaries as 'agents of imperialism.' He was fond of quoting Swinburne:

> We have done with the kisses that sting,
> The thief's mouth red from the feast,
> The blood on the hands of the king,
> And the lie at the lips of the priest.

Under Baker's expert guidance the night school flourished. It was a great advance on the old school but had still many disadvantages. It was held on the ground floor of what was actually a slum tenement. There were few desks so that pupils sat on benches or on the floor. There were no blackboards so comrades blackened the walls. The near-by rooms were occupied by poor white down-and-outs, by prostitutes and methylated spirit drinkers. Lessons would be interrupted by loud stamping from the floor above or by drunkards who forced their way in. We taught reading, writing and simple arithmetic and held occasional lectures and debates on general topics of working class interest. The teachers, as before, were enthusiastic white comrades. We were not expert in teaching but we improved as we went on. And our pupils were hungry for knowledge. I remember hearing one comrade trying to explain the meaning of the word 'monotonous'. He said it meant 'all on one note,' which left his hearers little wiser. But the chief virtue in our teachers was reliability, willingness to come regularly, once or twice a week, to cope with the lessons. Night passes were a great nuisance. Every African, if he wishes to avoid arrest after 9 p.m., must carry a special pass written and signed by his employer. Many white employers were not at all willing to sign passes for attendance at night school, specially a communist night school, so that the teachers had to write out these passes themselves. This was a laborious and time-wasting business. Later we had forms printed on which only the bearer's name, the date and a signature had to be written.

Of African leaders, apart from Thibedi, we now had a number who had joined the Party. Among these were two ex-school teachers, Albert Nzula and Edwin Mofutsanyana. Nzula was a natural orator whose talents were used not only in location meetings among Africans, but also in our Sunday evening meetings on the City Hall steps where he impressed white audiences. Also, from the ranks of African workers, we now had Gana Makabeni and Moses Kotane. Kotane, who had had little formal education, came to the Party through the night school. He proved himself an insatiable reader. No argument was too abstruse for him to tackle and he would turn up regularly with lists of difficult words for his teacher to explain. He became in the end a leading Party theoretician.

In country districts too the Party had made progress. At Vereeniging, refused admission to the location, the Party held a meeting outside which was attended by a great crowd. Several hundred joined, including many women. At Potchefstroom, where Thibedi had held a large meeting interrupted by the police who arrested him on a charge of inciting to hostility between the races, almost the entire location had joined the Party. These people were impressed by Bunting's defence of Thibedi, a defence which secured an acquittal. After the release of Thibedi, Wolton started a speech from a wagon on which the red flag was flying. He was attacked by a group of hostile whites. Natives came to his defence and general fighting ensued. White leadership has often been a hindrance to the Party, for

Natives, not without reason, are suspicious of all whites, even of those who claim to be their friends. But here they saw white communists attacked by the local whites whom they knew as their oppressors. As a result of all this the Party gained some two thousand members.

At Evaton and Ventersdorp branches had been established. I remember a meeting at Ventersdorp where I met John Marks another African teacher who had joined the Party. The meeting was typical of the usual C.P. or I.C.U. meeting in a rural location. It was held on a Sunday morning. The organizers had provided a table on which the speaker stood, flanked by two interpreters. The audience assembled gradually until a hundred or more were present. As usual a European member of the local police force was there with notebook and pencil to report any word which he thought might incriminate the speaker. I remember on this occasion introducing the new song Mayibuye which J.N. Tantsi of the African National Congress had helped me to compose. *Mayibuy'i Africa*—Let Africa come back was a slogan of the Congress and the nearest that Africans had come to formulating in their own language the ultimate aim of their movement. The song Tantsi and I had made went to the tune of Clementine.

Mayibuye!	Let it come back!
Tina sizwe esi ntsundu Sikalel'i Afrika eyahlutw' obawu betu besese bu'mnyameni.	We brown people bless Africa which was taken from our fathers when they were in darkness.
Mayibuye, mayibuye, mayibuy'i Afrika! Makapele namapase Sitoli nkululeko.	Let it return, let it return, Let Africa return to us! Down with passes. We demand freedom.

The tune was easy and all Africans are gifted in song. We soon had the crowd singing the words with a will and putting in their own harmonized variations. A memorable experience.

Soap-box oratory was all very well and I was able to help in the night school and also on the *S.A. Worker*, but what permanent place I was to find in this new scheme of things was a problem which grew daily more pressing. As to the work Benny Weinbren had offered me it did not materialize. The situation in the Non-European Trade Union Federation was not precisely as it had seemed to be when in Cambridge I had read Benny's optimistic letters. In fact the new organization was extremely loose. The central committee of which Benny was chairman was without funds and the new trade unions were as yet poor in financial standing. Also many of the secretaries of these unions did not approve the idea of a general secretary. I quite saw their point of view. If I had had private means I might have done something about this: organized some new unions, collected dues, built up the organization to the point where it could have afforded to pay me a modest salary. In later years other Party members did just this and made a good job of it. I felt, however, that trade union organization was not my line: I was not really, in spite of Weinbren's backing, the right man for the job. Also I had to earn my living.

For some months I busied myself with Party work, teaching in the school, making posters, speaking at meetings, but my funds were running low and I could not see what to do about it. In the end I went to Professor Moss and asked him if he could find me any post as a scientist. Moss was rather annoyed with me for my continued fanaticism for the Left movement. He had hoped that I might by this time have sown my political wild oats got it all out of my system and been prepared to live a steady life as a scientist. He did not fail to point out that it was not to promote soap-box fireworks that my scholarship had been given to me. I admitted this. However, Moss proved a good friend and negotiated with Dr Pole Evans, head of the Government Department of Plant Industry. I was offered a post as research worker in the Low Temperature Research Laboratory at Cape Town. 'This is a Government appointment,' said Moss, warning me. 'You will not be allowed to take part in political activities, and in fact this is the best thing for you.'

So I travelled to Cape Town at Government expense, my first experience of travel on a first-class ticket, and arrived there in time to start my new work on 1 December 1929. Research on problems of fruit storage was then a new thing in South Africa where the great importance of storage, especially in view of the time needed for transport to markets in Europe, was only just beginning to be recognized. The laboratory was a make-shift affair in Parliament Street. Later it was to blossom into an imposing and well-equipped building near the docks. My chief, Griffiths, was no biologist but a competent refrigeration engineer. I was put on to a rather dull routine investigation of the sugar-content of grapes and had to make weekly journeys to Paarl to collect my samples. I was disappointed too in the salary I was paid. This was about twenty-five pounds a month, less than I had earned as a junior lecturer at Witwatersrand University before I left for Cambridge. It was in fact the starting salary of an ordinary B.Sc. graduate and no allowance was made for my M.Sc. and Ph.D. degrees nor for my three years' experience of plant respiration research at Cambridge. I could not help feeling that I had sold my birthright for a rather mean mess of pottage, and so when opportunities offered for political activities in Cape Town I found I had no qualms in taking part in them.

The African National Congress was at that time very active in Cape Town itself and throughout the Western Cape Province. It was led by two young Africans of great energy and eloquence, Bransby Ndobe and Elliot Tonjeni. On Dingaan's Day, 16 December, at a large meeting held on the Parade, straw effigies of Hertzog and Pirow, leaders of the Government, were burned with enthusiasm. The meeting then formed a procession of over a thousand, which with bands and bright banners marched through the streets. I did not speak at this meeting but helped Ndobe to lead the march.

The problem of the influence of economic pressure upon thought and action is of course an old one in the revolutionary movement. Cecil Rhodes is said to have maintained that every man has his price. As I see it, it is mainly a question of the amount of importance one attaches to various freedoms. It is good to be free to express one's views and to cock a snook at a society that one considers reactionary, oppressive and unjust. It is good also to have money to buy food and clothes and housing and to spend on other desirable things. The reformer who has no private income and who is not supported financially by the movement to which he belongs is usually forced to make some sort of compromise.

Here I am suggesting that I might have been prepared to give up my political activity if my job in the civil service had proved more attractive. If I had been permitted to undertake real research there instead of routine records and if I had been paid a salary two or three times what I was receiving, would I have acted differently? I do not know. The point was that I felt a well-nigh overwhelming impulse to carry on in the movement and the fact that I was doing no useful work and being paid a miserable pittance for it encouraged me to give free rein to my desires.

I acted quite deliberately when I got into touch with Bransby and Tonjeni who welcomed me as a helper. They were then organizing the Dingaan's Day protest demonstration against a bill which Pirow, then the Nationalist Minister of Justice, had introduced in Parliament. This bill, an amendment to the Riotous Assemblies Act, would give the Minister full powers, without reference to the courts, to order any person to leave any area if he considered that the presence of that person in that area might lead to the creation of feelings of hostility between Natives and Europeans. This additional power which the Government now asked Parliament to confer on it was considered necessary in view of the failure of an earlier piece of legislation to curtail the activities of agitators among the Africans. The Hostility Clause of the Native Administration Act had made it a criminal offence for anyone to say or do anything 'with the intention of promoting feelings of hostility between Natives and Europeans'. Though many arrests and charges under this clause had been made during the past two years, the authorities had failed to secure any convictions. The Supreme Court had laid emphasis on the word 'intention'. It was laid down that mere criticism of the Government or its members was not an offence even if it did annoy the authorities and even cause feelings of hostility in some quarters. An example was the case against Sidney Bunting for speeches delivered by him in 1929 during his election campaign in the Transkei. Bunting won his case on appeal to the Supreme Court at Grahamstown. A consequence of this legal decision was Pirow's amendment to the Riotous Assemblies Act.

The choice of Dingaan's Day as the occasion for the protest against the new measure may require some explanation. On 16

December 1838, a commando of Voortrekkers had defeated the Zulu army of Dingaan at the Battle of Blood River in Natal. This victory was a turning point in the fortunes of the Voortrekkers and the anniversary of the battle has ever since been celebrated by white South Africans as a sort of national day. The suggestion, often made, that whites on this day celebrate the victory of civilization over barbarism, was now beginning to be resented by politically-minded Africans and from 1929 onwards the African National Congress began to hold its counter-demonstrations on that day.

When Ndobe and Tonjeni told me of their proposed meeting I made the suggestion that the protest might be made more dramatic by burning an effigy of Pirow. We had done this with great success at a meeting in Johannesburg shortly before I left for Cape Town. They thought it an excellent idea but wanted to burn two guys, one of Pirow and one of Hertzog, the Prime Minister. I helped to make the guys.

My participation in this meeting was almost certainly reported to the authorities. I had not made a speech but as I was the only white person who marched in the procession to the Houses of Parliament which followed on the burning of the effigies I must have been conspicuous. Towards the end of January, I duly received a letter from the Secretary for Agriculture, asking me to call on him at his office. He told me that it had come to his notice that I was engaging in political activities. He quoted the regulation under which such activities were forbidden to civil servants and gave me one month's notice of dismissal. My job would terminate at the end of February.

My experience of life as a civil servant had lasted just three months. I now had the awkward task of writing a letter to Professor Moss in which I tried to explain what had happened.

CHAPTER VII

The Happy Year

I WAS once more without a job. But I soon worked out a very clear idea of how I could find a permanent place in the movement. I wrote to Bunting and suggested that I should undertake the production of the Party newspaper in Cape Town. I had found a Coloured printer who was prepared to do the actual printing, the machining, of the paper at a reasonable figure, if I could bring him the forms on galleys ready made up in pages. I proposed to learn type-setting and to buy the necessary type. Bunting and the Party executive in Johannesburg were more than a little sceptical of my ability to do this, especially as I proposed to produce a weekly paper. However if the scheme could be carried out, they thought it would be an excellent thing. The *South African Worker*, nominally a monthly, had fallen much behind its schedule and was now appearing irregularly, at intervals of six weeks or more. The executive finally agreed to let me go ahead. I began to collect money for buying the type and also to learn something about type-setting.

The local branch of the Communist Party liked the idea of Cape Town becoming the publishing centre of the Party organ. It was, after Johannesburg, the most important branch of the Party. Nearly a thousand miles away from the head office it often felt neglected and ignored. The new arrangement, it was thought, would give more status to Cape Town.

I already knew the Cape Town comrades fairly well from my previous visits to that centre from 1925 onwards. The sheet anchor of the branch was Comrade Joseph. He had been connected with revolutionary movements in the Cape for a generation. Among the Coloured* comrades was John Gomas,

---

*Perhaps it should be explained that the term Coloured in South Africa refers to persons of mixed blood or to Malays or Hottentots. The Coloured people are chiefly the descendants of the slaves who were set free in 1834. They number over one million and live chiefly in the urban areas of Cape Town and Kimberley and in the rural districts of the Western Cape

who had joined the Party while on the executive of the I.C.U. which had later expelled him in the anti-Communist purge of 1926. Our chief African supporter was Josiah Ngedlane who ran the sub-branch at Ndabeni, the Native location about five miles from Cape Town.

An old Cape Town socialist, Ridout, had a newsagent's business in the suburb of Wynberg. In a shed in the yard behind his shop he had a cropper machine operated by a Coloured employee. Ridout supplemented his income from the newsagency by undertaking various small printing jobs. On Comrade Joseph's suggestion I went to see Ridout and he readily agreed that his man should give me a few lessons in type-setting. I practised furiously.

In the meantime I was making a number of new and interesting friends. The most exciting of these was Lancelot Hogben, then professor of zoology in the University of Cape Town. Hogben, at the height of his intellectual powers and in his most iconoclastic phase, was happily shocking the local philistines as well as some quite nice people in Cape Town. He had become the centre of a group of intelligent and charming people. One of these was Winifred Lunt, a lively girl from England, a mathematics teacher then taking a sabbatical year studying education at the University. I was later to marry her.

Hogben had named his house Xenopus, after the South African clawed toad, an animal now famous among physiologists. At Xenopus, Hogben, who had a great liking for drama, led me mysteriously aside, took up a rug in the dining room and showed me a cellar below. Access to this unattractive cavern was by lifting two planks of the floor. 'If ever you are on the run,' he said, 'come and hide here. Nobody knows about this cellar.' He told me also of the commodious boot of his splendid new car, a bright blue Nash which flashed conspicuously along de Waal Drive to and from the University at odd hours, for Hogben's physiology experiments required readings to be taken at intervals during the night. In this car I could, he

---

Province. The Malays are Muslims and are descended from political prisoners brought to the Cape from the East Indies in the eighteenth century. Later the Coloured people spread north and now, in 1965, there are many in Johannesburg where they are employed in garment making and in other secondary industries.

said, lie hidden in not too much discomfort and be secretly transported if need arose. I thanked him appropriately but privately hoped I should never have occasion to take up either offer. I have a great dislike of small confined spaces.

Hogben, in spite of his flamboyant enthusiasm, I considered too much of an individualist to make a good communist. He was at the time engaged in a controversy in the columns of the British *Labour Monthly* on the topic of dialectical materialism, his opponent being Clements Dutt. He was objecting to the attempt, first made by Engels, to apply the concepts of dialectics to biology. While I agreed with him and had indeed carried on this same argument with Willy Kalk in the days of the Y.C.L. when argument was the stuff of life, I did not now find the subject so interesting as he did, for I had long ago decided that many of the theoretical aberrations of Marxism were unimportant. Most of them, in my view, had little bearing on the practical aspects of the class struggle. But Hogben delighted in polemics, in all wordy war, in wit and subtlety. 'People will not ask the right questions,' he would say happily, 'because they're afraid of getting the left answers.'

He combined his leftist position in politics with strong opposition to religions, nationalisms and all such. He disliked flags and national anthems and did not care at all whom or how many he annoyed by his gestures of iconoclasm. Winifred, who had first met Hogben on a Union-Castle liner on a holiday trip to England, told me of an incident of the voyage. It seems that people on ships tend to become somewhat outside versions of their normal personalities. The ship's orchestra had the habit of playing God Save the King rather frequently, in fact at the end of every music session, often three times a day. Each time this happened everyone would stand, struggling up from deck chairs and rugs, and remain standing during the anthem. Many of the younger men, assuming solemn expressions, would stand at attention and salute. Hogben, however, remained seated or leaning on the bulwarks deep in conversation. This so greatly incensed some of his patriotic fellow-voyagers who in any case resented what they considered Hogben's intellectual snobbery, his exclusiveness in choice of companionship on deck, that they formed a plan to abduct him from his cabin at night and give him a salutary ducking in the swimming bath. Hogben was of slight physique, he would have resisted like a maniac and would almost certainly have suffered injury. But on board also were a number of his students from the university who, getting wind of this mischief, constituted themselves into a bodyguard so that for the rest of the voyage there were always some of them not far from Hogben while he was on deck and they took turns on duty outside his cabin during the night. The ducking did not happen.

Another provocative incident occurred at a University dance. Midnight took Hogben by surprise and found him dancing with his wife, Enid Charles, also a biologist. After the briefest pause the band struck up God Save the King and everyone on the dance floor at once assumed a respectful attitude. On which Hogben, abandoning his partner, made his conspicuous way across the floor to find a chair on which he sat until the national anthem ended.

Parties at Xenopus were rarely formal, almost never by invitation. What happened was that people dropped in, especially at weekends and then the most stimulating conversations would follow. As the hour grew later Hogben waxed more brilliant and outrageous. At such casual gatherings I met most of the Hogben set.

Of these Frederick Bodmer was probably the one from whom I learnt most. He was a Swiss, at that time lecturer in German at the university, also a serious student of politics. An eccentricity for which he was famous was his liking for renting some large tumble-down house, of which there were a number in the surburbs of Cape Town, and there camping in one or two of the rooms. By nature indifferent to luxury and unwilling to burden himself with possessions beyond bare necessities which included a bed and a frying pan, he led a life stripped of all trimmings, a life that was simple and even austere. It seemed to me a good life. In his bedroom was a narrow divan bed, always placed in the centre of the room, a few cushions, two or three chairs, a table for his typewriter, perhaps a cupboard, little else. Here we gathered for endless talk and argument, to listen to our host and presently to eat cheese and grapes, drink cocoa or Moulin Rouge, a cheap natural wine of the Cape. Bodmer was the ideal host, casual in his erudition, throwing off carelessly brilliant aphorisms in his oddly accented English. Here we discussed semantics as well as politics. Bodmer was already planning the book he was to write later, *The Loom of Language*, now a classic in its field.

At Xenopus, Bodmer, whose bohemianism suffered occasional lapses into an odd teutonic formalism, complained to Enid that the Hogben children did not accord him a proper respect. They addressed him as they heard the grown-ups do as 'Bodmer'. There were four children. Enid told the eldest, Sylvia, then nearly twelve, to say with exaggerated courtesy, 'Herr Doktor Bodmer, you seem to be an unassimilable alien.'

At Xenopus parties, Hogben, who shared my passion for Swinburne, would sometimes recite in his high clear voice with its languid faintly plaintive Cambridge accent long passages from memory, especially the verse.

> Thou hast conquered, O pale Galilean;
> The world has grown grey from thy breath,

Sometimes he would recite the whole of the chorus from Atalanta which tells of the mystery of man and which ends:

> They gave him light in his ways,
>   And love and a space for delight,
> And beauty and length of days,
>   And night, and sleep in the night.
> His speech is a burning fire;
>   With his lips he travaileth;
> In his heart is a blind desire,
>   In his eyes foreknowledge of death;
> He weaves and is clothed with derision;
>   Sows and he shall not reap;
> His life is a watch or a vision
>   Between a sleep and a sleep.

And indeed, though most of the Hogben set were biologists, a love of poetry was much in evidence. Here were Zoond and Zwarenstein, young lecturers at the university. Zoond, darkly handsome, was a pugnacious atheist. He would recite Rupert Brooke's poem of the cosmology of fish and end with dramatic quietness: 'There shall be no more land, say fish.'

Zwarenstein had a passion for the mountain and would lead small parties on Sunday climbs. We would carry with us lunch supplies of meat which we grilled over a fire, coffee and a bottle of Moulin Rouge. Zwarenstein always brought a book of poetry and would ask Muriel Johns or Winifred, whom we called Belinda, to read to us as we rested about the dying fire before the downward climb in the late afternoon. Muriel was a botanist, then working at Kirstenbosch, the national botanic reserve near the university. She had a lovely deep voice, a wealth of glorious dark red hair, a quiet reserved manner. Belinda had a lighter voice and less obvious beauty. She was a good climber and a lively companion. About us was the sun-drenched fragrance that was the breath of the mountain, the scent of pines and of the crushed maquis.

Other girls in the Hogben set were Laetitia Starke and Dora Weintroub, botanists then working at Kirstenbosch. Laetitia, we called her Starkey, had a lively wit and was a passionate non-racialist. Later she married, went to live in Buenos Aires, was lost to us. Dora, perhaps less clever, was gifted with a grace of living that can hardly be described. She had been a fellow student of mine in the old days at Wits, but owing to my poverty and shabby clothes and to my preoccupation with politics I had hardly known her then. Now she was like an incandescent glow of delight that illumined our doings. H., an authority on English literature, was often there at odd gatherings. I recall one party when H., a little high on Moulin Rouge, extemporized: 'Laetitia, I want to kish yer; Dora I want to gnor yer; Belinda, my heart is tinda . . .'

And at Xenopus I remember that we sang:

It's a long way from Amphioxus,
It's a long way to us;
It's a long way from Amphioxus
To the meanest human cuss.
   Farewell fins and gill slits,
   Welcome limbs and hair!
It's a long way from Amphioxus
But we've come from there.

Such idle moments are preserved in my memory like stills in

the swift-flowing sequence of happiness that was my life in those days.

Among those whom I came to know at this time were Cissie Gool and her husband Dr A.H. Gool. Cissie was a daughter of Dr A. Abdurahman, a South African Malay who, in the years immediately after the Boer War had gone to Scotland to study medicine. He returned to South Africa with a degree and a Scottish wife and soon began to play a leading role in politics. He founded the African People's Organization which became the Coloured wing of the Progressive Party.* Abdurahman was on the Cape Town City Council as member for Salt River, a Cape Town suburb and one of the few constituencies where Non-European voters were in a majority. He was prominent on the City Council and it was freely said that if he had been a white man he would have been mayor of Cape Town. As it was he had great power and was much courted by white politicians because of his influence with Non-European voters.

Of his two daughters, the older, Waradea, had like her father qualified in medicine at Glasgow. The other, Cissie, had married Dr A.H. Gool, the son of an Indian father and a Malay mother. His father had sent him to Cairo to be educated and from Cairo he had gone on to London to take his medical degree. The Gools were now famous for their hospitality and for their delightful parties. Cissie was beautiful, eloquent, much interested in Non-European politics. Later she in her turn became a city councillor. A.H. was gay and cynical, extremely well-read, an excellent art critic.

It soon became common knowledge among the Hogben set and all their friends that I was about to start printing a revolutionary paper. A number of them sought me out and offered financial assistance. It was for me a new experience thus to be offered help. One usually had to pursue and importune the fellow traveller when one needed money for the cause.

In the meantime arrangements for printing the Party newspaper were going rapidly ahead. I had acquired something of a type-setter's skill and now bought the type. The Party rented premises in Hanover Street, the main thoroughfare of District Six, Cape Town's Coloured quarter. There were two rooms on

*Not of course the Progressive Party of recent times which was founded in 1959.

the top floor of a two-storey building, a larger one which became the office and meeting place of the Party branch and a small one which became known as my bed-sitting room. Here I had my bed and my racks of type and other gear. The printer who did our machining was about a hundred yards away in an adjoining street. Carrying the made-up galleys to his place was no great hardship. I was fortunate in finding among our branch members Comrade Max a professional type-setter. He came twice in the week in the evenings to help me set. We trained a number of other comrades to distribute type, that is to put it back in the cases after use. Others came to work at addressing wrappers and to help with the folding and wrapping. Some of the older women specialized in this and acquired great skill. Also my friends of the Hogben set came to help.

A feature of the new weekly was its cartoons. These I made myself in the form of linocuts. The problem was not so much to execute the cuts, for I had always had some facility in drawing, as to think up a new subject each week. I had little time to think except at weekends. The cartoons were worth it, however, for they added considerably to the attractiveness of the little paper and as I cut the lino I encouraged myself by the thought that the space filled by a cartoon saved me so many hours of laborious type-setting.

We called the paper by its Xhosa title, *Umsebenzi*, which means The Worker. It was very small, only a single sheet of four pages. About half was in English, the rest in various Bantu languages, chiefly Xhosa and Sotho, with some Zulu and Tswana as well. I had studied Xhosa-Zulu and had little difficulty in setting in these languages. Sotho-Tswana have always been a mystery to me but by much practice I became quite good at spelling the words, though often I did not know what they meant. At first we had some difficulty in getting vernacular material but as the paper rapidly became known throughout the different provinces we soon had as many vernacular letters and reports as we could handle. Ngedlane proved invaluable as editor of vernacular.

We had a small but growing number of individual subscribers to the paper. It sold at one penny. Our chief sales were made by agents in the various locations who received bundles at sixpence a dozen and thus made a profit of a halfpenny on every copy sold. In the office I put up a post office map of South Africa, with black-headed pins to represent agencies. We began with a circulation of 3,000. By the end of the year we were approaching the 5,000 mark and sales were rising steadily. Five thousand may seem little enough for a paper which aimed at educating and organizing eight million people; but I knew each paper sold was read by many people and, anyway, this was only a beginning. The whole cost of producing *Umsebenzi* during this year was £5 per issue and this paid printing, postage and my own food and transport. I did not buy new clothes. It should be recorded that Sidney Bunting, still in Johannesburg, contributed regularly £3 of this amount, which he could ill spare for he was having a struggle to maintain himself, his wife and two sons.

I always look back on 1930 as one of the most thrilling years of my life. Never had I worked so hard but never was work more rewarding. My weekly routine was as follows. From Sunday night to Thursday morning I was occupied chiefly in setting. I knew I had to get a certain amount done every day if the galleys were to reach the printer on time. I often worked at night until I was completely exhausted and then flopped on my bed and slept at once. In the morning I collected mail from our post office box in the city, five minutes' walk from Hanover Street, did the necessary secretarial work and went back to setting. I never did any cooking but ate my meals, of cheese, grapes, peaches, milk, mostly out of paper bags while I sat on the bed. On Thursday morning I carried the completed galleys to the printer and in the afternoon collected the printed papers. Bulk parcels had to be made up and posted before 6 p.m. to catch the evening mail to Johannesburg, Durban and the other big centres. Failure to get them off in time would mean disappointment and reprimands from the north, for the papers had to arrive there by Saturday to be sold over the week end. The feeling of relief that I had on Thursday when I had carried the last set of parcels into the post office is impossible to describe. I then had my weekly bath in the public wash-house in Hanover Street, and having thus got rid of sweat and printer's ink, changed into clean clothes and went to the Gools for supper and to talk about things other than printing and politics. On Friday evening came the weekly branch meeting combined with the wrapping and despatch of individual copies to subscribers. Comrade Max and others stayed on after the meeting to dis and to start setting once more. On Saturday morning I spent a couple of hours selling the paper outside Cape Town station. On Saturday afternoon and Sunday morning there were often Congress meetings on the Parade where again I sold the the paper. Saturday evening I usually allowed myself off unless there was a special meeting at Ndabene or elsewhere. On Sunday I was free, free to climb Table Mountain, free to go to Clifton to swim and meet my friends. The Gools kept open house at their bungalow at Clifton. Life was strenuous but there were opportunities for relaxation, for the companionship of girls and young men, even for making love. I was no anchorite.

Selling the paper at the station entrance on Saturday mornings led to my first appearance in court. I usually took my stand at the Castle Street entrance and, standing just off the kerb, kept on proclaiming in English and in Xhosa that the workers' paper was for sale. On one occasion a young policeman stopped and watched me for a time. Evidently he did not approve of my behaviour and, after some exchanges, asked for my name and address. I subsequently received a summons to appear in the magistrate's court on a charge of standing on the pavement (side-walk) and obstructing the traffic. Fortunately, my friend S.A.R. had happened to be passing at the time of my altercation with the constable and he had stopped and listened. He appeared as my witness. His evidence showed clearly that I had not been standing on the pavement but in the gutter. I was found not guilty and discharged. But attendance in court had cost me some time. I thanked my witness and dashed back to type-setting.

And so with the grind of type-setting and the close routine of my days and making cartoons and friendship and some laughter, the weeks and months sped by and I hardly noticed their going. The Cape Town winter is a time of heavy incessant rains. I suppose that in 1930 the rains fell as usual. The odd thing is that I do not remember cold or rain. My memories are of sunshine on the mountain, of Belinda reading to us, of Starkey, of talk with Hogben, of the babel at the Gools, and then again of type-setting, type-setting which went on in my dreams, and of rushing to catch the post on Thursdays. Perhaps it is a happy thing that memory is selective.

CHAPTER VIII

End of The Cape Town Days

A FAULT that I have noticed in myself from time to time is a strong tendency to become deeply interested in the techniques incidental to some plan, often at the expense of real concern as to the ultimate aim. Association with Bunting should have been a salutary check on this fault for, as has been mentioned, Bunting was one who had to look at all sides of a question and think deeply before he could decide upon it. But often I would grow impatient of Bunting's careful delays and then I would anticipate his decision and plunge into action. What I was at this period trying consciously to do was to hasten the Africanization of the social revolutionary movement in South Africa. I have described elsewhere* in some detail how this process had been initiated by David Ivon Jones and Sidney Bunting during the first world war, at the time when the international socialists broke away from the South African Labour Party. The problem was to give voice to the aims and aspirations of the oppressed African masses and to link these with the more general aims of the world revolutionary movement, or in other words to express communism in the Bantu idiom.

In the first place we encountered the language difficulty. The Bantu languages, though in many ways highly developed with their almost Latin-style suffix and prefix grammar, were naturally lacking in the social and political terminology of a movement originating outside Africa and brought here in the first instance by white people. Our problem was similar to that of the early missionaries who had to translate the ideas of Christianity and the phraseology of the Bible into Bantu words. The process was facilitated, for both missionaries and communists, by the fact that the Bantu tongues readily absorb foreign words and Bantu-ize them. Thus Xhosa converts to Christianity soon added *i-Bayibile* and *u-Satan* to their voca-

*In *S.P. Bunting* and in *Time Longer Than Rope*.

bulary. But in other cases some existing Bantu word might be taken over and acquire a new and more specialized meaning. Thus *Tixo*, the name of one of the Xhosa gods, considered by some the greatest of their gods, became the Xhosa word for Jehovah. In Zulu, God became *uNkulunkulu* which means the Great-Great.

Prior to 1930 no one had attempted to systematize communist terminology in the Bantu languages, though the need for attention to this problem should have become apparent when, for instance, communist speakers to African audiences in the early days often found that their interpreters would render the word 'capitalist' by *ma-Juda*. Some found this rather shocking and in fact many of our supporters were Jews. Rebecca Bunting, Molly Wolton, Issy Diamond, Solly Sachs, Benny Weinbren, to name only a few leftist leaders, were Jews. However, it was natural enough that an African, unschooled in the ideas of Karl Marx, should think of capitalism in terms of his experience with the local Jewish storekeeper.

Noting this language stumbling-block and finding myself thus happily in control of *Umsebenzi*, I now set myself through the vernacular columns of the paper to devise Bantu language equivalents for the Marxist terms so frequently needed in our writing and speaking. My chief associate in this work was of course Josiah Ngedlane. Incidentally, we finally found as the Xhosa equivalent for the word 'capitalist' the term *ungxowankulu* which meant literally 'the man with the big bag'.

But as happened so often with me I dabbled in this problem, became keenly interested for a time then gradually lost interest and passed on to other things. However we did continue the attempt throughout the year in which *Umsebenzi* was published in Cape Town. To my knowledge no one else in the revolutionary movement in South Africa has tackled it since. However, in far-away Leningrad, our efforts were noticed. A Russian student of language, Academician I. L. Sneguireff, published two articles in the journal *Africana*.* One, dealing with 'Modern Economic and Social terminology in the Zulu, Xhosa and Suto languages' was based almost entirely on the vernacular articles

Africana. Academy of Science of the USSR. Transactions of the Marr Institute of Language and Mentality, vol. IX. Transactions of the Section of African Languages. Moscow 1937 Leningrad.

that had appeared in *Umsebenzi*. The second dealt with 'Revolutionary Songs of the South African Workers'. All of these were translations made by me or that I had inspired others to make of European revolutionary songs more or less adapted to African conditions. The Russian journal also reprinted a number of the *Umsebenzi* linocut cartoons. I do think that I had made a beginning but as with so many things I attempted in my life I did not carry it through. However, the problem of communication with Africans was one to which I returned in another way, later, in the night schools in Johannesburg and Cape Town.

The main political interest in the Cape now lay in the activities of the Western Province branch of the African National Congress with which we were co-operating closely. This organization was remarkable in that its leaders were mainly African and its rank and file largely Coloured. Native Africans, Bantu, were in a small minority in the Western Cape where they are not indigenous. History records that when the Dutch first occupied the Cape they found it inhabited by Hottentots only with Bushmen in the deep interior. It was only towards the close of the eighteenth century that the whites, in their eastward march, encountered the first Bantu in the neighbourhood of Algoa Bay. There has in general been some hostility and little political association between Coloured and African. It is therefore significant that Bransby Ndobe and Elliot Tonjeni had managed to organize under the Congress banner a great following of Coloured farm labourers in the country districts. They were actively circulating *Umsebenzi* in all Congress branches and we soon had agents for the paper in almost every important centre along what is known as the Garden Route between Cape Town and Port Elizabeth. The song Mayibuye also became well-known and was translated into Afrikaans the language spoken by many of the Coloured people. The Afrikaans version runs:

Ons bruin mense, seuns van slawe,
   Vra ons eie land terug,
Wat gesteel is van ons vaders
   Toe hul in die donker sug.

Gee dit t'rug nou!
 Gee dit t'rug nou!
Weg met al die slawerny!
 Pirow kan ons nie ophou nie:
Afrika sal vryheid kry.

>We brown people, sons of slaves,
> Demand our own land back,
>Which was stolen from our fathers
> While they were sunk in darkness.
>
>Give it back now!
> Give it back now!
>Away with all the slavery!
> Pirow cannot stop us:
>Africa shall have freedom.

In May of 1930 trouble broke out at Worcester, some eighty miles from Cape Town, when local whites broke up a Congress meeting. The great grievance of the Coloured workers on the Cape wine farms was the tot system, by which they were forced to accept a ration of wine as part of their wages. Temperance organizations had long tried, without success, to have the tots prohibited. There was also in the Western Province a certain amount of illicit kafir beer drinking which was not in the interests of the wine farmers. Feelings ran high on tots and on kafir beer. Frequent beer raids by the police were resented. A protest meeting was organized for the 4th of May in Worcester. The violence that broke out was probably initiated by local whites some of whom were armed. A black man was shot and killed. At the subsequent enquiry the Congress leaders gave evidence that armed white civilians had used their guns. More violence followed when the police entered the Native location and on this occasion five Natives were killed. Now the two African leaders of the A.N.C. were already in particularly bad odour among the farmers. It was said that they were agitators who were stirring up the hitherto docile farm labourers. In the excitement that followed on the riots Ndobe and Tonjeni went into hiding in the Coloured quarter. The local whites were searching for them and it was believed that they had pickets on the station to catch the two if they should try to leave by train.

We in Cape Town knew from the newspapers of the incidents of the riot but had no idea of the plight of our two comrades, till a Coloured woman approached me quietly at a meeting on the Parade. She brought a message from Ndobe and Tonjeni asking us to come and fetch them by car at eight o'clock in the evening on the following day. She supplied an address in Worcester and insisted that the car must be driven by a European since a Non-European driver would be conspicuous.

I at once recalled Hogben's offer of his Nash. This was a rather conspicuous car but that could not be helped. In fact there was practically no alternative for no Party member had a car in those days. I sent him a note explaining that I needed him and his car at 7 p.m. the following evening. I got back a cryptic typed message saying 'Rhodes Memorial 7 p.m.' The famous memorial is on the lower slopes of Devil's Peak and it is a lonely place after sunset. I took Johnny Gomas with me, since he knew Worcester and I did not. When we came to the meeting place the car was there with Enid driving. 'Lancelot thought it best that I should come,' she said. 'If there is to be trouble for either of us it had better be for me. Lancelot is the breadwinner.' She did not tell us that she had only just learned to drive, having got her licence a few days before. That I discovered later.

There are two ways to go from Cape Town to Worcester: a long roundabout route via Tulbagh and a shorter, rough road over the mountains via Bain's Kloof which was still about eighty miles. As it was important for us to reach Worcester at eight we went over the pass. It was a sandy loose-surfaced road, with a sheer precipice on one side. Though Enid drove extremely slowly the car skidded once or twice. It was now completely dark and long past eight o'clock. As we descended on the far side of the pass we had still quite a distance to go and we urged Enid to speed, which she did. Suddenly the car skidded and left the road. For a few moments we were travelling along on top of a fence knocking the posts down as we went. Then, by some miracle, we were back on the road. We were all shaken and Enid was trembling. We stopped and examined the car. A small side wind-screen was broken; otherwise there seemed to be no damage. 'I was told never to brake in a skid,' Enid explained. 'Had I done so we should have capsized.'

Presently we reached Worcester, then a typical country dorp with practically no lights in the streets. We saw very few people about. After some trouble we found the address and Johnny went into the house. But the two men were not there. They had moved on to another address. Eventually we found them and in this we should hardly have succeeded if I had not had the forethought to bring Johnny. We started back. There was no question of attempting the pass again and so we went the devious route by Tulbagh. It was a long road and Enid grew more and more exhausted. Occasionally she stopped and tried to sleep with her head on the steering wheel. We four big men sat there helpless. Not one of us could drive. We returned to Cape Town in the small hours of the morning.

One day at the Parade meeting I noticed among the audience a teenager who looked for all the world like the Tenniel drawings of Alice in Wonderland. I went to speak to her. She introduced herself as Angela Haden-Guest. Her father, Captain Haden-Guest, was a right-wing Labour member of the British House of Commons. Angela had apparently shown an embarrassing concern with ultra-Left politics in London and, hoping that in a fresh environment she would acquire some new interest, he had sent her on a long holiday to Cape Town where she had previously been on a short visit and where he had friends. But the poor captain had from his point of view made a bad blunder. I naturally introduced Angela to my Coloured friends. It happened that she was then staying at the Settlers' Club where Belinda was also living during this year. The Club secretary, who felt some responsibility for young Angela, consulted Belinda as to whether I was a desirable associate for the girl. Belinda replied that she did not think that there was any danger of my seducing Angela. However, a year or so later she was arrested during a strike of Coloured garment workers and deported to England. Angela was not the only member of the Haden-Guest family to join the revolutionary movement. Her brother was killed while fighting for the Republicans in the Spanish civil war.

During 1930 we were visited by an agent from Moscow. Actually he came officially on behalf of the Profintern, the Red International of Labour Unions. He spent only a couple of days in Cape Town and his sole contribution to the movement was an article which he wrote and insisted on my publishing in *Umsebenzi*. In this article he tried to put over the Party line in regard to the Native Republic slogan. Under my editorship, the paper had made no use of this slogan which Bunting and I considered so unrealistic. Instead we had made much of *Mayibuye!*—'Let Africa come back'.—which seemed not only much more attractive to the blacks but also much less repellent to the whites. The Moscow man, however, insisted on the real thing. So the long and tedious article, stiff with Comintern jargon, which as a journalist I disliked very much apart from my political views on what it said, duly appeared. But since it was written in the usual cumbersome Comintern phraseology I doubted if many people would read it. Probably it did little harm.

This agent was extremely nervous, a little fat man who seemed anxious to get his visit over as quickly as possible. In Cape Town he met no Party members except Johnny Gomas and me and one other. From him I learned something of the technique of illegality when I had to hand over a small suitcase to him. On his instructions I took the case to a tea-room cinema in Adderley Street and sat in a certain row on a seat next the aisle. He came in when a film was showing, grabbed the case without a word spoken and left by an exit different from the door he had come in by.

During the latter half of 1930 the Party's main concern was the working up of an anti-pass campaign, which was to culminate in a grand burning of passes on Dingaan's Day. The idea of destroying passes as a gesture of passive resistance to the pass laws was no new one. The African National Congress had first attempted it in 1919 when I, at the age of sixteen, had seen those torn papers laying all over Von Brandis Square. That effort had been abortive and had never been repeated, but the idea had remained. During the hey-day of the I.C.U. Kadalie had frequently proclaimed his intention of starting a pass-burning campaign. But he had never done so. Some of us believed that it was only what we called good-boy leadership which was preventing a general boycott of the pass laws and we held that if only Africans in really large numbers would destroy their passes the whole obnoxious pass system would collapse, for it would be impossible for the authorities to put millions of people in gaol.

Already in May *Umsebenzi* was proclaiming that passes would burn on Dingaan's Day and, as December approached, it seemed that there was going to be a big response, particularly in the Orange Free State where we had agents in all the towns and in most of the smaller dorps as well. The Party had sent Johannes Nkosi to Durban, where the I.C.U. rank and file were still very militant though restrained by Champion's cautious leadership. Judging by the rapid increase in *Umsebenzi* sales in that centre it was clear that Nkosi was making considerable headway. An 'anti-pass conference to prepare for Dingaan's Day' was convened by the Party in Johannesburg in October. Some 500 delegates, representing many organizations, were present and there were scenes of enthusiasm. Bunting in a letter to me described the conference but added, 'What is five hundred among so many millions?' He saw, better than we did in the Cape, that the thing was not so easy as it seemed. Events were to prove him right.

The Free State upsurge was effectively scotched by Clements Kadalie who suddenly appeared in Bloemfontein early in December and at a number of meetings denounced the impending pass-burning, saying the Government would find space in the gaols for the offenders. He did not seem to win much sympathy but he effectively destroyed the unanimity on which everything depended. In the event no passes were burned in the Free State. In the Transvaal nothing important happened. In the country districts where we had branches only the Party members destroyed their passes. In Johannesburg it rained heavily and the Dingaan's Day meeting was a failure.

Only Durban responded and responded magnificently. Thousands of passes were collected and burnt at a mass meeting on Cartwright's Flats. But here tragedy followed. The Durban borough police, the whites armed with revolvers and the Africans with assegais and clubs, attacked the meeting. Nkosi was struck down from the platform and a few days later died of his wounds. Three other Africans were killed also and many wounded. A reign of terror followed. Hundreds of Africans were arrested and deported. Many in Durban and the surrounding areas continued to destroy their passes but all the important leaders were now in prison. The movement did not spread to other centres. We had failed.

Waking and in my dreams I was haunted by the death of Nkosi. What had happened was strange and terrible. Born in Natal, Nkosi had come as a boy to find work in Johannesburg and at the age of fourteen had attended the Von Brandis Square meeting at which passes had been torn up. He had come as a pupil to the Party night school and had become a member of the Party in 1926. In 1929, as one of the few Zulu-speaking leaders, he was sent to Durban to work for the Party. There he would go to Champion's great I.C.U. meetings on Sundays on Cartwright's Flats and would sell his bundles of *Umsebenzi*. When Champion occasionally refused permission for this, Nkosi would write a sad letter to the editor of *Umsebenzi* expressing his bewilderment that Champion was so timid. Now at the pass-burning meeting on Dingaan's Day Nkosi was actually the speaker on the platform when the armed police made their attack. He stood his ground and urged the meeting to remain quiet and not to offer resistance. He was shot and struck and fell from the platform. Though thousands saw him killed no one was ever found guilty of his death. Comrade Krikst, who was present wrote to tell me about it. The twenty-four seriously wounded were loaded on to a wagon and driven to the police station and later to the hospital. As the wagon moved off blood was dripping from it. Four of the victims died. A hospital doctor, giving evidence later, stated that all the bodies were hacked all over by some stabbing instrument. Nkosi was just twenty-five when he died. He earned fame as the first African Communist martyr.

A week or two before these events, Douglas Wolton passed through Cape Town on his way back from Moscow. This was a significant event in the history of the Party. It also affected my own future. Douglas and his wife Molly had been among those who had welcomed and supported the Comintern thesis of 1928 which put forward the slogan of a Native Republic. When the Buntings and I had gone to Congress they had sent in a written minority report on the matter. They had both left for study in Moscow at about the time of my return from England and had there attended the Lenin school. Molly had stayed on in Moscow when Douglas returned.

END OF THE CAPE TOWN DAYS

Wolton had now come back armed with directives from the Comintern for the bolshevization of the Communist Party of South Africa. How detailed these directives were we were never able to discover. It was held by some members that many of the things he subsequently did were done on his own initiative and did not emanate from Moscow. But since these were afterwards endorsed by the executive of the Comintern I must assume that they were in line with the general spirit of his orders.

My own attitude towards the Comintern at this time was still a humble one. My experience at Moscow in 1928 had caused me to doubt my judgment and to develop a strong sense of inferiority in the presence of those erudite comrades who knew the works of Lenin and Stalin practically by heart and who spoke with authority about the various theses of the Comintern. However I came much later to understand that the trouble with Bunting and me at the Sixth Congress was not mere lack of erudition. We were in many ways much less ignorant than many of those who denounced us so loudly at Moscow and later in South Africa. Our trouble was an innate empiricism which made us prefer to reason from fact to theory rather than from theory to what ought to be fact. Bunting was always more consistent in his reactions than I was. When criticized he would stick to his commonsense point of view. In similar circumstances I became embarrassed. I wanted to believe that bolshevik theory and plain commonsense were the same thing. If what seemed to me commonsense did not square with bolshevik theory then it must be due to some stupidity or other shortcoming on my part. I was still in this mood when Wolton appeared in Cape Town.

He wanted to have a heart to heart talk with me and so we left the office where people were always dropping in and went for a walk on the slopes of Table Mountain. It was a perfect summer day and I found myself, as ever, enchanted and distracted by the windborne breath of the mountain. The fragrance returns to me still whenever I think of that talk. But my companion, the Moscow-trained fanatic, was hardly aware of our surroundings. He was much concerned about *Umsebenzi* which he said was not being run on correct bolshevik lines. Of course I had to agree with him that it was not good bolshevism to have the Party organ edited by a single individual who had no editorial board to control him and was responsible only to a committee a thousand miles away. I blushed when he referred to various political deviations I had made in articles in the paper during my period as editor. Douglas insisted that the paper should at once go back to Johannesburg where it would come under the direct control of the political bureau, and that I too should return to Johannesburg. With this proposition, amounting to orders, I could not, as one who strove to be a good bolshevik, disagree, though I did not want to leave Cape Town and though I knew that printing would certainly prove more difficult and costly in Johannesburg. While Douglas talked on and on of errors and deviations as we came down from the mountain, my heart began to ache with a dull pain as I began to face the prospect of leaving Cape Town.

Let me confess at once that my reluctance to make this move was owing not only to perfectly valid considerations of the increased cost and difficulty of producing *Umsebenzi* in Johannesburg but to my love of the delightful people I knew in Cape Town and also of the sunny beaches and the mountain on which I sometimes climbed on Sundays. However I said nothing of all this. I agreed. As so often I toed the line. I packed my type and *Umsebenzi* files and documents, said good-bye to my friends and took train to Johannesburg.

In any event the Hogben set was now dispersing. Hogben, with his family, took ship and sailed away to a professorship at Birmingham University. Bodmer would presently be on his way to a lectureship in London. Dora would be leaving Kirstenbosch. Belinda, her sabbatical year ended, was now deep in debt and was returning to Johannesburg where she had obtained a teaching post. The Gools remained and H. and Starkey and some others. But the happy year was over.

CHAPTER IX

First Expulsions

TOEING the line was at first not too difficult. I was still impressed by Wolton's easy mastery of Moscow directives and correspondingly aware of my own much weaker, as I thought, grasp of current communist theory. When Wolton spoke of the necessity of combating the right danger I had no thought of the planned expulsions which were to come. In any case, having obeyed the Political Bureau and transferred myself and *Umsebenzi* to Johannesburg, I became as usual at once absorbed in practical matters, the business of finding a printer, a room where setting could be done and comrades trained in this work, and the need to do all this at top speed so that the break in the continuity of *Umsebenzi* should be as brief as possible. All these activities filled my days and for some time I had little leisure to think of other matters.

I went home once more to the house in Bez Valley and there lived on sufferance. When my father indulged in polemics aimed at me I remained silent and for his part he made no attempt to control my comings and goings. As to not answering Dad this was by now the accepted family custom. Edna explained: 'It's no use trying to answer Dad whatever he says. It just makes him worse. You notice that Claud and Phil never utter a word. Dad wanted me to train as a pharmacist and work with him at dispensing. But I knew it would be impossible.' Edna had taken a secretarial course and was now in a good post. Enid was away in Barberton. Claud who had not taken to citrus farming was now back and running a filling station and garage near by. Phil was by now a clever mechanic and earning good wages. I foresaw that Phil would in time become the capitalist of our generation. Arthur had been unlucky in matriculation. He had failed first in Afrikaans and on rewriting the examination had failed in Latin. He had then gone to work for a wholesale firm of chemists. The house was full of the comings and goings of my brothers and sisters and their friends. Mum watched over the noisy talk which would die away so strangely when Dad pontificated. She welcomed visitors, served tea and cookies, carefully guarded peace in the home. But politics claimed me and I was not often there.

Disillusion came slowly. Again and again when decisions of the Political Bureau, of which I was now a member, seemed to me unrealistic or injudicious, I told myself that I was still politically naive and should make greater efforts to understand the Party line as supplied in overwhelming quantity by Moscow. The P.B. was dominated by the Imprecor trio, Douglas and Molly Wolton and Lazar Bach.

Douglas was a Yorkshireman and one knew it the instant he spoke. His broad accent seemed to become more so when he was on a soap-box and this served to increase the effect of stark sincerity of all his speeches. He was a fluent and forceful speaker and never at a loss to answer hecklers. He never spoke from notes. Indeed this was a rule with all our speakers.

His diminutive wife, Molly Zelikowitz, was a Lithuanian. She was petite, plump, pretty, dark-haired and bright-eyed, with a high colour which flamed higher when she was excited as she often was. This colour told its tale of her heart weakness. Molly was all pent-up energy like a coiled spring, all fire and fury when it came to public speaking which she loved. She was easily our most gifted orator, brilliant in repartee so that hecklers thus made to look foolish soon came to have a wholesome respect for her. She was intolerant of routine and never had patience to use any of her energy on office work. She could not endure contradiction, not even in the smallest detail. She had to be right, always right. Also she was somewhat vain, not only well aware that she had the gift of brilliant oratory but vain also of her own dainty person and pretty feet. I remember that on one occasion she and I were by arrangement to meet a certain Comintern representative in Joubert Park. Molly knew this man but I had not met him. When we were about to leave the office Molly suddenly said that she could not come as her feet were hurting her. She was suffering agony from new shoes which I suspected she had bought at least a half-size too small. I went alone and strolled about the park. I saw a man sitting on a bench absorbed in reading a newspaper. I sauntered past him whistling quietly The International. And so I encountered this envoy whom we knew as Russell. We sat and talked for about an hour. When I returned to the Party office I found Molly padding about in stockinged feet, moaning gently at intervals.

The third member of this trio was Lazar Bach. He too was small of stature, quieter than the others but no less forceful, very quiet of speech so that often one strained to hear him for what he had to say was always worth hearing. Brilliantly clever, he was a young Communist from Lithuania who had an amazing knowledge of Comintern doctrine and could quote Marx, Engels, Lenin and Stalin, chapter and verse, on any conceivable aspect of policy. He had that delight in intellectual subtlety which is so often found in Jews who have studied the Talmud as part of their early training.

All three were glib in Moscow theory and masters of Imprecor language. Almost all of Wolton's speeches and writings began with reference to 'the deepening economic crisis' and made much mention of 'the upsurge of the toiling masses'. 'Deepening economic crisis' soon became a nick-name for Wolton among our Native supporters. My own nick-name was 'he who goes there quickly', which did not displease me. All three wrote copiously and insisted that their long and well-nigh incomprehensible essays should appear in full in *Umsebenzi*. Molly's essays were slightly less stereotyped than those Douglas produced but the language she used was even more abstruse and she considered that the longer an article was the better, a view which as the editor of a small paper I could not share. But one could not influence Molly. Bach's writings were more concise but even less intelligible.

Under the pressure of these long theoretical dissertations which I could not refuse to print, *Umsebenzi* became virtually unreadable. Important news items in vernacular were crowded out. The circulation which had been climbing towards the 6,000 mark now slumped sharply. Also the paper, after the first five issues in 1931, ceased to be a weekly. It appeared fortnightly for a while, then at longer intervals. Within less than a year it had quite lost any popular appeal.

But all this did not happen at once. At first Molly was still in Moscow and it was Wolton and Bach who called the tune.

They insisted upon an African majority on the Political Bureau. I was included as I had shown willingness to learn. But Bunting, the founder of the Party in South Africa, was left out. Actually the African majority was only a mechanical gesture, more a manner of speaking than a meaningful reality. The new Native members, though continually and intensively coached in the theory and practice of the new line, the fight against the reformist danger, were in fact bewildered and always subservient. Their presence was unreal. They said little beyond expressing agreement with Wolton and Bach when called on to do so. These two were supported also by Louis Joffe, the hardworking treasurer who was a genius at collecting funds from sympathizers and who had clearly, as the irreverent commented, accepted the Comintern line for ever and ever. Because Joffe held the purse and paid functionaries each week many of the Native comrades regarded him as the real boss of the Party. His presence on the P.B. seemed to be due to the fact that he could be relied on to support the Imprecor trio on any issue. He never contributed any views of his own. He was not good at expressing ideas but acquired some skill at quoting Imprecor phrases.

At the end of February I was sent to Bloemfontein and then to Cape Town. In Bloemfontein it was my unhappy task to explain to the local branch members just why their leader, S. Malkinson, had been removed from the P.B. Malkinson could not understand why he had been dropped nor could his followers. They had written to the P.B. asking for an explanation. I am afraid that I made a poor advocate for I did not myself understand why it had been necessary to exclude the most active communist in the Free State. I explained that Malkinson lacked theoretical clarity, that he did not understand the new kind of Bolshevik Party that we were building in South Africa. Probably I said all this somewhat half-heartedly. Naturally I failed to convince them. After I left they sent another letter of protest to the P.B. and demanded Malkinson's reinstatement. Wolton and Bach then summoned a meeting of the P.B. and expelled Malkinson from the Party 'for fractional activities'. Thus the Bloemfontein branch was destroyed. In crushing the right danger Wolton was also smashing the Party. And this, though I did not heed the danger signs, was only a beginning.

In Cape Town, John Gomas and I threw leaflets from the gallery of the House of Assembly, on 6 March, the 'day of struggle against unemployment'. I was able to make a brief speech before we were ejected. I had time in Cape Town for a hasty glimpse of my old friends, Bodmer and the Gools, and then had to leave for Durban where I was to try to reorganize the branch which had been dispersed by police action following upon the Dingaan's Day incidents in which Johannes Nkosi had been killed. Earlier Gana Makabeni had been sent from Johannesburg to replace Nkosi but had almost at once been arrested, charged under the Urban Areas Act with being an 'idle, dissolute and disorderly person' and forthwith deported to the Transkei.

In Durban I now found an atmosphere of terror. No open meetings could be held. I rented a room in an Indian district and started a night school which soon attracted some twenty pupils. In this room I lived, mainly on sour milk and bananas which were cheap then, forty for a shilling, with occasional treats in the form of cheese. And here I held small gatherings, of the loyal and brave, not on any regular night of the week for I feared spies, but frequently. On Sundays I went to the large I.C.U. meetings on Cartwright's Flats and sold, with increasing difficulty, a few dozen of *Umsebenzi*. I also held meetings in Verulam and some other outlying districts. I earned a living, just adequate for rent, transport and food, by working for a comrade who had a vinegar factory where I was employed as chemist and performed endless titrations. I remember that this factory was acrawl with cockroaches of all sizes walking in layers on the floor. Cockroaches are partial to vinegar and wine. Presently a magisterial order banished me from the district. This I defied and was accordingly sentenced to a term in gaol.

This was my first experience of a hard labour sentence. Clearly it was difficult for the prison authorities to know just what to do with me in a gaol where nearly all the prisoners were Africans. As a white man I could not, they held, be sent out with Native labour gangs. So I was set to polishing all day a stair rail of rough wood, a surface that would not take a polish. I asked if I might work in the prison garden. This was permitted. But I found myself under the orders of two warders whose ideas about the lay-out of the garden differed. They gave me in turn contrary instructions. I spent much time setting plants in a certain place and presently digging them up again to put them somewhere else. Under such treatment the garden did me no credit. But at least I was out in the fresh air and moving plants about was much better than polishing that stair rail. The days went by.

When I came out from gaol the Durban F.S.U. committee met me with a finely lettered address which quoted a verse of Walt Whitman.

> Do the feasters gluttonous feast?
> Do the corpulent sleepers sleep?
> Have they locked and bolted doors?
> Still be ours the diet hard and the blanket on the ground,
> Pioneers! O pioneers!

I was much moved by this tribute but what followed was less happy. It chanced that Bernard Shaw was then in Durban and I looked forward to meeting him. The encounter was mismanaged. The Indian comrade who presented me, instead of saying that here was Eddie Roux who had just completed a term in prison for defying a banishment order, said something like: 'This is Dr Edward Roux who has been to Cambridge University'. To this Shaw replied, not unnaturally, 'Cambridge? Well, what of it?' and turned away with characteristic impatience. No one tried to explain my better claim to his attention.

This was my last evening in Durban. My usefulness there being at an end I was summoned back to Johannesburg where strange things had been happening.

It is a fact that, when any leading personality suffers expulsion from leadership in the Communist Party, it presently comes about that willy-nilly he is forced into a position where he is made to appear to be attacking the Party. Something of the kind had happened in the case of Malkinson in Bloemfontein and I was now to witness the working out of another such situation.

Bunting, though excluded from the Political Bureau and continually subjected to attack by the Imprecor bosses, his speeches misquoted and his careful replies denied space in

Umsebenzi, had remained through all this persecution a loyal member of the Party. And naturally, by reason of his long record of devoted service to the cause of the Africans, he had a loyal following of comrades and friends. But loyalty was now to be made increasingly difficult for him.

Wolton's plan at this time was that he and Bach should remain as far as possible in the background, not exposing themselves to undue risks, but keeping an eye on policy and tactics, while others, like Diamond and me and of course a number of the African comrades, should function openly as instruments of the Party and work to keep the Party in the public eye. I did not then think, nor do I now believe, that this policy was in any way an expression of cowardice on Wolton's part. He had shown many times and was to show again that he was prepared to face whatever might be coming to him. It was rather revolutionary realism. Why should the brains of the Party on whom everything depended be exposed unnecessarily to the dangers of arrest and imprisonment? But Bunting now smarting from ill-treatment, and Diamond the realist, did not see it in this light. Bunting snorted his contempt. Diamond still cynically recalls how on the occasion of the May Day meeting while he was speaking Wolton and Bach stood inconspicuously on the outskirts of the crowd, silent, listening to his speech and noting for future use against him all the deviations he committed.

It was not until September 1931 that Wolton and Bach were able finally to liquidate what they described as the right danger. For months, more than nine months, they had been busy working up their case against Bunting. Still Bunting remained in the eyes of the African rank and file, both inside and outside the Party, the great leader, the one they knew. All this talk of deviations, all the long-winded articles in *Umsebenzi* meant less than nothing to them. Charges of white chauvinism were equally unreal. Was not Bunting known as the man who defended Africans in court and asked no fee? 'He has a white skin but a black heart' was a typical African comment. And years later when Communists were selling literature in an out-of-the-way location, 'Who are you?' asked an old African. 'We are the Communist Party.' 'But,' said the old man, 'I know the Communist Party. He wears big boots.' Thus did the legend of Bunting die hard among those he had served. It was not easy to destroy this man.

But in September a resolution of the Political Bureau was published. This was a curious document. It began with a lengthy statement on the 'deepening world crisis', spoke of 'the right danger' and went on to list the names and misdeeds of six leading Communists who were thus notified of their expulsion from the Party. Bunting, chief victim of the attack, was accused of right wing deviations and of fractional activities against the Party. In defending Diamond in court in connection with the Frascati Restaurant case, Bunting had stated that the unemployed had entered the restaurant and asked for food in order to draw attention to the fact that they were starving. Such behaviour, he argued, was no more criminal than that of students out for a rag. Again, defending those unemployed who had been arrested in a fracas outside the Carlton Hotel, Bunting had 'appealed to the magistrate to have vision and to treat the prisoners leniently'. Also when Diamond was charged with contempt of court, Bunting had persuaded him to apologize to the court. Moreover Bunting had spoken on the same platform as members of the I.C.U. and African National Congress, thus 'compromising' the Communist Party. All these were right wing deviations. Bunting was forthwith expelled.

Others expelled at the same time were W.H. Andrews, C.B. Tyler, Solly Sachs, F. and Benny Weinbren. Of these four were leading trade unionists. Solly Sachs was secretary of the Garment Workers Union, the most consistently militant of all trade unions; but he had offended by organizing a picnic instead of attendance at May Day demonstrations. Tyler was secretary of the Building Workers Union in which he was accused of adopting a reformist line. Benny Weinbren, the lively founder and president of the Non-European Trade Unions Federation, was more difficult to attack but he was now accused of class collaboration. This meant that Weinbren was in favour of trade unions making use of legal machinery as far as possible to secure better wages and working conditions. Later Weinbren's policy came to be regarded as orthodox Communist strategy. Andrews, the most conspicuous figure of those expelled, was prominent in the white trade union movement. In the Trades and Labour Council he had consistently supported the cause of the Left and of

Native trade unionism. But Wolton was now able to accuse him of having spoken on the social fascist, that is the Labour Party and trade union, platform on Labour Day and of failing to obey P.B. directives in this matter. Finally F. was accused of inactivity in the Party and also of campaigning against the leadership. All were expelled. One whole number of *Umsebenzi* was given over entirely to explaining these expulsions.

Strange reading it made. It was with a heavy heart that I took my armful of the papers and sold them as usual on Cartwright's Flats on a Sunday morning in September. But I did sell them. Still I toed the line.

In December I was back in Johannesburg in time to witness the ugly climax of the anti-Bunting campaign. Bunting, smarting under injustice, aware that his legal devices had stood the accused in good stead in the court, denied any opportunity of replying to his accusers, had drawn up a statement defending himself and this, marked 'strictly private, for circulation among Party members only', he sent out to all members. He also addressed a letter to certain members inviting them to a private meeting in the Inchcape Hall on the morning of Sunday, 27 December. Inevitably a copy of this letter came into the hands of Wolton and Bach a few days before the 27th. They hastily called an emergency meeting of the Political Bureau. Now it chanced that a meeting of Ikaka labaSebenzi, Labour Defence, had been arranged for that same Sunday. It was decided to transfer that meeting to the Inchcape Hall and to begin it an hour earlier than the time named for the Bunting meeting. Bach undertook to bring along some stalwarts, members of the newly-established Jewish Workers Club and thus to ensure plenty of official support. These supporters were young men and women, mostly from Poland or Lithuania, earnest adherents of the Communist International but having as yet only a very limited knowledge of the movement in South Africa and of the events that had led up to Bunting's expulsion. They were told by Bach that Bunting was a traitor and that was enough for them.

Punctuality is not usually a feature of leftist gatherings which may start much more than an hour later than the advertized time, but on this occasion the hall was packed and the Ikaka meeting was in full swing when Bunting, Makabeni and others arrived. They were nonplussed. For a time they kept silent, too much taken aback to do anything. Then some began to shout: 'This is our meeting. Why have you taken our hall?' Fighting began here and there in the hall, chiefly between some of the Jewish workers and the Africans. Makabeni, normally the gentlest of men now a tiger in defence of Bunting, rushed out to find a stick. Others picked up chairs and swung them wildly. I and some of the less fanatical people on our side, that is supporters of the Political Bureau, intervened and managed temporarily to stop the fighting. But the Bunting crowd remained and would not be silent. In the end the meeting became a battleground with group fights everywhere and the Coloured owner of the hall appeared and ordered everyone to leave. In the next *Umsebenzi* this was reported under the caption 'Buntingites smash up Ikaka Conference'—'Agents of Pirow and Hertzog prevent Exposure of Prison Brutalities.' One sentence read: 'Thus the Bunting clique again clearly reveals itself as a definite agent of the Government to muzzle the workers and prevent any organizational work being done.' The sheer silliness of these words did not stop their appearance in print. I had no control of *Umsebenzi* then.

Against men who used such tactics Bunting stood no chance. The campaign against him went on relentlessly. It was carried into other organizations, especially the Friends of the Soviet Union. A special leaflet was printed denouncing him and this was handed out among the audience at an F.S.U. meeting by Party members who had ridden in seeming friendship in the same car with Bunting as they went to hold the meeting. A copy of the leaflet was handed up to him and at the beginning of his speech he made brief reference to it, thus playing into the hands of his attackers. The P.B. then instructed its fraction in the F.S.U. to demand a vote of censure on Bunting for thus making use of F.S.U. platform to ventilate his private quarrel with the C.P. Bunting was accordingly censured by F.S.U. committee, but in the course of the argument Bunting leaned across the table and asked a woman member, a newcomer to the movement, 'Do you think I am an imperialist bloodsucker?' This was Winifred Lunt then having her first experience of Party fraction work. She answered, 'No, it's ridiculous!' But she had to cast her vote against Bunting and for this naïve reply she later received a sharp reprimand from the P.B. and it was noted for future use against her. Further disorders at F.S.U. meetings were staged and duly misreported in *Umsebenzi* under such captions as 'Buntingites attempt to wreck F.S.U. meeting'. Inevitably the outcome was Bunting's expulsion from F.S.U. Although I was not in Johannesburg at this time and had no control over what was printed in the paper, still I was certain, from what I knew of Bunting, that his loyalty to the Party would endure, and that all the disorders had been devised purely to discredit him. It seems to me now that I ought to have taken some action in his defence though I do not see what I could have done effectively. Anyway I did nothing. Still I toed the line.

Though so many of us deserted Bunting there was one man who stuck to him through thick and thin. Gana Makabeni defied Wolton and the P.B. and openly championed Bunting's cause. But Wolton was not in a hurry to expel Makabeni from the Party. For one thing Wolton was trying to expose Bunting as a white chauvinist. It was hard to have to admit that an outstanding African leader was so strong in his defence. Another consideration was that Makabeni was the popular secretary of the African Clothing Workers' Union. However his intransigence showed no signs of abating and finally, in March 1932, he too was formally expelled from the C.P. on the ground that he had 'openly conducted propaganda in favour of Bunting and reactionaries' and had opposed efforts of the C.P. to secure the disaffiliation of the African Clothing Workers' Union from the 'reactionary' Garment Workers' Union led by Solly Sachs.

Wolton and Bach claimed that the rank and file of Makabeni's union remained loyal to the Party and the African Federation of Trade Unions. But in fact Gana had taken a substantial section of the union with him and it was not long before he once more had the entire union in his hands.

Gana's subsequent activities are a fine example of devotion and consistency. During the depression years 1932 and 1933 the African Clothing Workers' Union was in a bad way. But Gana stuck to his purpose. He obtained work as a labourer in a factory and conducted union affairs in his spare time. The Union weathered the storm and became one of the most successful of African unions.

In all this I remained silent. Shocked by the expulsions and revolted by the ugly manoeuvres employed to force Bunting to appear to be in the wrong, I still said nothing. I was in Durban, involved with a court case and presently in gaol. But my silence is my eternal shame. In any case protest would have been a useless gesture. The thing was done before I knew of it and of course the P.B. never reverses a decision. When I returned to Johannesburg I became once more editor and manager of *Umsebenzi* but now with Molly Wolton, a difficult co-editor, breathing down my neck. I crammed my days with ceaseless activity so that there was no time for thought, but at night, on my narrow bed in the house in Bez Valley, I slept badly.

And Bunting now began to age rapidly and presently suffered a disabling stroke, so that he could no longer work at his legal practice nor earn anything by playing the viola. He was not, in spite of Wolton's capitalist blood-sucker taunts, at all well-off. In court cases on behalf of Africans or Party members he had in general given his services without receiving any fee. And always out of his small income he had given regularly and generously to Party funds. He and Rebecca were glad to obtain a position as caretakers of a block of flats. He died in 1936.

Of the whole Bunting story I have written elsewhere* but I should like here to record that there were many in the movement whose consciences were troubled about the way in which Bunting had been treated. There was an uneasy feeling that his illness and death at the age of sixty-three had been a result of his expulsion, for it was said that this had so weighed upon him that his health had failed. As he lay in hospital dying it chanced that Gideon Botha, one of the few Afrikaner leaders in the movement, one time member of the International Socialist League and member also of F.S.U. at the time of Bunting's expulsion, lay seriously ill in the next bed. He called out, 'Bunting, Comrade Bunting, I did not vote against you in F.S.U.' The fact about Bunting was that he had undoubtedly worn himself out in service of the movement which he, more

*In *S.P. Bunting—A Political Biography*, by Edward Roux. Publ. 1944 by the author and distributed by The African Bookman. Now out of print. The whole profits from the sales of this book were given to the fund for the Sidney Bunting Memorial Scholarship at the South African Native College of Fort Hare.

than any other man, had created and which had turned and denounced him.

We all went to the funeral: old trade unionists and members of the I.S.L., people now long since outside the Party. Benny Weinbren organized the funeral and allowed four speakers. These were C.B. Tyler for the old guard, Gana Makabeni for the African workers, W. Kalk for the Party and I, as Bunting's friend and for the opposition within the Party. Gana, who loved Bunting, was too much overcome to say much. What I said was rather less tactful than was seemly on such an occasion of unity. I had first met Bunting when I was at school and he had rescued me from Cadets. With the formation of the Y.C.L. and my joining the Party in 1923 I came to know him well. I had worked with him and had shared in the struggle for the recognition of the Native workers. We had kept in touch at all times by means of long and detailed letters. I admired him greatly. I knew his intellectual honesty and his uncompromising moral need to act as his conscience dictated. His strong empiricism and his impatience with formal theory which led to no practical action were familiar to me. I shared his let's-get-on-with-it tendency. But I honoured too his need to think carefully before committing himself. 'This rage was right i' the main, That acquiescence vain' he was fond of quoting. In the main but not in any absolute sense was any particular political formula right or wrong. Affairs were not simple: one had to take the line of action that seemed best on the whole. Once having decided, he would act. He never compromised with his conscience. He never gave in. Something of all this I tried to say.

Umsebenzi published an obituary notice which said: 'The historical significance of the role played by Comrade Bunting lies in the fact that he realized the great importance of the Native masses in the anti-imperialist struggle and that under his leadership the Communist Party began to organize these masses for the struggle for their emancipation.' A fuller account of Bunting's role was promised for the next issue but this never appeared. It would, of course, have been awkward to write but this would hardly have troubled Wolton.

The Spark, the Trotskyist organ published in Cape Town, was more generous. At the end of a long article relating Bunting's life and work, his fight against white chauvinism and his final expulsion from the Party he had founded, we read: 'Bunting will always remain a living symbol in the South African revolutionary movement. For none was so beloved by the Bantu workers and peasants who, thanks to him, were drawn into the movement. It was they who most fully appreciated his great loving heart, the fine qualities of his character, his crystal-clear honesty as a man and as a revolutionary. This is not the time to recall his mistakes. Who among us is faultless and who does not make mistakes? The memory of Bunting will remain with us.'

One of the finest tributes to Bunting's memory was the founding of the Sidney Bunting Memorial Scholarship, at the Native College of Fort Hare. The money is subscribed annually by a group of Bunting's old friends. Unfortunately the capital sum needed to put this fund on a firm basis was not, I believe, ever raised.

The tragedy of his life was a double one. The Party he had built expelled and denounced him. This was tragic enough. The greater tragedy was that he did not understand why this child of his, this adored child that he had served so faithfully should turn and rend him.

Yet he remained a Communist. He died still believing in the Communist Party and convinced that mistakes by the local leaders had brought about his expulsion. Rebecca, who survived him, shared this view. She saw the whole anti-Bunting campaign as a personal vendetta on the part of a rival leader. She too remained a loyal Communist to the end.

My own belief in communism was to prove less enduring.

(Note: Rebecca is still around and in London).

CHAPTER X

Germiston Campaign

I SHOULD now, I think, put on record that despite the misery of the expulsions and the continued talk of right wing danger, life in Johannesburg was not all gloom. The Jewish Workers Club provided recreation and companionship on any evening. These young Lithuanian Jews, men and girls, were exuberant and delightful people. Many of them joined the Party and proved the most reliable of workers. Of these was Shochat, a theoretician, mercurial, eloquent, explosive, subtle as Lazar Bach, also the beautiful Hilda S., her friend Anna, Taivka the passionate 'little dove' and many others.

The Club premises a large room in, I think, Von Brandis Street were open every evening and thither Win and I went often to an atmosphere of lively cheer. The walls were adorned with brilliant posters which advertised the achievements of the U.S.S.R. Lectures were held regularly. And there we found at any time the sort of talk we liked. About us, as we engaged in heated argument which was not absolutely unlike the talk that we had both known in Hogben's charmed circle though always noisier and more furious, raged the various activities of the Club. Games of ping-pong, dancing to gramophone music, lively charades, coffee and cheese cakes—these are all mixed in my memory. And quietly in a corner two or four members would be playing chess. The Club provided great exercise in concentration. Usually we had to shout our arguments in order to be heard. And one happy by-product was that we acquired facility in pronouncing Russian words and names. 'Spasibo!' we murmured politely, 'Niet pravda!' we cried indignantly, and Birobidjan we babbled happily, Dnieprostroy, Azerbaijan, Novosigorssk, pyatiletka. Once we started to learn Russian but the class dwindled and died. Russian is a forbidding language.

On many occasions the members would organize skits which in true Yiddisher style mocked their own doings and even the exploits of the USSR. Also the members took much innocent pleasure in shocking their traditionalist parents and, more especially grandparents. They were not to be bound by outworn beliefs, not they! So on the Day of Atonement they arranged a Club picnic to Little Falls and there consumed ham sandwiches with almost ceremonial gusto. Later, some of them felt a little sick after this unclean meat but still felt the gesture had been worth it. No effete shibboleths for these clever, enlightened people! Alas, after thus conspicuously sowing their wild oats of defiance, many of them would slip quietly back into their ancient Jewish customs. We were presently to see how many of their marriages took place under a chuppah and how later they would arrange brismillah for their sons.

But now it was 1932 and they were in the first fine fury of revolt. With the light of freedom shining in their eyes they lived and worked and played and talked, especially talked, and gave us much delight. Bliss was it in that dawn to be alive. And from these radiant young people we built up a nucleus of loyal helpers who at a word would rally to defend the Party platform, form a crowd at a meeting, hand out leaflets, paste up stickers, also a group who came regularly once a week to single, fold, wrap and despatch *Umsebenzi*. Hilda would bring biscuits, Win made tea, the sessions ended hilariously. Always we laughed a lot, talked all at once when the work was done, argued, sometimes gave Shochat his head and at a late hour dispersed and went our ways. In my memory these evenings are pure joy. But Win, then in a difficult teaching post at Forest High School, occasionally protested. 'I have to keep those tough guys in order tomorrow. I do need a little sleep!' The others were mostly office-workers or artisans.

The Communist Party, now quite pure, announced itself as ideologically strengthened by the removal of the right danger. In fact it was much weakened, not only by the loss of hardworking leaders and their supporters who drifted away but also by the destruction in different ways of the Durban and Bloemfontein branches and the collapse of several smaller branches which had suffered neglect and a bewilderment which had not been dispelled by the heavy Imprecor-style explanations in *Umsebenzi*. However there was plenty of leadership. Molly was back from Moscow and in the background, Russell, the

Comintern representative whom I had met in Joubert Park, advised, exhorted, issued directives. The Political Bureau functioned at a furious pace.

In Johannesburg elaborate programmes were drawn up covering every field of activity. All Party members were subjected to the most severe discipline. New trade unions were to be built up. The African miners were to be organized, though, since these men were illiterate and lived in closed compounds so that we had no means of contact with them, how this could be done was not clear. Peasant leagues were to be started. Political training classes were to be compulsory for all members. Special day schools for Party functionaries were to be held from time to time. *Umsebenzi* was to be enlarged and its circulation increased tenfold. All was planned to the minutest detail. The whole Party was reorganized in factory, farm and street nuclei. Organized Party fractions were to function in all trade unions and mass organizations. Every committee, every member was to be given a definite task or tasks and an elaborate time schedule was laid down for their fulfilment.

The only trouble about all this was that there were now too few people to carry it out. Moreover, such forces as were available were still further reduced by a process called 'preparation for illegality.' Certain comrades were instructed that they were not publicly to identify themselves with the Party. They must remain behind the scenes, functioning on secret committees and directing the work. These secret functionaries had practically nothing to do but draw up gigantic plans which the over-burdened open functionaries strove in vain to carry out. At one stage practically all the open work of the Party was done by two of us, Joffe and me, though in the end neither of us was considered good enough to serve on the Political Bureau.

Joffe was a plump little man, cherubic in appearance, with a perky bouncing step and a certain tough innocence and enduring obstinacy which made him quite immune to argument. He had, said the irreverent, accepted the Imprecor line for all time to come. Win said that with his jaunty walk he was rather like Mr Pickwick. He was adept at extracting money from sympathizers who were often after a visit from him quite astonished to realize the extent to which they had been persuaded to express their sympathy. Joffe was at this time completely happy and fulfilled. He rejoiced in the comradeship of Wolton and Bach and would refer to them as 'the boys'. He enjoyed knowing that he was indispensable and invariably carried a neat black despatch case which was filled, as we supposed, with documents of the most secret. He took himself extremely seriously and lacked a sense of humour so that he was much annoyed on one occasion when the Jewish workers put on a skit at the Club and portrayed him, little black case, neat little paunch and all, talking of 'the boys'. He said, with offended seriousness, 'But this is dangerous. The police might get to know.' I laughed at him. 'Do you really think the police don't already know all about you?' This mollified him. What had hurt was the suggestion of ridicule. What comforted was the reassurance of his real importance. He was a good and loyal comrade.

I have mentioned that the Imprecor trio were all in their different ways effective public speakers but at this time of the undercover leadership it was only Molly who was a regular Sunday evening orator. I suspected that this was because she so greatly enjoyed speaking and putting odd hecklers to rout. Her audience enjoyed it too. Sunday evening meetings on the City Hall steps were lively also by reason of another brilliant soapbox performer in the person of Issy Diamond. Issy was no theoretician, right-wing deviations peppered his speeches, but he was always amusing and could make the crowd roar with laughter. He too had his ready comeback to hecklers. Other speakers were Gideon Botha who spoke simply and sincerely in Afrikaans and was seldom heckled, also Nzula who was brilliant but unreliable and sometimes John Marks. I also spoke fairly regularly but when not wanted on the soapbox I moved about among the crowd selling *Umsebenzi* to people who would buy the paper but complained that it was unreadable. 'As a paper it's good to light the fire with.'

It was on a Sunday evening that I saw standing in the crowd a girl whom I had known in Cape Town. I went to speak to her. 'Hello, Belinda!'

'Not Belinda now.' She smiled and was pleased to see me.

'Why not?'

'Cape Town is over. Things are grim. Now it has to be Winifred.' She bought a paper. 'Are you putting on an African speaker? I'd like to hear one.'

I went back to the platform and asked Nzula to speak next. He spoke as ever with assurance and competence and his easy control of English. No hecklers ever took him on. With his speech the meeting ended. It was a cold evening. It is not policy to harangue an audience that is shivering. I caught up with Winifred as she was leaving.

'Come up for cocoa,' she invited. 'I live near here.'

So I went with her to her room in Winchester House. This was then a rather grimy old-fashioned building with single rooms to let on the top floor. The rooms were cheap. We went up in an ancient creaking lift. Winifred made cocoa and opened a packet of biscuits. We sat on the bed and talked. The room was barely furnished. Curtains, a bed, a table, a chair, a queer Heath Robinson sort of wardrobe made of six orange boxes which were set on end, three at each side and between them a space with a hanging rod across and a brown paper cover to keep off dust. There was a divided cretonne curtain in front and the boxes at one end contained food supplies, cups and plates, at the other end clothing. There was also a cabin trunk and a sewing machine. I thought of Bodmer's room.

Winifred apologized. 'I'm still rather hard up after Cape Town.' But I admired the room and the independence it stood for.

'Why did you come to South Africa?' I asked her.

'Well, it's stupid really. I had bronchitis. I kept on having bronchitis. My doctor said it was just a bad habit and I ought to snap out of it. I should go to a dry climate for a while. Then at Wembley I saw the South Africa pavilion and there was a display of Ericas, quite lovely. And a notice said that there are more varieties of flowers on Table Mountain than in the whole of England and Wales. So I thought I would come here.' I began to like this girl. A mass of Ericas seemed to me a good reason for wanting to come to South Africa. She went on. 'And then there was this job at Roedean. I hadn't a hope but I applied. They looked down their noses at my Lancashire accent but I got the job. I suppose I was the only applicant.'

'How did Cape Town happen?'

Her eyes were shining now.

It was the most incredible luck. I met Hogben on a ship

going home on a trip to England. He was talking to Professor Campbell who said something quite stupid. This was tourist class and we were sitting at a long table at tea time. No one had spoken to me but I chipped in and said "What a piece of teleology!" and Hogben smiled at me and we went on talking. It was really because of Hogben that I decided to take that year off from teaching and study at Cape Town. I had some money saved but of course not enough. That's why I'm in debt now. But it was worth it.

And again I liked her and the bare shabby room.
Then she was asking me about myself and I told her of my life, of the house in Bez Valley, of being locked out, of bugs in Braamfontein, of Wits University and of Cambridge and then of *Umsebenzi* and why I had had to leave Cape Town. She was not one of the girls who had come to help me then and the story was new to her.

We talked and talked and I left just in time to catch the last tram to Bez Valley. This was the first of many evenings I spent in talk with Winifred after the Sunday evening meetings. These were sometimes in some café with Benny, Willy and others, but more often in her room because it was cheaper. 'I cycle to school,' said Winifred, 'because that way I save two fourpences every day.' She was then teaching at Jeppe Girls High School.

I too had to think about fourpences.

Or sometimes we talked poetry and I would recite long passages of Swinburne. She was fond of quoting Browning. 'The poetry you love forever is what hits you when you're about sixteen,' she said. We disputed over Gerard Manley Hopkins whose verse she admired and I did not. She was in love with the words and the syncopated rhythm so great a contrast to Swinburne's measured melody. What put me off was the philosophy of the poems: especially I disliked the 'Wreck of the Deutschland.' 'But you can't ever have everything,' she protested. 'You can't expect a poet to have your ideas.' I conceded this but still could not like Hopkins.

Also, rarely, on some Sunday afternoons, we managed to walk together on the koppies where we botanized. Her degree had included botany as well as mathematics which was the subject she now taught. These scrambly walks were the sweetest rest from politics.

And, as I have mentioned, we went often together to the Jewish Workers Club.

But Sunday evening meetings, though often enough quite exciting, were mere routine. The serious work of the Party at this time was with the unemployed. On May Day of 1931 Diamond led a huge demonstration of white and black unemployed. They shouted the slogan 'We want bread' and tried to enter the Carlton Hotel. The police intervened and arrested some of the leaders. As a result of this Diamond was sentenced to a year's imprisonment and in the early months of 1932 he was still in gaol. It was up to others to organize the unemployed.

I shared a little in this work when I had time but it was carried on in the main by Molly, by Gideon Botha and by certain of the African comrades. It says much for Molly's forcefulness and charm that she, a Jewess, proved so popular with the white unemployed who were mostly Afrikaners. However with her round face and high colour she did not look Jewish. The problem was always to get white and Native unemployed to march together in a demonstration. A meeting of the whites would be held outside the Labour Exchange while African speakers went to tackle the crowd of Bantu near the Pass Office. At some time, pre-arranged, the two meetings would be brought together to form a procession to go to various authorities and demand relief. These marches began well but by the time they arrived anywhere it was found that most of the whites had vanished. Only a handful of white supporters remained to give some semblance of united action.

Such demonstrations were attempted regularly with varying success but on Christmas Eve things went well. About a hundred persons, nearly one-third of them white, walked in procession with a wagon. They appealed to various businesses, to butchers, bakers, grocers, for gifts of food for the workless. They did not meet with many refusals. A load of good things was piled on the wagon and these were shared out among all who had marched.

But on the whole the Party was having heavy going. In May Douglas Wolton went to gaol with a sentence of three and a half months' hard labour. This was on a charge of criminal defamation and arose from an article in *Umsebenzi* of the previous September. In this article Wolton had alleged that in

Krantzkop Gaol the Dingaan's Day prisoners held there had suffered ill-usage. It seems probable that most of the allegations were strictly well-founded but in court some witnesses were easily led into contradicting themselves and the magistrate was able to reject most of the evidence. One witness, at the end of his evidence, removed his shirt and showed the scars on his back. The case was taken to appeal and the judges handling the offending issue of *Umsebenzi* found also a linocut by me. This showed a black man drawing a wagon on which sat a fat white farmer. By the side walked a policeman with a long whip and in front was a missionary holding a leading rein. The caption was an extract from a speech made by a Nationalist: 'I submit that the Native is happiest when he works for the white man.' This was one of my more ambitious efforts. The judges held that this cartoon was itself an incitement to race hostility. The appeal was lost and Wolton went to gaol.

Towards the end of the year the most exciting events took place in and near Germiston location. This location had up to now proved too difficult for the Communists to tackle. The superintendent had rigorously insisted that no one not resident there should enter without a written permit. Now in September 1932 a vacancy occurred in the parliamentary constituency of Germiston. This was at the time of the gold standard crisis. The Nationalist Government was trying to keep on gold. The English pound had been devalued and the South African pound, based on gold, was worth about £6 in London. This suited the South African reserve Bank and certain South African capitalists but it did not suit the Chamber of Mines who were still paying wages and buying supplies in this country at the rate set by the undevalued pound. The S.A.P., led by Smuts, was trying to force the Government off gold. The by-election in Germiston thus became of critical importance. The previous member had been a Nationalist.

The Communist Party now decided to enter the election with an African 'demonstrative candidate.' Africans had no vote in the Transvaal nor were they allowed to stand for election to Parliament. But most of the inhabitants of Germiston were Africans and the Communists maintained that if these had votes they would return a Communist. So J.B. Marks was nominated and the campaign went ahead. We tried to hold a public meeting for whites on the Germiston market square but this was broken up with some violence by Nationalists. Some meetings held at the railway workshops, where the workers were mainly English-speaking artisans, had more success.

But the main objective was to reach the Natives in the location. Risking capture by the superintendent, Communists entered the location and handed out leaflets calling meetings on vacant ground just outside the location. The burning grievance in the location was the lodgers tax. Under the Urban Areas Act municipalities are entitled to levy a tax on all persons over the age of eighteen, not being tenants or their wives, who live in a municipal location. The tax in Germiston was half-a-crown a lodger a month. Tenants had built their own houses on plots for which they paid a monthly ground rent. Now in addition a tenant had to pay tax for members of his own family once they reached the age of eighteen. In this time of heavy unemployment the people were not able to pay. To catch the illegal 'lodgers' the police made frequent rough raids in the small hours of the morning. So to avoid being caught and imprisoned many young persons, men and women, would leave their homes at night and go to sleep out on the veld. Transvaal nights can be bitterly cold.

Here was a genuine grievance and the Party made the most of it. Huge crowds turned up to our meetings which were held usually on Sunday mornings just outside the location. The meeting on 16 October stands out in my memory.

On that day we set out early. It was a lovely morning with the brilliant sunshine and high clear sky of the high-veld spring. A sympathizer had provided a motor lorry and on to this we piled, speakers, interpreters, an assortment of stalwarts from the Jewish Workers' Club and girls in their bright cotton frocks. On the way we laid our plans. Our supporters were to stand in close rank round our platform facing the audience and were not to leave their places whatever in the way of disturbance might develop amongst the crowd. In retrospect there seems something of quite splendid absurdity in our journey that morning, some thirty young dreamers, starry-eyed, a lorryload of laughter, setting forth to defeat the oppressors of the toiling masses.

Outside the location we set up a borrowed table as platform

and our guard took up their positions. We put up a red and white banner. A large crowd gathered quickly and the meeting began. As chairman I spoke first and was followed by Molly. Jeffrey Movene was interpreting. We spoke mainly of the lodgers' tax and of what, under communist leadership, the people could do to combat it. The crowd listened quietly and there was no disorder. But presently a number of police arrived. These included some plain clothes detectives well-known to us, also two officers in uniform, Captain Brown and Lieutenant Fourie, also a number of African police and other African good boys who mingled with the crowd. At least they tried to edge their way in but found the people densely packed. On the outskirts, by pushing and shoving, by offensive remarks, they managed to raise small scuffles here and there. Some of our young stalwarts, eager for a scrap, seemed about to break away from the platform cordon. 'Keep your places!' Hilda reminded them. The scuffles died down.

The police were now in some difficulty. They could not order the meeting to disperse as it was not being held within the location or on a road but on a stretch of waste ground. Also since it was not disorderly they could not claim a breach of the peace. So they began themselves to interrupt the speakers. To be heckled by police in uniform was a new experience for us but Molly was more than a match for any policeman. Soon she had the crowd laughing at the slower-witted police officers. The next thing they tried was to order an African to speak from the edge of the crowd, urging them to stop listening to this nonsense and to go instead to watch the football game which was in progress in the location. But the people chose to stay and hear the talk about the lodgers' tax. The police then demanded the pass of our interpreter. Now on the way, riding on the lorry, we had discovered that Movene, in disobedience to Party instructions, had no pass. The cordon stood firm and the police could not easily get near to take Movene. Molly continued to speak in her clear strong voice and we all pretended not to hear the demand for the pass. Some plain-clothes men, Europeans, pressed forward close to the cordon and one of them drew his lighted cigarette across the faces of three of the girls. At the same time they shouted in rhythm 'Shut up! Shut up!' And their unofficial supporters now began to succeed in penetrating the crowd and in starting scuffles here and there. The meeting became a rough and tumble and Molly's voice could no longer be heard. Also Movene, more and more distracted by the confusion and noise, was no longer capable of interpreting. The end was inevitable. The police reached the platform, pulled Movene down and arrested Molly and me.

We were led off struggling to the accompaniment of boos and jeers from the crowd which followed to the police station. On the way we saw a European standing by the road. He laughed and made some comment. Two white police in uniform ran towards him. He fled into a hut and closed the door. The police followed and pulled the door open. People outside could see through the open door that the police were striking the man about the head with their swinging handcuffs. Then they closed the door. After a few minutes they came out.

The arrested Communists were charged with 'resisting arrest' and with 'inciting feelings of hostility between Natives and Eueopeans' and also, in the case of Movene, with a Poll Tax offence. In our turn we proposed to lay charges against the police of unlawfully shouting and breaking up a public meeting and also of assault upon a number of women who had stood in the cordon about the platform. The cases were referred to the Attorney-General and he, wisely from the point of view of the authorities, allowed the matter to drop. But this was a hollow victory.

On nomination day it was found that there were four candidates in the field. Besides the Government and S.A.P. candidates, there was a Labour Party man and also an independent. I had been given the task of making the nomination of our Communist candidate, the Native J. B. Marks. I waited until the four white candidates had been duly nominated and then rose up and made my demonstrative nomination. The magistrate, looking astonished as well he might, heard me with grave attention and then turned up a passage in the electoral regulations and read it aloud. He added a few words of explanation of the reasons why Marks could not be accepted as a candidate and ended by saying he had taken note of the matter. From our point of view this was all much better than it might have been and the incident was well reported in the press.

However, for me at the moment the outlook was not healthy.

I saw that I was surrounded by a crowd of extremely large and furiously angry young men, mostly Nationalist Afrikaners as it seemed. My problem was how to get away without being lynched. For a while I sat where I was and thought things over, making no attempt to move. One of the nominated candidates, J. N. Strauss who was later to succeed Smuts as leader of the S.A.P., seeing the position, spoke to the police and they, grudgingly enough for they too were angry, took me into a room to wait. Some little time later they ordered me roughly to be on my way. They told me to leave by a back door of the building. Foolishly, I thought this not a bad plan. In the event it proved an idiotic thing to do. Clearly some of the Nationalist toughs had expected just this, possibly tipped off by the police, and a number of them had gone to this exit. I found myself in an alley with groups of angry young men at both ends. Behind me the door closed against any attempt to return. Choosing what seemed the less dangerous group I ran full tilt at them and managed to get through under a rain of blows. Once clear I ran for my life. As I have said earlier, I am no runner but fear now lent me an unnatural turn of speed. I managed to shake off the pursuit. But now I did another idiotic thing. Instead of making for the crowded streets of Germiston and so to the main station, I ran out of the town and took shelter in a coppice which was part of a large plantation and there stayed hidden among the trees. I could hear my pursuers crashing past in various directions. Then for a long time I heard nothing. I waited for a while longer and then emerged with caution. Still I saw no sign of danger and looking about me found that I was quite near Driehoek Station. There, thought I, I could find safety on a train. This was my final folly of the day. My tormenters had evidently sent out groups to wait for me at probable escape points and no sooner was I on the platform than five or six of them appeared. With fists and feet they attacked me, pummeling and buffeting and trying to drag me away from the station while I clung in desperation to the ironwork of the footbridge. I think their numbers were some hindrance to them, some help to me. While they were hitting me some station officials stood and watched with interest. But a train came at last and I managed to get on. I was not pursued further.

Back in Johannesburg I was met by a group of Party members

who took me to a doctor's surgery. Here I was patched up and bandaged. In fact, apart from some severe bruises on ribs, shoulders and shins, and one deep cut from a fist blow on my cheek, I was not much hurt. I had received a valuable lesson in what not to do when pursued by a mob. However, owing to my bruised ribs and arms, I was not able to make the usual linocut cartoon for *Umsebenzi* and this Win undertook, her first attempt at a linocut. She drew an African boxer in the ring, his hands fettered behind him by chains labelled Pass Laws, being punched hard by his opponent who was Pirow the Minister of Justice.

And indeed, before election day on 30 November, the Minister of Justice issued an order to five leading 'reds' to leave the Witwatersrand for a period of one year from 12 November, thus hitting hard at our various activities. Those thus banished were Issy Diamond, Douglas Wolton, Willy Kalk, Solly Sachs and I. All except Sachs, who had been recently expelled, were Party members. Wolton, now out of gaol, was not in Johannesburg at the time. Though Sachs was no longer a Party member it was he, more than any of the others, who was undermining the Government's chances in the Germiston election. There had been a strike of garment workers in Germiston and most of these girls were Afrikaners. They, their brothers, fathers and husbands, had probably supported the Nationalists in previous elections. But during the strike the police had used much brutality in dealing with demonstrations and on one occasion mounted police had ridden down a girl striker. Sachs was the militant and popular leader of the Garment Workers' Union. Issy Diamond was a popular leader of the unemployed, Kalk was a trade union organizer, Wolton had annoyed the authorities by his allegations of prison brutalities, and I had played a part in affairs at Germiston location. The banishment orders neatly removed us all from the scene. Pirow aimed to kill several birds with one stone.

In the event it did not happen that way. We all disappeared from the Rand for a few days, Issy leaving his barber's shop, Kalk and Sachs their trade union offices, I my work on *Umsebenzi*.

The Party had a plan for me. The ban began from noon on 12 November, which was a Saturday. Shortly before noon a meeting was started on the City Hall steps. Recent events had roused public interest and a large crowd soon gathered which suited our purpose well. I was put on to speak, instructed to pause dramatically while the Post Office clock struck its leisurely twelve strokes and then to continue speaking for a few minutes. In the crowd were the inevitable plain clothes men and some uniformed police. They stood there nonplussed while I went on with my speech after the hour of noon. It seemed that no instructions had been issued to them. They made no move to arrest me and by delay they lost their chance. I went on speaking for nearly ten minutes more then ended my speech and left the platform. Molly at once took my place and began to divert the meeting with more than her usual brilliance while I slipped away amongst the crowd and so to a car which stood waiting in President Street. Swiftly I was driven away.

Thus began a period of hide and seek played with the police. During this time I successfully stayed hidden. I shall not say just where but it was in a flat quite near the centre of the city. The sympathizer who gave me house room lent me also shirts to wear and a distinguished suit sufficiently unlike my normal casual khaki shirt and shorts. Also I wore a hat. In fact I went about disguised as a gentleman. It felt extremely odd. Standing before a looking glass I tried the effect of shaving off the centre of the line of my eyebrows which was continuous above my nose. This did not seem to make much difference. I wore glasses also, of plain glass slightly tinted, and this helped to conceal in part the still quite visible wound on my cheek. Walking was another thing. I managed to disguise my normal swift and slightly off-balance stride and to assume a slower and steadier pace. This was made somewhat easier than it might have been by a still swollen knee from my adventure at Driehoek and even more by the fact that I had in general nowhere to walk to, no reason for hurry.

My chief discomfort was the enforced inactivity. The daily papers were delivered and I read them exhaustively noting reports of the police search for me and finding other political items of interest. After that what to do? I had not brought any books and I missed the piles of writing paper that normally I took for granted. I read all the books in the flat. I sauntered in Joubert Park, feeling uncomfortable in my hat. I thought of a way to get a message to Win. At this time she was taking a course in bookkeeping at Thorlund's Commercial College. In theory she attended three evenings a week but in practice, having decided that she could follow the text quite well by herself, she went only when she had work to be corrected. I took a chance. I called at the College on Tuesday afternoon and left a note addressed to her. It read, 'Where the sundew wasn't, 7–30 Wednesday.' This meant a spot on the koppie opposite Roedean where once we had thought we saw sundew. There I went early and waited. I had no way of knowing that Win had received the message. Also I guessed that since my disappearance she would have been trailed by detectives. Actually this trailing was not skilled and we were usually aware of it and able to shake it off when we wanted to. On this occasion Win jumped on to a Twist Street tram as it was moving off from a stop and she felt confident that she was not followed. From the terminus she walked to the koppie.

We scrambled up the rough slope to the height and there I spread my mack. My hat, which I now took off, had alarmed her. 'Oh, Eddie, you don't look like you!'

'I am me. But terribly bored. What's been happening.'

'Everything. Nothing. You feel like you! You looked like Toerien.'

'What's Toerien been up to?'

'Not much really. They're baffled. They trot round after us and lurk in doorways. Raincoats and soft hats. Like pantomime spies.'

'S–sh! Laugh quietly.' I wanted to hear more.

'Well, they went to Bez Valley to try to catch you there. They looked in cupboards and under beds. Your sister made up a Pimpernel rhyme. "They seek him here, they seek him there. Detectives seek him everywhere. Is he up a chimney or under a bed? That demned elusive Roux the Red".'

'Yes, I read that rhyme in the R.D.M. Which sister?'

But this she did not know. She had not then met my family.

I heard later that it was Enid who had devised this jingle. Toerien and another plain clothes man had gone to the house in Bez Valley. In the boys' room they pounced on young Arthur who had gone early to bed and lay muffled in covers with only his hair showing. They seized him by the hair and pulled him out of sleep. After this my father, much diverted, invited them to a glass of beer in the kitchen and discoursed long with tongue in cheek. He detested my politics but my present police-baiting antics were much to his taste.

I wanted Party news. How had the Sunday meeting gone?

Magnificent! I've never seen such a huge crowd. I sold fifteen dozen easily. Only one snub: a man said he wanted it to wrap fish in. Molly spoke and M. and Gideon. Then Molly again. She had them eating out of her hand. She put the Party line, how the Government is out to silence the toiling masses and these banishments are a sign of fear. She poked fun at the detectives and got everyone laughing. But I wish Issy could have been there.

I wished this too. I thought how often Issy, our liveliest speaker, was neglected and his gifts despised. He was not long out of prison and now, banished, he was on the run and his business suffering.

'Joffe says he'll collect you for some lunch hour meetings. They'll send a car for you.'

'You didn't tell Joffe you were meeting me?'

'Of course not. I told no one.'

'That's my girl!'

'Hilda says she loves you.'

'I love her too.'

'Niet pravda! No one but me.'

Below us on Houghton Drive the sleek cars purred by and lighted the road so that we looked down on a brilliant stage.

Time sped by. Win ran to catch a last tram. I had to let her go alone while I followed more circumspectly walking with my new careful step.

Twice more during my hiding period I met Win by arrangement and once we met by accident, but how and where are best not recorded.

And twice the Party sent a car to collect me, first warning me by telephone. I hastily reverted to my khaki shirt and shorts and was taken to factory lunch hour meetings, then after speaking, whisked away and back to my hide-out. But this game could not go on much longer. It was decided that we should end it by a dramatic arrest: I should speak at a public meeting and let the police take me openly. And so it fell out but in the meantime Solly Sachs, who was always quick to get the law to work for him if this could be done, had made an application to the Supreme Court to test the validity of the banishment orders. The matter thus became *sub judice* and all the banished persons returned to Johannesburg pending the decision of the court. This went against us but an appeal to the Appellate Division with the usual law's delays, prevented the order from being carried out for another ten months. In the meantime Smuts had become Minister of Justice and he withdrew the ban imposed by Pirow.

In Germiston the by-election proved an overwhelming victory for the South African Party. The Nationalist candidate came second, the other two nowhere. The Party collected votes for their demonstration candidate and declared that Marks would have been elected if African votes had been allowed. This was only an estimate for in the conditions of confusion and terror in the location it was not possible to collect all the votes.

The campaign in the location continued but meetings of residents were now regularly broken up by the police and their good boys and arrests followed. Men, women and even children were charged with public violence and some were sentenced to imprisonment. We had to give up holding meetings.

In January we tried again. About six of us, Party members, on this occasion without a bodyguard, started a meeting on a Sunday morning. No notice had been given of this meeting and the crowd gathered slowly. As soon as we had a few hearers, a gang of African men arrived armed with heavy sticks and, led by one nicknamed Mac who was a Native sergeant of police in the location, set about the meeting and drove the Natives away. Two white police looked on with approval. When asked to stop the assaults they refused and said, 'You people came here at your own risk.' Black and blue, their soap boxes smashed, their banners torn, the Communists managed to escape. The affair was reported next day in the *Rand Daily Mail* under the caption 'Communists not wanted!'

Later in January one more protest meeting was attempted in the location. Residents gathered to protest against the police raids to catch the illegal lodgers and also against the smashing up of meetings. This meeting was broken up by the police, led by the superintendent himself flourishing a revolver. Shots were fired and some eighteen Africans were wounded. An old woman died of her wounds.

Turton, the superintendent, was subsequently acquitted on a charge of culpable homicide.

This was the final act in the Germiston campaign.

CHAPTER XI

Party Discipline

It is hardly possible, I believe, for any person who has not actually been a member of the Communist Party to understand the tremendous scope and power of Party discipline. This was a rule, often harsh and always unyielding, to which all members submitted. The rule covered our every activity; in effect one had no private life but in every detail must serve the Party. To learn the perfect obedience required was at first a hard lesson. What was it that caused so many of the young and intelligent thus to surrender their freedom? It is always ultimately a choice of becoming accomplice by consent or of joining in revolt. The choice of revolt may stem from a deep feeling of guilt and from what Ignazio Silone has called 'that pride which makes poverty and prison preferable to self-contempt.' A feature of our loyalty was that every act of sacrifice and self-denial served always to bind us more strongly to the ideal we served. Hardship could not weaken resolve but strengthened it. No member could conceivably be tempted from the Party by any lure of luxury or pleasure. And this is the grand error of those who think to fill empty churches by making the seats more comfortable or by providing jazz music. It is not pleasure or comfort that is man's deep desire but meaning.

Now, since presently I was to marry this girl from England, I want to tell how she came to join the Party. In her days at Liverpool University Winifred had been inclined to rebellion and had been a member of the lively Debating Society and of the small and despised Fabian Society. But the latter was a rather dim and gently reformist organization which held occasional lectures and whose members learned to sing the Red Flag. In South Africa Winifred was deeply shocked by her first experience of a South African train with its segregated coaches, for whites, for Indians, for Natives. This was the train which bore her to Johannesburg to her post at Roedean. Roedean, that distinguished private school, proved to be a little enclave of England and she felt, after three years, that she knew Johannesburg hardly at all. So when, in 1931, she was no longer at a boarding school she chose deliberately to live in the centre of town. She now saw the colour bar in action and disliked what she saw. But it was not until later in the year when I was away in Durban that she decided to join the Party.

It happened on a Saturday afternoon that she cycled to a meeting for Natives on a vacant lot in Ferreirastown. She stood observing, writing an occasional note of what the speakers said. These were Kotane, Mofutsanyana and others. Joffe came bouncing across to ask her what paper she represented. She told him she was not a reporter. When the meeting ended the small band of Communists began to push their wagon with its banners along Fox Street towards the Party office. Winifred rode away but, noticing a group of police waiting in a side street, she turned back and was in time to witness a vicious attack on the Communists. The police swung staves to good effect and also smashed up the banners. Next morning Winifred went to the Party office and there met Kotane, his head bound with a clean bandage through which blood was still seeping. She met others but remembers especially Kotane. She decided then that she must join the Party and asked Joffe if there were instruction classes she could attend. Joffe thought she was a spy.

Her first experience of a class was unfortunate. Arriving a few minutes late she found the office in darkness and thought that the class must be elsewhere. She waited about for some time and presently saw a group approaching. Here came Joffe and Douglas Wolton and some others coming late to the class. This was the first time she was aware of Party casualness in matters of time. And of all these things she wrote and told me.

At this time Moses Kotane was well on his way to being our cleverest African theoretician, possibly sharing this distinction with Marks. He had begun by learning the meanings of difficult words, was now fluent in English, a voracious reader and accurate exponent of communist writings. He was an adequate speaker but a better writer. Sometimes it was Kotane who would conduct the instruction class.

There too was Edwin Mofutsanyana who had come from

Potchefstroom with his wife Josie Mpama who was our only African woman leader. Mofutsanyana was thoughtful and reserved, gentle, slow of speech, never a good soap-box man and never eloquent in explaining Imprecor directives. He was loyal and accepted the Imprecor line without question.

Winifred was presently assigned to work in the Friends of the Soviet Union and in the night school. It was as a member of the Party fraction on F.S.U. committee that she had her first experience of having to obey orders which she disliked. As a newcomer to the movement she did not know much of Bunting's record of devotion to the Party but she was aware of integrity in him and was disgusted by sordid manoeuvres which tricked him into seeming technically in the wrong. In letters we exchanged I spoke of political necessity and the need for obedience to leadership. But away in Durban I did not learn the whole truth of what was happening until much later.

In 1932 when I was once more in Johannesburg we were able to argue more effectively than in letters. Does the end justify the means? I said that ours is a bolshevik party and we must trust our leaders. It was an issue that we never resolved. But Winifred had, as I had, a strong inclination to immediate practical activities. We both plunged into various tasks that lay to hand and presently the argument was forgotten.

Lazar Bach replaced me in Durban and attempted to build up Native trade unions there, also to found small local branches of the Party. In these attempts he had a little success but the various organizations soon collapsed and towards the end of 1932 Bach was recalled to Johannesburg.

Here work among the unemployed continued and the Party was strengthened by the coming of two Africans from Pretoria. These were genuine workers, rather rough proletarians, not tribalist but location born. Both were effective speakers; both were sincere and filled with enthusiasm for the cause. Later this enthusiasm declined and sincerity became corrupted as they were drawn into the struggle for power within the Party where factional manoeuvres were now rampant and were, if we had had the wit to perceive it, a symptom of dissolution and decay. Peter Ramutla had already suffered a year's imprisonment on a charge of vagrancy served on him while he was addressing a meeting. Stephen Tefu, rather the cleverer of the two, proved himself competent and fearless in work with the unemployed, which apart from the work in F.S.U. and some unions, was for some time our main activity.

The Party ran a soup kitchen in Ferreirastown and organized the unemployed to collect food and money for the purpose. This was soon stopped by the authorities who began to arrest men on charges of holding illegal processions. Tefu was arrested.

In this year came Gideon Botha, an Afrikaner who had once been a member of the I.S.L. He was a vital person who had lived strenuously. He had been a hobo in America and had there met Jack London. In South Africa he had worked on the mines and had played a part in the strikes of 1913, 1914, and 1922. Later he had gone into the country and had come to have a liking and respect for Africans. He now returned to the left movement and became the leader of the white unemployed, also a speaker in Afrikaans at our Sunday evening meetings, also a member of F.S.U. As our only Afrikaans-speaking leader he was in a position of strength and was able to steer clear of factional activities. It was he who later, when Bunting lay on his death bed, was to call out his disclaimer of having voted against Bunting in the F.S.U.

These men were my comrades. When Bach was recalled, Douglas and Molly Wolton left for Cape Town. The Comintern man, Russell, had already gone, so that of the Imprecor set there remained only Bach and since all direction fell to him he was kept busy and had no time to stifle *Umsebenzi* with long theoretical essays. I saw my chance to make the Party organ once more a readable newspaper.

Umsebenzi was now enlarged and presently became again a weekly. Soon its circulation began again to climb so that it once more outdistanced its chief rivals, *Umteteli wa Bantu* and the *Bantu World*. Later I happily made a linocut cartoon showing a race in which some four or five Bantu newspapers were the horses with *Umsebenzi* well in the lead. The increased circulation was in part owing to a change in policy which I initiated. Since the end of 1930 the Party had concentrated, though not very adroitly so far as *Umsebenzi* was concerned, on the Bantu workers and peasants, but now I tried to capture the interest of the Bantu intelligentsia. These were teachers, ministers of religion, clerks, minor officials, a few traders. It had been

Communist policy to call them reformist and good boys. *Umsebenzi* now carried informative articles and much discussion of problems such as the new Bantu orthography, 'what should we call ourselves, Bantu, African or Native?', matters of health and education. Presently we found we were in touch with a number of African teachers who became subscribers and even agents.

Also we now started a small monthly magazine, *Indlela Yenkululeko*—The Road to Freedom. This was edited by Winifred and largely written by her and by me; she typed the wax stencils which we duplicated; finally we folded the sheets, stapled them together in a bright cover and sent the magazines off to various centres and especially to students at Fort Hare then the only Native university college in South Africa.

We had found that attacks upon religion did not go down well with Africans though rationalism did gain a few converts. Criticism of some missionaries and of the average white Christian was more acceptable. The Bantu could easily see that many churches practised a colour bar, their members being Christian in name but not in deed. The African would say: 'They told us to shut our eyes and pray; when we opened our eyes we saw that the white man had taken our land.' Yet of the white men with whom the Natives had daily contact many of the missionaries were clearly their most sincere friends. So, reluctantly for the Communists greatly relished anti-religious propaganda, we abandoned these attacks and concentrated instead on a more constructive approach to the thoughtful among the Bantu. This was work I enjoyed and Winifred shared my enthusiasm. *Umsebenzi* and *Indlela* prospered and we felt we were getting somewhere. For a time I was left free to follow my bent though on the P.B., of which I was presently again a member having been removed earlier because of my vacillations in respect of the campaign against Bunting, Bach did not fail to rebuke me for the right-wing deviations committed in *Umsebenzi*.

During this year Winifred and I came up against Party discipline. I was told that as a dedicated revolutionary I ought not to marry. She was told that as a petty bourgeois intellectual she was the wrong sort of wife for a revolutionary leader. We discussed the matter. 'The trouble is,' said Winifred, 'that my father was haberdasher to Mr Spurgeon.' But I said, 'It's not what our fathers were but what we are now, you and I, the kind of thing we like doing. We are condemned as right-wing intellectuals whatever we do or don't do. If we don't marry there'll be scandal and you will not be able to teach any more. A pity, because you do it well.' And other things were said. So in the end we disobeyed and were married in a registry office with no friends present. Later we let it be known that we were married. We rented a small house in Anderson Street. When I went to the landlord to take this house he objected that it was not a suitable house for a white person. I had in the end to tell him that I was a Communist and wanted a place where Non-Europeans could visit me. So we got the house and one room was given over to type-setting. This work was done chiefly by me and by Sepeng, a lively Basuto who was one of our brightest interpreters. On the platform he was not content with words only but would render in mime what was said. To us he was Sepeng the merry, the good companion. From the house Sepeng and I had to carry galleys to the printer and there I had to make up the forms ready for printing. Often I found myself working against time. I remember that one night as I toiled late, alone in the printer's shop, trying to have everything ready for next day, Win came walking quietly to bring me a banana, to tell me it was long past midnight and to urge me to come home and get some sleep.

And presently we allowed ourselves a sort of busman's honeymoon. This was in winter but I planned a camping trip which would include visits to Fort Hare college. We had to do things cheaply. I took a large packing case and set an axle below it with two small wheels. I fixed also two long strips of wood at a slant and with a crossbar for towing. This we loaded with too many items of camping gear and some provisions. Well-oiled this contraption ran smoothly enough on city streets but was not strong enough for what we wanted of it. We took train to East London and there on the platform I assembled the cart and we set off. I thought it would be pleasant to travel by the sea and so we went along the shore. This was our second mistake: we made plenty more. I had not anticipated the softness of the sand. The wheels sank in, the going was heavy. We made our first camp on a rocky beach where there was no fresh water. For some reason we had with us a cabbage which we proposed to cook for supper. We tried cooking it in sea water but had to throw it away and make do with a slice of bread. Our trip was a series of such mishaps but in between troubles were some lovely moments and the rest from directives and deviations was something I needed even more than I had realized.

So our days went by in arduous travel and with nights of bitter cold. Always the problem was to find water. Once we came upon a woman, caretaking a closed factory, who was making jam. She said she had more fruit than she could use and gave us a huge bag of guavas and filled our water bottle. The guavas were heavy so a mile or two further we camped to enjoy a feast. And that night we heard a strange sad cry, 'A-hoo! A-hoo!' and the sweep of heavy wings as an owl flew up the valley. That night our water bottle froze and split neatly in half. We went on to Hamburg where the axle finally buckled and the wheels came off. Here we rested for a day while I bought a donkey and Win found some sacks and made saddle bags. Then we turned inland towards Peddie and our going was through the ancient arid land of the Ciskei.

Max was a large donkey, a gelding, and I suppose as donkeys go he was not unusually obstinate. Until now I had always thought that tales of luring a donkey on by means of a dangled carrot were just tall stories. But we found that if one of us walked ahead with an orange on a stick Max would mend his pace. The orange had to be at one side for he was blind in one eye. We had bought oranges in Hamburg and every now and then we rewarded Max with one. Poor beast, he was always thirsty as we were. Each evening when we camped we had to search for water, water for Max, water for ourselves; we never found enough.

Often Natives came to sit by our fire. 'Where from?' they asked. We told them Johannesburg. 'Hau!' A pause to consider this, then 'Where to?'

'Alice.'

'Hau!'

Then, 'How many children?'

'No children.'

'Hau! Too young?'

This made Win laugh. She offered tea which she poured into the tin mugs they carried. They wanted a gift of coffee but we had none. We gave them some tea and sugar.

And next morning one came with a little water in a tin. Muddy and ill-smelling the water was not attractive but it was a precious gift.

And so Max plodded his wilful way and we suited our going to his pleasure. Till then when we saw a man beating a donkey we had thought of cruelty to animals but now we learned the hardship of travel with a donkey. To walk at his slow pace exhausted us. Sometimes, hardening our hearts we thwacked him with little mercy. May God, in whom we don't believe, forgive us. Once we came to a place where donkey droppings lay fresh in the road. Max stopped, smelled carefully, then lifted his head and let forth his ancient discordant bracketing cry. We urged him on but he stood still and again he brayed in ageless melancholy. No donkey answered. We gave him an orange to help him to bear his grief. He took the orange but when he had resumed his slow gait he would still now and again stop, raise his half-blind head and call again his cry of sorrow.

We came at last to Alice where, with permission, we camped by a lovely river and here we rested for some days. From this camp we went to hold meetings at Fort Hare. These were talking parties with the students who came to join us sitting on the grass. They told us of their life in college and of how they were disciplined and treated as schoolboys. We told them of the movement and of *Indlela Yenkululeko*.

By this time we had become notorious and were followed by detectives. Back in camp we found one, a local country bumpkin, who sat a few feet away and watched our every move. This became annoying.

'I heard you had a donkey,' he said.

'Yes, we did have one but he's gone and now we have another.'

A long silence followed while he thought this over. Then he said, humbly, 'I see what you mean about the donkey.'

Presently I persuaded him to go further away, to leave us in peace to wash and prepare for the night. I promised that we would not run away.

Indeed we were both extremely tired. We had sold Max for fifteen shillings. Energy, time, money and opportunity had all run out together. At Blaney we took a train. 'Poof! We stink,' said Win. We were dirty and thought of the lovely city where clean water ran out of taps. Win added, 'This is the oddest honeymoon I ever had!'

Back in Johannesburg we were soon to hear news which was a shock to us all. In Cape Town the Woltons had been active in a tram and bus workers strike. They had organized a militant group of strikers to harass the union secretary who was, they alleged, trying to negotiate an agreement which favoured the bosses. Douglas was arrested and charged under the Riotous Assemblies Act and the Industrial Conciliation Act. He was not allowed bail and was thus effectively silenced for the duration of the strike. Later he was sentenced to three months' hard labour. This was his second spell in gaol within eighteen months. It was clear that the continual arrests and imprisonments, the hectic life they led and the financial difficulties which were the lot of all revolutionaries were having a depressing effect on the Woltons. Molly had a weak heart. Her doctor had ordered her to give up public speaking which she greatly enjoyed but which exhausted her. Their daughter, now about seven years old, was having no sort of home life, being left in the care of a succession of women comrades. When Wolton came out of gaol he found a letter from his brother in Yorkshire offering him a job on a Yorkshire newspaper and also a home for Molly and the child. The Woltons yielded to temptation, packed their few possessions and left at once for England without bothering to notify or ask permission of the Political Bureau in Johannesburg. This was a gross breach of that Party discipline that they had so fanatically imposed on all members. Everyone smiled. To Bunting and the other expelled it seemed evidence of the insincerity of the whole campaign of denunciations and expulsions. Diamond said, 'I told you so!' Bach was silent. My own view was that the Woltons had literally driven themselves to breaking point. The only pity was that so much of the harm they had done was irreversible. On the whole what I chiefly felt was relief and I thought happily that now with these doctrinaire fanatics out of the way we might be able to get on with some real work in the Party.

Some time earlier two African members of the P.B. had been sent to Moscow for further training. One of these was Nzula. Brilliant but unreliable in his personal life he was addicted to drink, and vodka was to prove the cause of his death. He fell down one night in a frozen street and there lay for some hours. He died of pneumonia.

Thus the P.B. was much depleted. From Cape Town John Gomas and Josiah Ngedlane were summoned. In Johannesburg Moses Kotane and I were once more brought in. We had been excluded previously for various right wing deviations. As editor of *Umsebenzi* this was inevitable for me but Bach did not cease from pointing out my continual right wing deviations. For a time Bach tried to keep the Party on the old line of struggle against the right danger but he was now in a real minority.

Our next campaign was against the pick-up van. Of this I wrote in *Umsebenzi* in November.

> At any time of the day or night, but mostly during the week-ends when people are not working and are visiting their friends, the police come in a motor van. They go to any populous locality, jump out of the van and arrest anyone they can lay their hands on. The arrested persons are bundled into the van, often seriously assaulted in the process, taken to the lock-up and brought before a magistrate the next morning. There is no difficulty in laying charges—it is always possible to find that any African man or woman at any time falls foul of one or other of the thousand and one oppressive laws and regulations that constitute the glorious heritage of South African civilization. The magistrate sentences them in batches of ten or twenty at a time. Usually fines are imposed with alternative imprisonment and every effort is made to get the prisoners to pay up. We even know of cases, and are prepared to substantiate them by witness, where people who had money in their possession when arrested preferred to go to gaol rather than pay fines, and where the police have practically forced the money from them and refused to allow them to serve sentences.

Umsebenzi went on to allege that the main motive for the pick-up was economic, an attempt to swell the revenue brought in by the police department. We advocated the formation of defence committees in the locations to combat the activities of the pick-up van.

In December 1933 the slogan was 'To Hell with the Pick-up!' and large posters with these words were pasted in prominent places in the town. A cartoon in *Umsebenzi* showed a pick-up van with members of the government as police in charge of the van. Dingaan's Day was announced as a special day of protest against the pick-up and police brutality. Mass meetings were held on this day, both in locations and on the City Hall steps. For speeches delivered at some of these meetings I was arrested and charged with incitement to violence.

In court, conducting my own defence, I was able to draw attention to the reign of police terror to which the Native people of South Africa are subjected. I said that

> bands of armed hooligans are terrorizing the people in the locations. In the ordinary course one would appeal to the police for protection but in this case we cannot do that for the police are themselves the hooligans. I have shown that the police authorities are fully aware of what is going on. It is significant that though many articles have appeared in the press asking for a commission of enquiry into police brutality the Government has done nothing about it. In the circumstances I think we are justified in calling upon location inhabitants to defend themselves against these assaults and even to arm themselves if necessary.

Evidence I wished to call as to brutal actions by the police was not allowed. Winifred was able to state in evidence that I had ended my speech with the words, Workers of the World, Unite! But this did not save me. I was sentenced.

The case was carried to appeal. The Supreme Court held that my own account of what I had said was enough to condemn me and also that the poster 'To Hell with the Pick-up!' for which I admitted responsibility was in itself an incitement to violence. So presently I went to gaol, this time in Johannesburg, to do four months' hard labour.

Here conditions were quite unlike the set-up in Durban gaol. The chief difference was that there were a good many European prisoners. I offended, accidentally in the first place but thereafter in obstinacy because of the crude manner in which I was rebuked for insolence in failing to say 'sir' in every sentence when replying to a gaoler. I was punished by some days of solitary confinement on spare diet. After this the governor of the prison had me up and spoke reasonably to me. 'You will appreciate,' he said, 'that in a place like this we have to insist on certain forms of respect to warders. One of these is saying "sir". It will be best if you will accommodate yourself to this rule. I have no wish to make things worse for you.' I could not but agree. I said, 'I will try—sir!'

The problem of just what hard labour to give to Europeans in our South African gaols must always be an awkward one. My hard labour now consisted in a latrines assignment. I had to scrub and clean out lavatories and also to cope with night sanitary buckets from the cells, clean these and have them ready for return. An unsavoury job, much less pleasant than my labours in the garden of the Durban gaol. The days and weeks went slowly by. I knew that during this time Win was due to have her baby. There she was in the Queen Victoria Maternity Hospital, a stone's throw from the prison where I was cleaning foul buckets and not able to comfort her.

I first saw my daughter when she was three weeks old. My mother had gone to invite Win to come to live at the house in Bez Valley during the last days of her pregnancy and after the child was born. So when I was released I went straight home and found my daughter in a pram in the back garden. I looked long at the baby. She had a firm little mouth. I said, 'Oh Win, she's a lovely little girl.'

So there in the girls' room for the first time there were three beds, for Edna, for Enid now home and nursing at the Kensington Sanatorium, for Win and a cradle for the baby. All the boys were home too and Mother was once more surrounded by a large family. Win had endured much anxiety and was now not very well. We stayed there for some weeks.

Then back to life in town, this time in two rooms in Harold Building in Harrison Street. These were large rooms and had huge windows. They would have been just the thing for an artist's studio. We lived in the inner one and the outer was a sort of office. Here we held our *Umsebenzi* wrapping parties with the baby asleep in the next room. I went on with my crowded life but Win, for a time, played Party work more quietly. She kept *Indlela* going and worked in F.S.U. and also earned some money by giving private lessons in mathematics to schoolchildren and in English to one or two members of the Jewish Workers Club who were, we heard later, rounded up by Joffe to help our finances. From sympathizers we received gifts of baby clothes, of a baby bath and cot and blankets, of pyjamas for me, of stockings for Win. It seemed that our breach of discipline was forgiven and forgotten.

And during the last months of that year, astonishingly, we acquired a car. This came about as follows. Edna came one day to ask us to lend some money to Phil. This had to come out of Win's savings on which we were then living as well as on the small amount I earned as a Party functionary. We cheerfully agreed to lend the money but Phil was slow to repay. One time when we mentioned the balance still owing Phil said that he had bought an old car for £3 and proposed to do it up and sell it for £25 which he would then pay to us. We had doubts as to the end part of this plan and Win suggested that we take the car in payment. This was an ancient 12 h.p. Renault with a sloped-back bonnet like a Paris taxi. It was we were told the only car of its kind in the country and spare parts would not be easily obtained. Tyres were an instance of this for the correct size was in centimetres and we had to take the nearest approximation in inches. So if we turned too quickly an outer cover might come off and trap the inner tube, like a pink balloon, between tyre and rim. Win had not driven for many years, not since she left England, but she set to and achieved a driving licence. At Christmas we went in the car for some twelve days camping at Swartkop, a brief holiday more restful than our over-strenuous Ciskei venture.

Presently it proved a fortunate chance that we had this car for in January, when Alison was eight months old, Win was offered part-time work again at Roedean where the vice-principal arranged hours so that Win could do things for the baby before going to work. We found a maid, a most beautiful Zulu woman named Kate, to care for the child for a few hours each day. And soon we moved to a small house in Ameshoff Street not far from the rooms where I had once lived with

Willy Blumberg. And in our new house on a Sunday morning as we still lay in bed Alison said clearly her first words: 'Hello, Mummie!' She was a darling baby.

CHAPTER XII

More Expulsions

EVENTS in North Africa, Italy's invasion of Ethiopia, roused Africans throughout this country to heights of political awareness never before achieved. Many Bantu now realized for the first time that there still existed in Africa an independent country where black men lived and were ruled by their own king. They were inspired by the thought of black men defending their land against white aggressors. Haile Selassie became their hero overnight and his pictures were pinned up in their homes. All Bantu newspapers now experienced an unprecedented boom. The circulation of *Umsebenzi* passed the 7,000 mark and I saw the opportunity to start a new paper. This was *Umvikele Thebe* —The African Defender, which was published in the name of Ikaka labaSebenzi—Labour Defence. *Umvikele* was a monthly of eight or more pages lively with news and pictures of the doings in Ethiopia. I obtained the loan of blocks for these pictures from leading newspapers in Johannesburg. In its columns we spoke of the Italian imperialist aggressors but included local news also and did not fail to make use of our slogan, Workers of the World Unite!

Umvikele had an immediate and tremendous success. Its editions of 10,000 copies were always completely sold out. For the first time in newspaper history a paper, carrying no advertisements, paid for itself by sales alone. *Umsebenzi* agents handled sales and we sold on the streets in Johannesburg. Each Sunday, Win and I would go to some likely spot, near Prospect Township or Western Native Township or Sophiatown, and sell all day. We would carry with us some fifty dozen, a heavy armful, stand a little distance apart, cry our wares and sell until we had none left. At about two p.m. usually, hunger overcame us and we took a few pence from our now heavy pockets and bought doughcakes at a Native eating house. These were large flat tasteless cakes of fried dough which we ate hungrily and helped down with a cup of tea. Later, weary and weighed down by small cash, we took tram for home.

Umvikele, however, had a short life. When presently it became clear that the black men were losing the war, the reaction was terrible. All Bantu newspaper sales sank not merely to their former level but far below. The new paper died.

All this was in fact one more instance of my tendency to immerse myself in practical activity. I was thinking more of *Umvikele* than of what was going on in the Political Bureau but presently disputes there forced me to take notice.

The new era of comparative reasonableness in the Party which had come in unobtrusively with the defection of the Woltons was not destined to endure. We reformist elements in the P.B. were at first timid and unsure of ourselves, uneasy in our release from sectarianism and possibly fearing more interference from Moscow if we moved too far to the right. We did not, for instance, deal with Bach as he and the Woltons had dealt with Bunting. We allowed him to remain on the P.B. and I for one argued that he should be kept there because of his theoretical knowledge and his value as a critic.

But Bach did not merely play the role of critic. He quietly set about strengthening his position. He was as ever supported by Louis Joffe who, as financial secretary in a party that now consisted almost exclusively of paid functionaries, was a powerful ally though his grasp of political theory was but a mechanical acceptance of instructions from Imprecor as relayed by Bach. And Bach continued to harvest weekly his crop of deviations in the columns of *Umsebenzi* and in the speeches and activities of various comrades. In particular he was presently able to accuse Moses Kotane of bourgeois reformism. This was because Kotane had put forward the suggestion of forming a united front of Non-European organizations, a sort of all-in association in which the Party should not thrust itself too openly into the picture. Kotane maintained that the Party inevitably destroyed every united front mass organization by blatantly taking control and dominating its policy. This he considered bad strategy. We had all seen it happen in the Friends of the Soviet Union which after a promising start had not flourished. Kotane argued that a united front to be successful must be a real unity in which Africans could act and make decisions and feel that they had genuine power and control.

Bach did not stop at rejecting and criticizing Kotane's proposal but found in it evidence of a fundamental deviation. The trouble was, he said, that Kotane's interpretation of the slogan of the Native Republic was incorrect. So now once more the slogan controversy flared up but at a different level. It was no longer a question of being for or against the slogan which by now we all in theory accepted, but of being for or against a certain interpretation of the slogan. Kotane, who by now could quote chapter and verse of Imprecor and of the writings of Lenin with a facility equal to that of Bach, held that the original formulation of the slogan was correct, namely that the Native Republic was a stage towards a workers' and peasants' government. But while the Comintern representative had been in South Africa a change had come about so that the Native republic was now synonymous and synchronous with the workers' and peasants' government: the idea of stages had been jettisoned. It was this new version which Bach now insisted on. And he now argued that Kotane's plan for a united front not blatantly dominated by communists was evidence of his lack of understanding of the Party's true role as guide and leader in all workers' organizations. It showed Kotane's lack of faith in the leadership of Imprecor.

Details of the controversy would weary the reader. Indeed they wearied us and we became exhausted by a series of stormy debates in which not only the P.B. experts but all members of the Party were involved and which went on often through the night into the small hours of the morning. To me it seemed that many of these subtle theoretical arguments were so many red herrings employed as a cover for disagreements and rivalries over the practical work of the Party. Some of us took the line that Bunting should not have been expelled, that the trade unions had been alienated by an extremist sectarian Party leadership, that the members of other organizations had been driven away by our narrow intolerance. We argued that the whole campaign against the right danger was not relevant in South Africa, was not justified by conditions and had been ill-judged and destructive. We questioned whether the Party should continue to domineer in mass organizations, antagonizing fellow-travellers in the unions and in F.S.U. In particular we said that Joffe should not try to play the dictator in the newly-formed Anti-Fascist League. In reply we were accused of promoting the unacceptable doctrine of South African exceptionalism, of special pleading, of failure to understand the over-all situation.

One particular issue of dispute was the question of the Party night school. This had been dead for some years and to some of us it seemed that it would be a good idea to reopen the school and to try to make Party headquarters once more a living centre of daily activities. We would organize lessons, lectures and friendly gatherings. But this Bach stigmatized as a social-democratic deviation. 'Not because I am opposed to the school as such,' said Bach, 'but because the proposed reopening has been put forward in such a way as to suggest that there is something wrong in the bolshevik system of organization of the Party.' These subtleties were quite beyond the comprehension of some of his less sophisticated followers and one of these, Peter Ramutla, shouted furiously at me, 'Over my dead body you get your night school!' The night school opponents did not choose to remember how certain most valued comrades, notably Johannes Nkosi and Moses Kotane, had come into the Party through the school.

In any case genuine theoretical differences came to be quite obscured at these sessions by a number of trivial and ridiculous taunts. It had seemed good to me to write a statement of the views upheld by Kotane and others. This was some nineteen pages long and we had it duplicated by a commercial firm and circulated privately among all members. For this we were accused of betraying Party information to outsiders and this was all that Bach and Joffe would say of the statement. They would not discuss its contents. Then Hilda was accused of trying to poison members by brewing tea in a rusted tin. Winifred was condemned for using the word 'thrift' when she should have said 'soviet economy.' There was no depth of pettiness which was omitted at these miserable sessions.

Within the P.B. matters came to a climax but that body was evenly divided between the Bach faction and the supporters of Kotane. However, fortune favoured Bach. Back from Moscow came suddenly two comrades who had been sent for training.

These at once assumed their seats on the P.B. and, without consideration of the matters at issue which were indeed by then a sordid tangle of accusation and counter-accusation, gave their votes for Bach's interpretation of the slogan and condemned the whole outlook and criticisms raised by the opposition.

So in September 1935, four years after the expulsions of Bunting, Andrews, Solly Sachs, Weinbren and Tyler, disciplinary action was taken. Some half-dozen of our more vociferous supporters were expelled from the Party on a charge of having attacked the line and leadership of the Party and of having worked to sow discontent in the ranks of the Party and of mass organizations sympathetic to the C.P.S.A. These included some of our best and most devoted workers, among them Hilda, Anna and Shochat. Kotane, Ngedlane and I were removed from the P.B. and *Umsebenzi* was taken from my control. Issy Diamond was suspended from Party membership for three months for having associated with elements that had been conducting factional activities against the line of the Party. Winifred was not mentioned but against her Bach and Joffe had been organizing a technique of isolation. When she called a meeting of F.S.U. committee Joffe privately instructed every member not to attend. She was in effect no longer able to do anything as secretary of F.S.U. She now gave up trying and concentrated on her teaching and care of our child.

The statement in *Umsebenzi* which announced the expulsions ended with the words, 'Now that the situation is clarified, we sincerely hope that all those who have been previously confused will now see their way clear to following the Party line and leadership.'

But apparently many Party sympathizers were not at all clear, for the leadership found it necessary to call a special public meeting at the Jewish Workers Club, at which Mofutsanyana on behalf of the P.B. made a speech explaining and justifying the expulsions. At this meeting, in defiance of Party discipline, I made a speech in reply, defending those who had been expelled and demanding their reinstatement. I was also able publicly for the first time to make a declaration of faith in Bunting, to express my deep regret for my compliance in his expulsion and my silence during the discreditable attacks that were subsequently made on him.

Bunting was present at this meeting. I met him a few days later. He spoke with his usual gruff sincerity. 'We were glad to hear your confession,' he said. We spoke of the future of the Party. Bunting held that no progress could be made until the bad elements were removed. They were still in the saddle and their grip was stronger than ever. But I was full of hope that the new line expounded by Dimitrov at the Seventh Congress of the Comintern would bring about a change of policy. There was no more talk in Moscow of the right danger and the people's front was the plan. The chief danger was now sectarianism. This was a truly dialectical swing. It appeared that practically all the parties of the Comintern had made sectarian leftist mistakes thus tending to isolate themselves from the masses. In view of Dimitrov's message I hoped the Comintern would now admit its mistakes in South Africa, remove Bach and Joffe from the leadership and reinstate expelled members. I hoped even that Bunting might be brought back. But in this I was being naive as ever and nothing like this happened.

Kotane, Gomas and I had sent an urgent telegram to Moscow stating that the sectarian leadership was splitting the Party just when the Italian attack on Ethiopia made unity more than ever essential. We asked the Comintern to intervene. To counter our appeal the P.B. sent a representative, a Russian comrade named Richter, to Moscow.

In reply to our telegram Moscow requested more information about the split and suggested that representatives of the opposing factions should go to Moscow to explain the matter. Bach went at once and an African comrade was sent some weeks later. I did not go. Win said, taking off Ramutla, 'Over my dead body you get your ticket to Moscow!'

It was months before any reply was received from Moscow and then it was simply: 'We are not interested in discussing past mistakes. Here is the new line. Get on with it.' It was clear that bolshevik self-criticism was demanded only of those who found themselves in minority opposition to the official line. In fact some said: 'The Comintern does not make mistakes. If mistakes were made in South Africa it was because instructions were not carried out or because Moscow was misinformed as to the situation in South Africa.'

And Bach was never to return. He became mixed up with the

purge and anti-Trotskyist trials. We heard later that he had been officially expelled and banished to some rural area. Rumour had it that he had been shot. Richter too fared badly and was expelled. Perhaps going to Moscow to explain had not been such a good plan. I remembered how in 1928 Moscow would not listen to us.

It now happened that I was in effect marooned. I was never publicly expelled but suffered the same kind of isolation treatment as had ended Winifred's work in F.S.U. I was excluded from work on *Umsebenzi* and foresaw that deprived of its editor-manager and of the active working-party members who had met weekly to fold, wrap and despatch, the paper would soon decline. I was no longer a Party functionary; my help was not wanted. My days, once so tight-packed with strenuous work for the Party, were now a desert of an emptiness more exhausting than any toil. When the expected answer from Moscow failed to deal in any way with the reality of South African affairs, I realized that my period of service was indeed ended. Hammer and sickle had rejected me. I remembered then how on a Sunday morning in 1921, on the roof of the Trades Hall, in radiant sunshine and in the purity of enthusiasm we had founded the Young Communist League. I knew that the efforts of some seventeen years of my life now counted for almost nothing.

The dream was over, the vision had faded. Was it for this that Nkosi had died and Bunting had suffered? It was not easy for me to face the situation. I saw that to the Comintern bureaucrats the achievement of African freedom was as nothing. Our South African party was as a pawn to be played and sacrificed to the needs of central power policy. When the general struggle was declared against the right wing danger; South Africa too had to exhibit this danger. Policy dictated to us from Moscow had no relevance to our needs in which the leaders were simply not interested. No account could be taken of the different stages reached in different countries but all were rigidly and mechanically treated in the same way. The party in S.A. in the name of an unreal struggle against non-existent right wing dangers had now destroyed her most loyal servants. I could not forgive what had been done to Bunting nor my own unwilling part in this. I made one resolve: that presently I would make what amends I could by writing a life of Bunting to pay tribute to a great and sincere leader. But for the moment, lacking dream and vision I could not begin even on this. I was lost in emptiness and could not think what to do next. When I did bring myself to do anything, it was too late.

In April 1936, the Hertzog-Smuts government in a joint session of both houses of parliament had passed the Native Representation Act. This provided that the Cape Native franchise should be abolished and in its stead Native voters should be put on a separate register and would vote independently for three white members of Parliament to be known as Native Representatives. These representatives would not be allowed to vote on matters of finance or affecting the constitution. Also the Native 'electoral colleges' would choose four senators to represent their interests in the Senate. Further a Native Representative Council was to be set up consisting of Africans to be elected.

The Communist Party which should have attempted to compete found itself lacking in suitable candidates, both black and white. The most prominent African member was Edwin Mofutsanyana but he was not well-known. Honest Edwin was a loyal member but a poor speaker and not popular with the masses. However the Party put him forward as a candidate in the Transvaal. In the other three provinces they were not able to find a candidate. In the Cape parliamentary elections the Party had no white leaders known to the Africans; while candidates for the Senate were required to have fixed property to the value of more than £500. In the event they ran H.M. Basner as candidate in the Transvaal and Orange Free State constituency.

In the case of candidates for the three Cape parliamentary seats a provision of the new law required them to have been resident in the Cape for at least two years. As soon as I knew this I thought that I might have a chance. I hastily packed and took train to Cape Town leaving wife and daughter. I hoped that presently I could bring them to join me in the Cape.

But this my final attempt to remain in the political field was of no use. In bits and pieces, chiefly by my stay in the Cape in 1930, I just failed to achieve this residence qualification.

In these elections Margaret Ballinger scored a notable

victory in the Cape Eastern circle. In spite of being a woman she gained a huge majority. She became one of the most courageous and effective members of Parliament. In Cape Western the successful candidate was D.B. Molteno who also distinguished himself as a member. The Transkei returned the moderate G. K. Hemming.

In elections for the Senate, Basner was defeated by Rheinallt Jones of the Institute of Race Relations, but in the second election in 1942 Basner improved his score and was elected.

Mofutsanyana was not elected to the Native Representative Council. This was an advisory body whose advice was in general ignored by the Government. In 1946 it was to adjourn itself for this reason.

But now I sought a job and found one as a municipal baths attendant. I earned £10 a month and knew this to be inadequate to maintain my family. For the present Win and Alison must remain in Johannesburg where Win now went to live in at Roedean. She and the child lived in a cottage in Roedean grounds.

And in December they came to stay with me and I met again my delightful daughter. I arranged that we should stay in a room in a small house in Salt River. At nights we put a screen round Alison's crib and usually went out for a walk as soon as she was in bed to give her a chance of falling asleep. And sometimes we heard her singing little songs to herself. One of these I remember:

> Roedean school, Roedean school.
> They play tennis ball,
> They play cricket ball,
> I shall play when I am older,
> Roedean school.

Later Win and I discussed our personal problems. We both felt that time was slipping past and that marriage a thousand miles apart was not satisfactory. We decided that Win should give up her post at Roedean and come to join me. I could not see exactly how I should earn a living and considered it hardly possible that I could make any kind of return to the scientific world, but I thought of journalism and that we would manage somehow. In the meantime I had ceased to write: even letters were difficult. My life had contracted to the confines of one small room where I brooded over my actions and inaction and asked myself at what stage I should have acted differently. I did not like the answer I found. Presently I began to write my life of S.P. Bunting.

CHAPTER XIII

Fruit, Fish and Family

WHAT happened next was astonishing.

At that time in a laboratory in the chemistry department of the University of Cape Town a group of talented young men were at work on various most exciting lines of research. These were post-graduate students now working for the degree of Ph.D. In control of their various activities was Professor Smeath Thomas whose manner of rule was to give the researchers a good deal of freedom. Dr W.S. Rapson, lecturer in the Chemistry Department, supervised the work. And one of these young men was C.J. Molteno, a cousin of the Donald Molteno mentioned in a previous chapter. For some reason, though his initials were C.J., we knew him as Peter. Donald, Peter and Eddie had met in London at a time when Eddie was leaving Downing College and Peter was about to go up to Cambridge to that same College. And now Peter was working on research at U.C.T.

Another worker was Izak Donen who was engaged in research on plums and grapes, their healthy growth, disease resistance quality in relation to various nutrient treatments, storage potential and satisfactory ripening under storage conditions. This last was of special importance to South African economy in view of the necessity for early harvesting caused by the long distance train transport and the three weeks' shipment period from South African ports to the United Kingdom. Donen, a biochemist, found himself at times handicapped by the fact that he was not trained as a botanist. Various others of the young researchers encountered the same difficulty. 'What we need in this set-up,' said Donen, 'is a really good botanist. Not a systematist but a plant physiologist.' Here Peter remarked that he happened to know of an expert in plant physiology who was at present working as a baths attendant at Claremont. Donen was interested but cautious and suggested that he should meet the man.

So Peter brought Donen to meet Eddie Roux where he was at work. What Donen saw was a man with a strong thoughtful face, much sunburned and dressed casually in khaki shirt and shorts, engaged in sweeping aside floods of water splash. What Roux saw was an alert young man, with bright dark eyes and hair already receding into future baldness. Peter, grinning happily, presided over the encounter. The outcome was that Donen appealed to Smeath Thomas to take on this extra man and Smeath Thomas, ever willing to promote the wealth of research in his Ph.D. laboratory, applied to Pretoria for a research grant for Roux, in which he was supported by Sir James Carruthers Beattie, then principal of the University. The grant was made and though not a large sum was better than Roux could earn by cleaning up in swimming baths. He gave notice to the baths department and went up the hill to the University of Cape Town. The quite incredible had happened and Roux was once more in the world of scientific research.

In the laboratory he worked mainly with Donen and here his Cambridge work under Blackman proved the perfect foundation. Besides the work on the respiration of Kelsey plums and Peregrine peaches, on which Donen and Roux contributed a paper to the *Biochemical Journal* in 1939 and Roux a paper to *Annals of Botany* in 1940,* the partners developed an interest in methods of pruning grape vines. The methods used were traditional and had never been subjected to any statistical survey of the relative effects on crop production of different methods. Research was begun in the large vineyards of K.B. Quinan at Somerset West and was planned as a long-term project. This happy partnership continued until the outbreak of World War II which put a stop to a good deal of fruit research.

In the same laboratory Sholto Douglas was also at work on grapes and Otto Papst was investigating the organic content of vine shoots at various stages of growth. Of course, since Roux had spent some years with hammer and sickle, all these workers were younger than he. When I asked him what he was doing he would reply happily that he was a sort of general lab assistant. However, in addition to the work on fruit ripening and storage, Roux and Molteno had the idea of investigating the vitamin A content of certain South African fish liver oils,

*See Appendix II for Roux's scientific papers at this time.

a sideline which was to have important consequences for both these young men. They found, as they had anticipated, that these oils in the livers of fish caught locally were in fact much richer than the imported cod-liver oils from northern oceans. Molteno continued with this interest and formed a company, C.J. Molteno (Pty.) Ltd to exploit these oils. Roux was still working mainly on fruit respiration problems.

And presently, as we had planned, I left Roedean and came with Alison to join Eddie and we lived in a small house in Upper Constitution Street on the edge of District Six and just below de Waal Drive. This was a poor district, quite suitable, for certainly we were poor, and our house was the middle one of three joined on both sides to the next houses. Bugs came marching in through the walls. Our neighbour on the right was the superintendent of the three houses and also of certain flats. His wife was a Coloured woman and his two little boys were obviously Coloured with their kinky hair, dark skin and neat little faces. They were about Alison's age and the three were often together in our minute front garden. We had three small bedrooms and here came Kotane to live with us. He was still in the Party and was now working in Cape Town with John Gomas. Our neighbour the flat superintendent was quite rabid on the matter of segregation of Natives. He held that all Coloured belonged with the white community but that the Native must be kept in his place. Noting the comings and goings of Kotane, he descended upon us one morning, perhaps to complain of our harbouring an African. However, it chanced that morning that Kotane who shared in all our doings had taken himself a bucket and soap and with glum deadpan face was diligently scrubbing the stairs and kitchen floor. Plainly his status in the house was that of a servant. We did not correct this impression. The superintendent retired baffled, for the times he had noted of Kotane's comings and goings were not those of a servant. We let it go by default for we thought it was none of his business what friend slept in our spare room.

Presently Alison, now five, wore a diminutive gym tunic and attended a nearby primary school.

A post was advertised at Zonnebloem College. The subjects mentioned were mathematics, English, biology and hygiene. Kotane said I should apply. But Zonnebloem, the oldest school in the Cape, was now a training college and secondary school for Coloured students. I doubted whether I would be acceptable for a post there, the more so since I spoke little Afrikaans (and that with a Lancashire accent, said Eddie) and also the school was controlled by the Anglican Church. However, I applied, was interviewed by the principal Mr Hogwood and got the job. This caused a change in our living arrangements. I found a Coloured maid, Nettie Marais, who came daily from Claremont. She was a lively cheerful person with a real cockney idiom of speech which gave us much pleasure. She was a careless cook and when occasionally, if I had to be late home, she cooked our dinner and I ventured to make certain suggestions, she would answer indignantly, 'What's it metter? It's all foot.' We all became fond of Nettie and she stayed with us for years, in fact until we left Cape Town.

My work at Zonnebloem was heavy. This was not only by reason of the lack of cultural background of most of the pupils but also because there were nine teaching periods in the school day which seemed very long. The tall windows were unshaded and when the hot afternoon sun streamed in my pupils and I were often in danger of falling asleep despite the harsh sounds of the horns blown by fish vendors in the street nearby. But the work was a challenge and full of interest. I admired the determination of many of the students who were getting their education under difficulties. In my first year at Zonnebloem the head boy was a thin exhausted-looking young man of twenty-seven. Throughout his schooldays he had in alternate years attended school and taken time off to earn money. When I knew him he was working some evenings in the week as a waiter somewhere in Sea Point. One evening it chanced that Eddie and I with friends went to the restaurant where he was employed. He gave us a great welcome and led us to the best table. He addressed me as Madam, as all Zonnebloem pupils did but with no subservience. This was quite in the Roedean manner. Before my Roedean days in my first school in the centre of Liverpool I had been always 'Please, miss'. This waiter-student had by his efforts paid school fees for a younger brother as well as for himself. His ambition was to be a teacher. This he never achieved because he had now a wife and young family and a teacher's salary could not compare with the earnings of a good waiter.

In the end he died of consumption to which the Cape Coloured people are particularly susceptible. I think that, though his eyes were anxious, he was one of the happiest people I have ever known, certainly one of the bravest. He was not clever but a born student.

Presently we moved to a charming little house called Sunnyside. This was near the University, in Rondebosch, in a street that led down to the Liesbeek River, which would overflow and flood our floors in winter rains. In our garden was a fig tree and lots of grass and a few flowers. And from this house Eddie walked up to the university by the path followed by Kipling's cat that walked by himself. Alison went to Rustenburg Junior School and I made her summer uniforms of blue tobralco.

As to happiness it is hard, looking back, to pinpoint it, to say here or there or then. We had been happy in the strenuous days of hard work in service of the Party. Now, that vision lost, our happiness had a different quality. It was quieter. Eddie was fulfilled in his work in the lab and in the evenings he wrote his life of Bunting and also political articles for *Trek*. I enjoyed my efforts at Zonnebloem and Alison was our delight.

In September 1939 the coming of World War II put an end to this peace. The Smartt Memorial Scholarship which Eddie had held for a period now ended and money for fruit research grants was no longer available.

In the meantime Molteno's company had flourished greatly and had been bought up by Irvin and Johnson who with the National Trawling Company had formed a new company, Vitamin Oils (Pty) Ltd, with Molteno as managing director. Peter now asked Eddie to join in the work of investigating and exploiting the liver oils of all fish caught locally. These oils of comparable potency to oils previously obtained from Japan now became of vital importance to the U.K. where they were used medicinally and to fortify margarine.

Research was carried on in a laboratory in the I. and J. factory in the Docks area at Cape Town. This was a place of maximum security and all who entered had to show a special pass. Peter recalled that the Docks police always treated Eddie with great respect and he thinks that this was owing to the fact that Eddie had had some difficulty in securing a pass. It seemed that the police, noting the name Roux, thought that here was a man with Ossewa Brandwag leanings.* Though manager of Vitamin Oils Peter was never ushered through the Dock gates with the friendly smile accorded to Eddie.

The factory reeked of fish and even of putrid fish. Eddie and others who worked there would discard their ordinary clothes which were shut in a special cupboard and don working overalls. But nothing, no cupboard, could keep off that fishy smell. When Eddie arrived home each evening he stank of fish. He would bath and change again but still there was the smell. And on the trains between Rondebosch and town he would travel third class to avoid giving offence to the sensitive noses in the better coaches. Once a week workers at I. and J. were given a present of fish and Eddie would bring home a long parcel of a magnificent kabeljou or hake or sole. It was up to me to cope with these fish which were delicious, but smells put me off and I soon lost my enthusiasm for fish.

But fish were a gold mine and the work expanded. Hake liver oil was rich in vitamin A and hake was the fish most commonly caught in the trawls.† Soon a new name was wanted for this liver oil and for quite a time we used our ingenuity in devising one. All our suggestions were rejected. The patents office stipulated no name ending in –ol. In the end it was Russell Ovenstone who found the name Ocean Gold. This was actually a name used in Australia for an oil sold for feeding to chickens. Hutchinson, a Manchester man, the practical and resourceful secretary of Vitamin Oils was enthusiastic for this name. The oil was put on the market as 'Ocean Gold for young and old.'

Other fish liver oils were investigated and in shark livers an oil was found rich in vitamin A and having no trace of vitamin D. This was an advantage since doses of vitamin D are in general unsuitable except for the young.

Fish used for research were kept in cold storage chambers. Each of these little rooms was supplied with a door opening device which could be operated from within. One of these devices was defective. So one day, having gone in to collect material, Roux found himself locked in, someone passing outside having closed the door. He knew he had not long and

---

*Ossewa Brandwag, a strongly nationalist Afrikaner organization.
†For Roux's scientific papers on the hake see Appendix II.

at once began to swing a large stiff-frozen fish to try to hit the door-opening mechanism. This was in total darkness and it was not easy to aim. In this he might have succeeded though his chances were not good but, by chance someone opened the door from outside. Telling me the tale that evening Eddie said, 'I have never been nearer to death, not even in Driehoek.' He added that the faulty door catch had now been repaired. He still looked pale at the memory and I said, 'Let's have wine with our dinner, wine that maketh glad the heart of man.' I opened a bottle of Moulin Rouge, the cheap burgundy of the Cape. We finished the bottle over our quite mediocre meal. Eddie said that he would not write that evening. Nor did I feel like facing corrections of school exercises. Early to bed.

Perhaps the most fishy story of all was what we always referred to as the Mossamedes muddle. This happened later but may be told now. Early in 1946 an attempt was made by two Portuguese firms to set up a vitamin oil extraction plant in Portuguese Angola. Roux was asked to make a preliminary survey and went to Angola for one month. There he investigated the vitamin content of liver oils obtained from sharks, tuna and other fish. This could not be done with the precision now achieved in Cape Town but was carried out in an improvised laboratory using a hand mincer, a primus stove, a chemist's balance and weights and certain chemicals taken from Cape Town. With these somewhat primitive tools estimates were made of the amounts of vitamin A present in the livers of locally caught fish. The sharks' livers were on the whole disappointing though some varieties yielded good results. The result of this pilot survey was a recommendation that only a small factory should be built.

In the lab Roux struggled with the language difficulty but presently acquired some knowledge of Portuguese and was able to train Mario Frota in the work of analysis and to hand over to his care before leaving.

It was on the journey north that Roux encountered an odd set-back, I think at Lobito Bay. When he went to the hotel where accommodation had been reserved for him and gave his name, it seemed that no one knew anything about him. Midday came and everyone relapsed into the afternoon siesta. Roux found a patch of shade and sat down to think things over.

Presently, having printed his name clearly on a page of his diary he returned to the hotel and showed the word ROUX. On which they protested, 'Why did you tell us your name was ROO? Now we see it is RUKS.' This was surprising for Roux had thought that the French pronunciation of his Huguenot name which is the custom in South Africa would be easily recognized.

Other visits to Mossamedes followed. One was made from Johannesburg in December 1949 when Roux spent a month in further investigation and in improving the knowledge of Mario Frota who was finding the work difficult. The lab clearly needed a good technical assistant.

On this occasion on board a Portuguese liner Roux experienced a gargantuan Christmas dinner which went on for hours and at which the main dish, considered the utmost delicacy was prepared from bacalão, dried codfish caught in the arctic circle. Bacalão is a national dish eaten on Fridays and festive occasions. Later at Porto Alexandre, which owes its very existence to the abundance of local fish, at a ceremonial dinner this same dried cod which had been transported some 6,000 miles was again the main course. Bacalão is a fish about which the Portuguese are very sentimental.

Mossamedes itself is in an arid region in the desert of the northern Namib. It is a forbidding coast and has nothing to commend it save the wealth of life in the sea. The river Bero flows visibly once in six years. Rain falling on mountains a hundred miles away flows west but the streams run dry long before they reach the coast. Beneath the sands of the dry bed of the Bero river there is water which the settlers have tapped and use to irrigate their fields of maize, sugar cane, bananas and oranges. The richest fishing area lies to the south at Baia dos Tigres where a sand spit nearly forty miles long encloses a magnificent harbour. But at Tigres there is no fresh water and water has to be brought there by boat. Another fishing port is Porto Alexandre which is in a region of extreme desert. One sees there a few stunted bushes and occasionally the desert plant *Welwitschia mirabilis*. Water is piped to Alexandre from a river bed twenty miles away. The small settlement is sheltered from the encroaching sands by a grove of casuarina trees. All trees must be watered by hand for some years after planting and even then only about one in three can survive. At Tigres there is one tree, again a casuarina, much loved and cherished by the settlers.

Roux went once more to Mossamedes in July of 1950. He had been vexed and distressed to learn from the company of the dismissal of Mario Frota without anyone having been trained to replace him. This affair remained a mystery, in part veiled by the obscurities of the Portuguese tongue but also, Roux felt, deliberately unexplained. Roux never met Frota again. In the event this loss was overshadowed by the fact of serious seasonal fluctuations in the vitamin content of shark oils. The falls in vitamin now made the proposed factory a more than dubious proposition and with the development in the U.S.A. of techniques for synthesizing vitamin A it became clear that the venture must be abandoned.

These comings and goings involved us in one awkward bit of travel timing. In December of 1946 I left for England where my father was seriously ill. At the time the Union-Castle liner sailed from Cape Town, Eddie on a Portuguese ship was nearing home. We missed each other by about twelve hours and I found small comfort in sending a greetings-farewell message from one ship to the other. On another occasion I remember that Alison and I waited on Cape Town quayside for the arrival of the Jão Bela. It was a shining day and we watched the lovely ship as she drew slowly nearer. As she paused and waited suddenly a mist spread over the water. Ourselves still in sunshine we could see above the mist the upper decks of the liner. We saw a launch put out from the quayside and make towards the ship and the tip of its small mast remained just visible. We saw the little boat shoot a long way past the bows of the Jão Bela, then presently make a wide sweep and return to the ship. Then the mist was suddenly gone and the Jão Bela docked and Eddie was with us once more.

But at the time of which I am writing the Mossamedes muddle was still in the future. In the fish period our finances improved steadily and presently we counted things up, took several deep breaths and decided to buy a house. Sunnyside was delightful in fine weather but in winter rains we found it tiresome to be so often flooded. It seemed injudicious to live so near such a wayward little river. But with our savings and a building society loan we still had not enough money. I thought of Professor W.F. Grant under whom I had studied philosophy of education in 1930. He had shown himself kind and sympathetic. I asked him to help us. In perfect trust and generosity and asking no security, he lent us £400 and this we contrived to repay within two years. He had refused to charge interest but we managed to pay a meagre four per cent. We felt that he had made an outstanding gesture of friendship.

The new house, though now when we return it looks small and shabby, seemed then a splendid place. It was the largest house we had ever lived in, having two sittingrooms and three bedrooms. It faced west. I remember that the first night we slept there, with open bedroom door, I woke early and saw the first rays of the sun come slanting in through the back windows making the passage, cream painted, glow like the inside of a daffodil. It was a lovely house. We must give it a lovely name. When we came there it was called Murthly. I sang a jingle: 'Of paying for Murthly, we haven't an earthly!' Alison joined in and sang, 'But we will pay, some day, some day.' Eddie said we must change that name. We wanted a name like Xenopus, the name of Hogben's house. Not the name of any fish, though our fortunes were founded on fish, for we both felt that hake and kabeljou were not lasting features of our lives. Eddie thought of Euglena, the name of a small swimming organism which has a brilliant red spot, light sensitive and considered to be the first beginnings of the eye. Euglena, true eye cavity.

And in Euglena, with its small front garden and the enclosed patch of grass and garden at the back, we were happy for some years. Alison loved the garden. She would come running in, crying, 'Mummie, come see the little love!' and I would go out never knowing whether I should find a chameleon or a koggelmannetjie or a praying mantis. Once it was the first anemone that had opened, a miracle of brilliant scarlet enamel.

And Alison must have a cat. We found in a pet shop a pretty black Persian kitten and she named him Benito. But as is the custom with cats presently Benito had kittens and became Benita. After that it seemed there were always kittens about the place. One of these, especially loved, we named Henry and he went with us when we moved to Johannesburg. Another, Tigger, also petted and adored, died miserably of biliary fever, and Alison grieved long. Indeed she grieved as little girls do over many creatures. She found a dove and wanted to keep it. I said that it would die. 'Why die? Why, why? Why will it die?' 'I don't know why, darling. I think it just wants to die.'

'Oh no! How can anything want to die?'

But next morning the dove was dead. Alison wept and I recited to her the Keats poem:

> I had a dove and the sweet dove died.
> And I have thought it died of grieving.
> O what could it grieve for? Its feet were tied
> With a silken thread of my own hands' weaving;
> Sweet little red feet! Why should you die—
> Why should you leave me, sweet bird! Why?
> You'd lived alone in the forest tree,
> Why, pretty thing, would you not live with me?
> I kiss'd you oft and gave you white peas;
> Why not live sweetly as in the green trees?

Alison learned the poem and wrote it in a little book that she kept for special thoughts. This book was private. We were never to look into it. But sometimes she would show us a page with a poem written out or a drawing or a piece of prose that took her fancy. On an early page was a painting and the lines:

> The Owl and the Pussy-Cat went to sea
> In a butiful pea-green boat.

Much further in the book was a page where she had drawn a tawny striped cat with yellow eyes and had written a verse that Eddie often quoted, a verse by his favourite poet:

> Stately, kindly lordly friend,
>   Condescend
> Here to sit by me, and turn
> Glorious eyes that smile and burn,
> Golden eyes, love's lustrous meed
> On the golden page I read.

Later she came across some of T.S. Eliot's cat poems but these she did not care for and there was no drawing of Macavity Cat. 'Why not?' I asked her. She said, 'He doesn't really love cats!' I said, 'But he makes quite clever poems about cats, don't you think?' 'Yes, clever! But that's different!'

In these days Alison became in love with the subtlety of words. Once she said to Eddie, 'You are very unnoticeable: you never notice anything.' When we laughed she went away and had a session with her dictionary, and thereafter played the trick deliberately to make us laugh. 'You are most objectionable: you are always objecting to things.' And another time, 'You are just not memorable: you never remember anything.' And on the main road to Cape Town there was a robot where no road crossed. 'Why a robot here?' she wanted to know. Eddie explained it was slow-down robot to reduce traffic speed. 'Oh, I see,' said Alison, 'a slobot.'

It became apparent that she had some talent for drawing, painting and design. At her school she was one of a few who were chosen to attend a special art centre for children held on Saturday mornings. Here she painted to her heart's content, made soap models and potato-cut stencils. Eddie found his lino-cut tools, laid aside since the days of *Umsebenzi*, and showed her how to use them. She made some pleasing lino-cut prints. On Saturday afternoons she would go often to Rondebosch Common, sit on the grass and make sketches of the tall pines, or by the Liesbeek she sketched a pattern of overhanging trees. She drew the outline of Table Mountain, a cluster of dry poppy seedheads in our garden, a chameleon clinging to a grenadilla vine. She tried again and again to draw Henry but the results did not please her. And from these sketches she made her lino-cuts.

When Christmas drew near she would retire to her bedroom to make presents and cards. On the door she put a notice: 'Xmas is near but dont come in. Anybody comming in will be priked with a pin.' She was never bored, never aware as are some children of long stretches of time to be filled. She read voraciously and wrote her stories and poems and made plays to be acted with her friends. As I remember these days it seems we were often laughing, always laughter was at hand.

Nettie was with us and would talk often to Alison. Her son, Peter, was to be confirmed. To Alison this was a mystery.

'Tell me, Nettie, what is this confirmation? What happens?' And Nettie would launch into an account of what she thought happened. 'Well, all the girls they wear wite, wite soes and stockings, wite dresses and wite weils. But no joolery bcause the bissop he doesn't like joolery. And the boys wear dark with wite sirts. And the bissop he put his hands on their heads and he say "Yap yap yap . ." (here Nettie could not imagine the words spoken) and then you is in the tsurts.' Alison would listen enthralled to this tale and in the evening, when Nettie had gone home to Claremont, she would repeat the talk with incomparable mimicry. We laughed but warned her, 'Always be kind to Nettie. She is good to you.' Alison agreed but said 'Still I find this confirmation funny! Poor Peter! I love Nettie but poor Peter!'

And the lovely days made years and the years flowed by and were gone.

The one great sorrow was news that came in a telegram from Johannesburg. Edna had died suddenly. Edna was Eddie's beloved sister, beautiful and kind. It was she who had spoken to him of family affairs, had persuaded him to come home, had urged him to avoid quarrels with their father. She had married but her life with Paddy had been difficult. She was reserved and proud and when she died, of diabetes, no one had even guessed that she was ill. Eddie grieved that he had not known of her troubles, that they had not written to one another. None of the Rouxs was given to much letter-writing. Eddie's mother would write only when she had something to say and always the letters were crisp and businesslike and she would sign herself E.M. Roux.

Alison was in her final year at Rustenburg Junior School when we knew that we were to leave for Johannesburg. At the same time I knew I ought to go to England. We decided that she should try for a scholarship to Roedean. This she duly did, suffering from a feverish cold at the time. I said 'Never mind, dearest. Have a smack at it. If you don't win, it doesn't matter. Then you can go to Jeppe, your father's school.' Her chief competitor was Rachel Coke, a clever child at Herschel School where by this time I was teaching mathematics. I thought that Rachel would do better than Alison for her abilities were of a more measurable kind and I considered her a good examination performer. What happened was that they tied for first place and Roedean increased the scholarship award and gave half to each of them. Alison was now all set for the white walls of Roedean, the old-fashioned djibbeh uniform and all the British public school tradition. Our friends said how could we, who believed in equality of opportunity, send our child to such a nest of privilege. Eddie replied that Win thought Roedean a good school and I said that I would like every child to have such a good education but did not see why our child should not.

All this coincided with my own need to get to England quickly. Twice or three times we sent Alison off to Johannesburg on the train. Each time we would cheer ourselves by a farewell dinner party in the station restaurant. Alison did not cry but in the brave letters she wrote there were tears. I thought what a hardhearted mother I was thus to leave my daughter and what a silly wife to leave Eddie. Our married life had consisted so much in hardship and separations that it seemed the merest folly to leave him now. But I went. My father died and I was there with my sister and brother. My mother, gravely ill, recovered her normal health and I was able to return to South Africa.

Of Eddie's life I sometimes think as of a river. At first it tumbled, turbulent and swift, over rocks and through rapids and by deep and narrow channels, then it broadened to a calm still flow between quiet meadows. Our life in those years seems in retrospect to have been such a placid reach. We had time for friendships which hitherto we had but snatched precariously.

Of our good friends one, Edith Stephens, was a near neighbour. She was then living in retirement from her lectureship in botany at the University of Cape Town. Her house called Hazeldene, rather like ours, was round the corner in Belmont Road. With an adroit throw one could have tossed a biscuit over our back hedge, a tangle of neglected myrtle, across an intervening sanitary lane and into Edith's well-cared-for back garden. She did not visit but liked to have visitors. We went often to talk and to admire the beautiful garden she had made with its series of ponds in which she cherished assorted tadpoles and goldfish and other fish. About these ponds was a wealth of unusual vegetation which made passers-by stand and stare.

She was busy on collecting and classifying species of edible and poisonous fungi and after a while produced two small books, beautifully illustrated, to guide the amateur.

Her workroom was phenomenal. On two sides the walls were lined with books. In the centre was her working table, large and piled high with books and papers, in fact so large that only rather thin people could walk round it. From this table rose here and there, like miniature skyscrapers in some ancient low city, more bookshelves well filled with books of reference. Dear Edith! Most serene, most versatile, most delightful of companions. I feel now that death has taken her that we did not value her enough. But we did love her.

Then there was Barney Heffer who had come to South Africa on the death of her husband—of Heffer's bookshop in Cambridge. Here with her young son and her friend Mary Maurice she was devoting herself to establishing an English country dance movement in Cape Town. In this we joined with enthusiasm. Eddie became if not expert at least nimble in Morris dance. I was in a running set and we ran till my muscles ached. Barney, wayward and beautiful, who moved in grace, was our friend in those days. Sometimes Eddie, who loved his violin, would fiddle to our dancing.

The Stohrs were also our friends, Fritz the psychiatrist and his wife Elsie Hall the world-famous pianist. In Johannesburg, in 1929, Fritz had lectured me most severely over my choice of male playmates. But indeed I had not much choice. He now approved of Eddie. Fritz was a dear and his casual conversation was witty and rewarding.

Alice Allen we knew through the night school. She was a brilliant teacher of English and was then teaching at Wesley, a Coloured school in Salt River. Alice had abundantly that special quality of kindness and sincerity which Eddie had also. She was vitally alive and on easy terms with life and with people in a way that made her the perfect companion whether on a mountain climb or in an evening's talk. Happiness crowned the hours we spent with Alice.

Old friends were there too, the Gools and Muriel Johns, though Starkey had married and gone off to South America. If our days had not the splendour of the times with Hogben and Bodmer, our happiness was more calm and steady.

CHAPTER XIV

Three Books Were Written

IT was in 1936 when Bunting died that Roux resolved to make what amends he could by writing the story of Bunting's life. He worked steadily on this in the years that followed but found that it took some time to collect the material. He had been still a schoolboy at the time of their first meeting when Bunting was forty-three. Thereafter he had known Bunting well in a friendship of shared enthusiasm that endured for twenty years. But in this period Bunting seldom spoke of his past. So for the earlier years Roux had now to write to or visit a good many people, not only Rebecca Bunting but also Colonel F.H.P. Cresswell, Adv. F.A.W. Lucas, K.C., Charles Mussared, Philip Roux and S.A. Rochlin. Rochlin had preserved an exhaustive collection of political records and these proved invaluable. From the material thus obtained Roux pieced together some account of Bunting's early days. Of the later years Roux had himself intimate knowledge from soon after the time of the founding of the Y.C.L. Also to check his own memory he had files of *The International* which Bunting had edited and of *Umsebenzi*. Handling these memories proved difficult for reasons which Roux foresaw. He had worked in close association with Bunting and had come greatly to admire him. At times when they were not together, as when Roux was at Cambridge and later when he was in Cape Town, they had exchanged long letters in which they discussed all political developments. This association had ended only with Bunting's expulsion from the Party which had been followed by a period of partial estrangement when the older man was failing in vigour and communication ceased. But after Roux's public confession of regret for his compliance in the expulsion, made at a meeting at the Jewish Workers Club early in 1936, a measure of friendship was restored. It seemed that Bunting forgave Roux and they spoke together of the future of the

Party. What might have come of this will never be known for in fact Bunting was then already near death. The difficulty over reporting these years was no longer lack of knowledge, for Roux knew the story very well, but that the issues were so highly controversial.

It must be true, as Roux held, that the story of a life should be written white hot while memory is bright but this necessarily involves other people still living, still indignant, still with their own views as to what happened. It is clear that no one was in a better position than Roux to tell the story of Bunting's life but this did not save him from finding that many people, including Rebecca Bunting, did not agree with his report. Indeed Rebecca remained loyal to the Comintern to the end and held that all the evil that had come about in South Africa had been due to the self-seeking machinations of the Woltons and of Bach. Others said that Roux because he had loved Bunting too well—but how can one love too well for understanding?—was not the one to write such a book. But in fact, in writing of the man he had so much admired, Roux was able to achieve a high degree of objectivity.

The book, *S.P. Bunting—A Political Biography* appeared in 1944, published by Roux with the help of Issy Diamond, Benny Weinbren and other friends of Bunting, in a limited edition of 500 copies. It is long ago sold out, and if, as Africana, it is to be found on the shelves of some collectors it is there prized for its rarity rather than for its content, the story of a great life.* To me this seems sad. How soon are good lives forgotten! Of Bunting there may be mention in some political encyclopaedia of the future but of those who remember him and value his work there are always fewer as the years go by. Since I am now trying, as well as I can, to write of another life that I hold worthy to be remembered, I make no further apology for quoting here Roux's own words in the preface to the book.

> The circulation of the manuscript among a number of persons who had known Sidney Bunting and who had played some part in the events recorded, resulted in a controversy as to whether it should be published at all. Some members and sympathizers of the Communist Party felt that it would do

*Reissued 1970 by Frank Cass & Co.

harm to that organization and urged that it should not appear, or at least should be rewritten in such a form as not to cause offence. Others, including a leading official of the Party, were equally emphatic that it would not harm the Left movement and urged that a knowledge of the Party's past, including mistakes and shortcomings, was essential to a correct understanding of the movement. It is necessary, they said, to learn from mistakes of the past. My own opinion is that the book should appear, because there should be an account of Bunting's life and no one else is likely to write one, while I have been in a unique position to do so, As to rewriting the manuscript so as not to offend anybody that seems to me an impossible task.

The book is largely an unvarnished record of the facts and Bunting wrote so much that I am able to give his story largely in his own words. I have not refrained from commenting on certain matters nor have I been able to avoid bringing my own affairs into the narrative to some extent. Some orthodox communists may quarrel with this book and opponents of the Left may imagine that it provides confirmation of their views. To the former I would say that no true revolutionary can afford to be ignorant of the history of his party and that here he may find valuable information on how not to conduct political affairs. To the latter I say that the Communist Party in South Africa is still the only political organization of any consequence in this country which fights in season and out for the political, social and economic emancipation of all the people in South Africa. That is a virtue which should weigh more with liberal-minded and intelligent people than any present shortcomings or sins of the past.

The Bolshevik movement has demanded and obtained from its servants a peculiar and extreme form of loyalty. It has demanded from deviators, even when condemned to death, confessions which have puzzled and amazed the world. The force which made Soviet Russia a first-class fighting power which broke the Nazi armies before Stalingrad and is now clearing them from Soviet soil is based on a degree of unity almost unbelievably thorough. The means by which this unity was achieved may have shocked some of us; but in Russia at any rate their ultimate efficacy cannot be called in question. Sidney Bunting was an Englishman whose loyalty to Bolshevism was proof against denunciation and expulsion. In this he was a true follower of the Bolshevik tradition.

In fairness to Mrs Bunting I must state that she does not agree with much that I have written both as to the character of her husband and with regard to the Communist International and its role in South African affairs. Readers will understand that my comments, such as they are, are my own responsibility.

This book is offered as a tribute to the memory of a great man whose contribution to the cause of racial freedom in South Africa was unique.

These sad brave words were written in humility and contrition. The little book sold and the proceeds were duly sent to support the Sidney Bunting Memorial Scholarship at the Native College of Fort Hare. Now that the Bunting story is slipping into oblivion I welcome this opportunity of mentioning his name. I regret, though it was not important, my own small part in the campaign of persecution when I gave my vote against him in F.S.U. I did this mechanically, without understanding, and never, never is there any way of making amends.

Eddie Roux wrote on almost every day of his life. Most evenings were given to this work. At times when the Bunting story was held up while Eddie awaited reply from someone he had consulted he would turn to writing the political articles which appeared regularly in *Trek* a fortnightly magazine which was then edited by Benny Sachs. Some of these articles were based on research into the past and were part of the material of a work begun in 1935, a political history of the black man in South Africa, his battles, the organizations he built up and the personalities that played their part in this struggle.

In such a history the writer's knowledge may be at first hand, or he may rely on original sources such as newspaper files, letters and other documents, or his facts may be at third hand, extracted from previously written history. Roux's book contained necessarily all three kinds of writing though all the latter part, some two-thirds of the whole, related events which he had himself participated in or witnessed, a fact which makes this one of the most vivid histories ever written.

In the earlier chapters he told of Makana the prophet, leader of the Xhosa people in the early nineteenth century, how he led them courageously and how finally he surrendered himself in the hope of thus gaining peace in their lands. Sentenced to life imprisonment on Robben Island, Makana and some others managed to escape in a boat which made for Blaauwberg strand some four miles away. The heavily laden boat overturned in the surf and Makana was drowned. His followers refused to believe that he was dead and for long they were saying Makana will return, in a phrase that has now become proverbial in their language with the meaning of hope deferred. And then the strange story of the young girl Nonqause, a black Joan of Arc, who was in her turn a prophet of Xhosa nationalism. She was sixteen when she had a vision of the spirits of the dead who gave orders that all cattle were to be killed and no land cultivated. On a certain day millions of fat cattle would spring from the earth and fields of ripe corn would appear, two red suns would rise and the sky would fall and crush all white men for ever. Those who saw the cattle slaughter and the neglected lands felt they were witnessing the suicide of a nation. On the appointed day one sun rose as usual and swept across the sky to its setting. The Xhosa now realized their doom. Some 50,000 died of starvation. Others reached the colonists and were given food and work. Nonqause fled and hid for many months, later changing her name, marrying and begetting descendants. But the might of the amaXhosa was ended.

Roux wrote of the early Cape liberals, of the rebel Thomas Pringle, of Dr John Philip and Dr van der Kemp who shocked even his fellow missionaries by his marriage to a slave woman. The doings of Pringle and of John Fairbairn who put up a struggle for the freedom of the press, also of Andries Stockenstrom who opposed the white settlers' treatment of Hottentots, Bushmen and slaves; all these were of special interest to Roux and he saw these men as outriders in the long struggle for emancipation of the Non-European.

Of the later nineteenth century liberals in the Cape, including John Tengo Jabavu, editor of *Imvo Zabantsundu*, of Rose-Innes, Sauer and Merriman and of Jan Hendrik Hofmeyr, Roux wrote also, and of the tragic betrayal of their cause in the Act of Union of 1910, a surrender to which they consented in the interest of a united South Africa. Only W.P. Schreiner fought against the colour bar to the bitter end.

The terrible story of heroic effort, of anguish and betrayal, lives again in the pages of Roux's book. He describes the rise of the Order of Ethiopia, the various poll tax rebellions, Gandhi's campaign of passive resistance and above all the rise of the I.C.U., the Industrial and Commercial Workers Union of Africa, under the leadership of Clements Kadalie. Founded in 1919 the I.C.U. (I see you—white man!) became a political mass party of national emancipation. Its numbers grew until in 1928 Kadalie was able to claim that he was the leader of a movement a quarter of a million strong. He was a powerful orator and was able to rouse enthusiasm and inspire courage in those who had been hopeless. The great need of the Africans has always been for leadership and this Kadalie gave them. On the crest of this mounting wave of hope rode Kadalie, secure and confident, admired, respected and flattered by Europeans, drunk with the heady wine of success. But for a complex of causes in which the main ingredient must have been a desire, conscious or unconscious, to arrest that moment of time and so remain forever borne forward on the acclamations of the multitude, he was unwilling to carry out the mass resistance he had promised. Later! Later the time would come. He failed to understand that the time had already come when he must act or lose all. The mounting wave crashed but not against the barriers that held the Bantu in misery but to fall among the rocks and pools of intrigue, incompetence, mismanagement and dishonesty. Kadalie, failing to take the current when it served, had lost the venture. But of this tragic tale of Kadalie the most tragic feature is that the opportunity he thus squandered was unique in the story of the black man's struggle for freedom in this country. Black leaders will arise but it may be that never more will it fall to the lot of any leader to enjoy a trust so absolute as was given to Kadalie.

In this period and from then on Roux shared in many of the events narrated and some of these as they concerned his own life have been told in this book.

He finished the history in 1939 but the outbreak of war prevented any attempt at publication. The story had ended in 1936, the time of Roux's rejection from the movement.

Later he added some chapters to bring it up to date in 1946.

For some time Roux had been trying to find a title for his work. He had the journalist's ambition for a neat phrase and sought a title which should convey at once the anguish and the ultimate hope of the emancipation movement. On the title page he had quoted: 'The West Indian slave, anticipating Einstein's transfusion of the categories, made a proverb: "Time longer dan Rope". That might well be taken as the motto of Africanism.' Lord Olivier, in *The Anatomy of African Misery*.

And it was in a casual talk with our friend, Dr Anna Böeseken who had been a fellow student of mine in 1930, that we found the answer. 'There is your title,' said Anna, 'Time longer than rope.' This seemed exactly what was wanted.

The book was published by Victor Gollancz in 1948. The last words of this first edition were: 'Time is on the side of the Bantu and time is longer than rope.'

The third book written in this period concerned the problem of communication. Roux had already, in 1930, begun vocabulary studies and had discussed the problems with Bodmer. It was his aim, then chiefly in the columns of *Umsebenzi*, to express political ideas in words which would be familiar to African readers. He found that to write simply was not simple.

He had first encountered this problem in the early 1920s in the course of his political and trade union activities among urban Africans in Johannesburg. At mass meetings in general three languages were used: English, Zulu or Xhosa, Sotho or Tswana. Sometimes a speaker in English would use expressions unfamiliar to the interpreters and Roux, who knew a little Zulu, was at times aware of an incorrect rendering. This made him discipline his own choice of words and try to use the simplest possible. Similarly in writing he tried for simple words and simple short sentences, avoiding if possible all relative clauses. This was his aim during 1930 when he succeeded in making *Umsebenzi* the most readable of papers for Africans. In 1931 and thereafter he was not able to induce the chief contributors to translate their long essays from Imprecor jargon into simple words. Nor would they use short sentences. The damaging effects of their abstruse articles were at once reflected in falls in the sales of *Umsebenzi*. Roux set about making an exact study of the whole question of vocabulary.

To do this he hit upon an ingenious and valuable technique. Using at first the pupils of an African night school in Cape Town, he would spend about ten to fifteen minutes of a session in comprehension tests on these just-literate Africans, those who had passed standard III, mostly taught in mission schools. The tests were carried out as follows. Sentences were written on the blackboard containing the words to be tested which were underlined. Having first made certain that all other words in the sentences were understood, Roux next asked the pupils to indicate any of the underlined words which were unknown to them. Their understanding was then tested by asking them to make sentences using the words. An early test was made using the words: cord, rope, string.

C. K. Ogden's Basic English was not known to Roux until 1935. When it came into his hands he thought at first that here at last was just what he had been looking for. He began at once to experiment with Basic.

Basic English provides a small vocabulary, 850 words, of great defining power. In this it is a tour de force in word economy. In addition Ogden had sought to eliminate what is recognized as a great difficulty in English, namely the wayward variety of verb forms. In Basic only eighteen verbal forms, called operatives, are permitted. These are: come, get, give, go, keep, let, make, put, seem, take, be, do, have, say, see, send, may, will. All other verbs are eliminated. For 'know' one must say 'have knowledge of', for 'love' 'have love for' and so on.

However doing away with normal verbs involves an increase in use of prepositions and, having some experience as a teacher of English to foreigners, I pointed out that a very great difficulty in transition from one language to another is always the correct use of prepositions. To say 'put an end to' instead of 'finish' or 'make use of' instead of 'use' is not really making English simpler. In Basic past participles are permitted for these are counted as adjectives. One may not say 'I telephoned'; but 'I was telephoned' is good Basic. As with any limited vocabulary circumlocutions are inevitable but in Basic these are multiplied by the strict exclusion of ordinary verbs.

In the night schools Roux endeavoured to persuade the teachers to learn Basic and to teach in that tongue, but some could not and some would not and all were volunteers. One had to remember that the chief virtue in a teacher in a night school was that he could be relied on to turn up regularly. However, Roux himself tried to teach in Basic.

The test with cord, rope and string, gave comprehension figures of 30, 95 and 100 per cent. 'Cord' is a Basic word of great defining power but the other two proved better known. Another example is 'error' and 'mistake' with scores of 30 and 100. 'Error' is a Basic word. An even more striking instance was fusnished by 'complete', 'end' and 'finish.' Of these 'complete' has the greatest defining power, 'end' is the simplest word, but 'finish' is the word known to all Africans. 'Missis, the coal is finish.' 'But John, why didn't you tell me yesterday?' 'Yesterday the coal not finish. Today coal is finish.' Similarly 'join' scored over 'connection', 'tool' over 'instrument', 'find out' over 'make a discovery'.

These experiments made by Roux in the Cape Town school were repeated and results confirmed by Jack Lipman in the larger Johannesburg night schools.

Also in writing in Basic in the *African Defender* Roux met with difficulties. Copies of every issue were sent to the Orthological Institute in London and Mr Ogden's assistants went to some trouble to return them with errors corrected, so that the standard of the Basic steadily improved. But the difficulties were not lessened. Kotane, editing the vernacular section of the paper, always interested in problems of philosophy or semantics, tried his hand in the new discipline but came to question its value. 'Why can't I say "They use the Black Man to take the nuts out of the fire"?' he asked. Roux would explain that in Basic 'use' is a noun only, and he must say 'They make use of the Black Man . .' 'But everyone understands it the way I wrote it,' Kotane would argue. 'What is the use of our sticking to Basic if the people understand us as well or better if we don't use Basic?'

But Roux did not give in easily. He wrote a small book, *The Mayibuye Reader* a general knowledge reading book for Africans, in Basic. This he submitted in manuscript to the Orthological Institute for correction of errors. It was published in 1938 and was used as a reader in the night schools in Cape Town, Johannesburg and other centres. The little book at once roused a controversy among the teachers some of whom raised the same point as Kotane had made. The anti-Basic section won the day and though the reader continued to be used this was rather for the value of its content than for the manner of its English. In the end Roux came himself to be convinced that Basic despite its virtue of defining power was not the answer to his problem of communication with just-literates in South Africa. It was not so much defining power of words as day to day talk that was needed.

There is a sense in which Basic, though planned on semantic lines, seriously restricts the semantic power of English, a language in which nouns such as farm, dog, place, draft, house, and adjectives such as rough, perfect, damp, clean, may without change of form serve as verbs, such verbs being of standard modern form with past participles ending in -ed. The total prohibition of verbs in Basic destroys this semantic virtue.

But apart from any particular criticisms of Basic that may be made, as that under the most favourable conditions the language it produces is stilted and not strictly good English ('Have you love for me? You have knowledge that I have love for you.') the trouble seems to be that Basic is just not a joining-on language. It cannot work on what is already there. If it were given a clear field and could start from the beginning with learners who knew no English, it could achieve much comprehension in short time, but it cannot build on existing random knowledge. And in South Africa there is never a clear field: always the missionary, the storekeeper, the boss, have got in first. And of what they have done communication plans must take cognizance. It seems that Basic with its rigid frame cannot do this, cannot adjust. There is a sense in which Basic is too unreal, too much a blue print, almost too good to be true, too perfect to be useful here and now. And Roux, after defending Basic for some years, finally came to acknowledge this.

In 1942, addressing a meeting of the Joint Council of Europeans and Africans, he said, in Basic:

An African comes to my door and says: 'I have a desire for work.' I make answer: 'The work in the garden is completed but if you still have a desire for work in the month after this, come and I will make an attempt to give you work.'

And then in everyday casual speech:

An African comes to my door and says, 'I want work.' I answer, 'The work in the garden is finished but if you still want work next month, come and I will try to give you a job.'

And then:

Is 'have a desire for' really more fundamental than 'want'? I do not have a desire for bread, I want bread. I do not 'have a thought', I think and what I think is a thought.

In this talk Roux went on to advocate his own system of Easy English.

Following upon the comprehension tests which had led to rejection of some 200 Basic words as being totally unknown or insufficiently known to urban Africans, Roux had gone on to construct his Easy English word list, a general purpose vocabulary of 1,000 words, for which he claimed no great defining power though he held that for everyday use the list was adequate. Since in the tests he had rejected some 200 Basic words chosen for their defining power he felt that these must be replaced by a rather greater number of words of less defining power. So using the 650 Basic words not rejected together with 350 words from various sources he made the vocabulary of Easy English. In choosing the 350 words he made use of Michael West's defining vocabulary of 1,150 words, Hornby and Palmer's Thousand-Word English, the Oxford English Course of 2,000 words and the Interim Report on Vocabulary Selection, 2,000 words.

In general in these systems the choice of words had been determined by a study of word frequency in written English. But all words were submitted to comprehension tests in the night schools, for the fact of frequency in written English was no guarantee of comprehension by just-literate Africans.

Finally a few words were gleaned from the Bantu Languages themselves, as poyisa, tshipu, demesha, joyina, which gave police, cheap, damage and join as being well-known.

Simplified English is sought for different purposes. It may be wanted as a working speech for foreigners, as a lingua franca for world use, as a universal language for scientists, or, as Roux needed it, as a means of communicating knowledge to Africans.

Many attempts at constructing an international language have been made with varying success. It seems that Hogben, in Interglossa,* achieved what is probably the nearest approach to a semantically perfect world language. He described it as an attempt to apply semantic principles to language design. It was not based on English. The words of Interglossa are formed from internationally current Greek and Latin roots, the minimal grammar is based on word order. The result is a language of strange beauty easily understood by scientists. Here in Interglossa are the words of the first three verses of the twenty-third psalm.

> U Theo eque me Ovi-pe. Mi post habe pan necesso Re. An date preparo mi Clinica in plu chloro Agri. An acte controlo me Pedi littora paco Hydro.
> An date sano mi Logo. An acte dirigo Mi a Via de Verito pro an Nomino.

In the original:

> The Lord is my shepherd. I shall not want.
> He maketh me to lie down in green pastures: he leadeth me beside the still waters.
> He restoreth my soul: he leadeth me in the paths of righteousness for his name's sake.

In Basic:

> The Father is my sheep-guardian. I will not have need.
> He makes me to have rest in green fields: he is my guide beside quiet water.
> He puts my body and mind right: he is my guide in the way of right acts because of his name.

In Easy English:

> God is my shepherd. I will not want anything.
> He makes me lie down on green grass. He leads me beside quiet water.

Interglossa by Lancelot Hogben, Pelican Books, 1943.

He keeps me in health*: he leads me on the road of doing right because of his name.

However, though the problem of an international language is a fascinating one, the growing use of English as a lingua franca in Africa was what concerned Roux. Having at first welcomed Basic as the solution to his problem of writing comprehensibly he had come to realize that for ease of communication with Africans the defining power of Basic mattered less than the actual familiarity of certain words and that verb elimination meant foregoing the known usages of everyday speech.

Thus Roux's Easy English was made, with no special grammar but based empirically on the words of daily speech. Embodying the results of his comprehension tests Roux now made a *Handbook of Easy English* with a list of 1,000 useful words. Except for the restriction of using these well-known words and avoidance of difficult words Easy English is normal English. The handbook was intended for the guidance of speakers and writers who wished to be readily understood by the greatest possible number of Africans. It was published by the African Bookman in 1944.

Roux wrote also a book *Why Not Easy English?* in which he set forth his aim, described his researches and discussed the rival claims of other restricted vocabularies. This he submitted to various publishers.

But the little book was unlucky. It happened that in 1944 Winston Churchill gave his blessing to Ogden's Basic English. It is difficult to believe that Churchill had ever tried using Basic. In an article in September of that year the *New Statesman and Nation* expressed doubts as to whether Churchill with his probable vocabulary of 250,000 words would find it easy to express himself in Basic. If he wanted to say 'we will fight them on the beaches' he would have to say instead 'we will make a fight against them on the edges of the land.'

And 'twice in my lifetime the long arm of destiny has reached across the ocean and absorbed the entire life and manhood of the U.S. in a deadly struggle' would become 'Two times in my existence the long arm of history has been stretched across the

---

*The reader will note that the word 'soul' gives trouble in all these versions.

sea and has kept all the living things and all the males of the U.S. in a fearful fight.'

However, writing in Basic can be clear and may have an almost biblical beauty of restraint. A letter commenting on the article suggests that Churchill's extravagant and over-elaborate verbiage, his Gibbonish, would benefit by submission to the discipline of Basic. Both mockery and defence seem wide of the mark. Basic was not designed as a strait jacket for English when spoken to the English but as a vocabulary to convey the maximum of meaning within a minimal word range.

Roux's objective was different again but Churchill's blessing thus given to Basic was perhaps the deciding factor which prevented the publication of *Why Not Easy English?* The timing was unfortunate.

Roux now wrote in Easy English *Harvest and Health in Africa*, *Education through Reading*, and notably *The Cattle of Kumalo*.* With L. D. Lerner he wrote the four books of the *A B Adult Readers*. He edited the Sixpenny Library of some fourteen booklets dealing with topics of interest to Africans. Last he wrote the little story *James Mabeta goes to Sea* which appeared in 1949. This was intended as extra reading for students of the A B Readers. It is written in the present tense and illustrated by drawings made by Alison Roux. It was published by Sir Isaac Pitman. Alison was then fifteen and was later much displeased with the drawings she made. But we thought them good.

In spite of the rejection of *Why Not Easy English?* Roux did not consider that the time spent on this project had been time wasted. For one thing he had himself learned a good deal of how to write simply.

But now his tendency to turn from one interest and move on to other matters asserted itself. Easy English was laid aside, the typescript and all records stored in our large filing cabinet, possibly to be used in the future, more probably to be forgotten.

*For list of books in Easy English see Appendix I.

CHAPTER XV

The Academic World

THE fair lands of Frankenwald, field research ground owned by the University of the Witwatersrand, lie some fourteen miles to the north of Johannesburg, east of the Pretoria road. Fair is a manner of speaking though, when the wind stirs those ancient grasses which may have grown undisturbed since grass began and their rippling waves are lighted by the rays of the setting sun, the lands of Frankenwald have a serene beauty. This is in part a beauty of loneliness, a calm peace the more impressive by reason of its nearness to the fret and turmoil of a great industrial complex. Actually Frankenwald is on some of the poorest soil of the Transvaal, its grasses are the harshest of indigenous grasslands and the area suffers extreme cold in winter by reason of the masses of cold air which flow down into the Jukskei valley. Frankenwald thus offers a challenge to the ecologist and knowledge there hardly won may be richly fruitful on gentler, more fertile, lands. So it seemed to young Professor Phillips when he founded the Research Station there. So it seemed to Roux when, forsaking fish, he joined the Frankenwald team of scientists.

The first meeting of Phillips and Roux was at a congress of the South African Association for the Advancement of Science held in Pretoria in 1926 when the young forestry expert, then Research Officer of Indigenous Forests, Knysna, and already beginning to be known for the imaginative power and scope of his ideas, impressed the gathering by his contribution of several outstanding papers on aspects of South African forest ecology. There John Frederick Vicars Phillips, distinguished graduate of Edinburgh University met Edward Roux, his junior by four years and then in his M.Sc. year at the University of the Witwatersrand. The meeting was a happy one. The two young men discovered a common interest in ecology and a passion for soil conservation.

More important was the meeting of Phillips with Jan

Christiaan Smuts, a former president of S2A3. South Africa's world famed politician and philosopher, the author of *Holism*, was himself a keen amateur botanist and his special interest was in grasses. Smuts was impressed by Phillips and in their discussions on ecology his insistence on applying the principles of holism had a profound influence on the younger man.

Phillips gained his D.Sc. (Edin.) in the following year and in that same year accepted the post of Ecologist and Deputy Director of Tsetse Fly Research and Reclamation in Tanganyika. Four years later, in 1931, he was appointed Professor of Botany at the University of Witwatersrand and there found in the lands of Frankenwald an ideal field for the study of highveld grassland. Ecology is essentially, as Smuts and Phillips insisted, a study of the whole environment, comprising not only climate and all physical factors of the terrain but all animals and plants, all forms of life and the complex of their interrelations. For such a whole Phillips had a word: biome.

Frankenwald was then a large area of veld, some 2,600 acres, which was chiefly the estate given by Alfred Beit with the addition of some land purchased by the Transvaal Government. The land had been donated for purposes of research, and in 1922 the Government handed it over to the University. But its area was presently diminished. In 1934, at a time when the University was in desperate need of money, 1,600 acres were sold to the firm African Explosives and Chemical Industries Ltd. Phillips protested but the land was sold. He managed, however, to obtain a grant of £4,000 of the purchase price and with this money built a small laboratory, nucleus of the Research Station which was officially opened by General Smuts in 1935.

In fact Professor Phillips was not ill-pleased with the 1,000 acres that remained. The area is divided into two roughly equal portions by a tributary of the Jukskei River. The Jukskei, itself tributary to the Crocodile, is too much contaminated by chemical and human effluent to be of value in ecological research, but the little stream that flows through Frankenwald is pure and provides an instance of aquatic vegetation in a region of grassland. About it the veld is mostly undisturbed, that is it has never been ploughed or cultivated, and here Phillips began his long term studies and experiments on pasture, grazing and the conservation of the veld.

A.E.C.I., the largest manufacturers of fertilizer in South Africa, now had an agricultural section, founded in 1929 under the direction of T. D. Hall. Their estate of Modderfontein marches with the lands of Frankenwald and Phillips invited Hall to co-operate in field experiment. Thus began a long period of valuable research in which the applied scientists of A.E.C.I. worked with the pure scientists of the University.

The second World War somewhat slowed down the tempo of the work at Frankenwald but with the end of the war came a unique opportunity to do something on a really big scale in the cause of soil conservation. Smuts was then Prime Minister and it was with his blessing that Phillips set up a course for ex-service men to train them in soil conservation, water conservation and the preservation of the veld. He established at the University a School of Ecology and Pasture Management.

The ideal leader for such an enterprise, Phillips possessed gifts of imagination and sustained enthusiasm, also the eloquence that persuaded others of the importance of the work and the power of inspiring in students an enthusiasm and devotion comparable to his own. He was also a practical man who could see at once what was needed and had the knack of getting things done quickly. The Government, then drafting a Soil Conservation Act, was prepared to grant money. A new large laboratory, dormitories for students and a communal mess room were built at speed. Frankenwald was ready to receive the ex-service men. Teachers were needed and Phillips now recruited a useful team. Seconded from A.E.C.I. came Dudley Meredith to lecture on agronomy and R.E. Altona on crop and pasture management. S.J. Smuts who had distinguished himself at Vlekpoort, an experimental conservation area in the Eastern Cape, came as agricultural engineer. A local veterinarian, J.G. Boswell, gave lectures and demonstrations in animal husbandry. A.O.D. Mogg, formerly of the Pretoria Herbarium, led student excursions into the veld for study and identification of grasses and other flora. Joseph Protter came from work on cotton in Swaziland to devise methods of teaching soil science. From the Civil Engineering Department of the University came lecturers to give a course in surveying, while botany was taught by members of the Botany Department. Frankenwald was now a vital entity filled with young enthusiasm and at its centre was the restless unquenchable spirit of John Phillips and the steady devotion of his wife Jean.

A plant physiologist was lacking and Phillips now recalled the young man, Edward Roux, whom he had first met at the S2A3 Congress in 1926. He considered it a great loss that Roux had been side-tracked from botany and during the years 1930 to 1946 had made little contribution to the science of plant physiology. True there had been a paper in 1936 on a 'Combustible Soil from the Witwatersrand' which Phillips had himself communicated on Roux's behalf, also certain papers on the metabolism of peaches and plums, finally some papers on fish; Phillips had noted these with interest and now did not hesitate to offer Roux a senior lectureship in the Botany Department.

And so after an absence of seventeen years Roux returned to botany and to his abiding interest in soil conservation. Other interests, as Roux has written, tended after a time to fail him but guarding the soil from erosion was bound up with his love of this ancient eroded land. Certainly it was clear that he no longer cared excessively for fish. We packed up and left our beloved Euglena and our Cape Town friends and went our ways. Alison to Roedean, Eddie once more to the house in Bez Valley and I to England. With Eddie, in a wooden box with slatted side, went Henry our cherished half-Persian cat. A full year was to pass before we were again together in Johannesburg.

At Frankenwald Roux found in Phillips an inspiring leader and in these young ex-servicemen the most rewarding students he had ever known. Since the new Field Research Station lacked equipment and field facilities for the necessary work, Phillips sought and found farmers who willingly placed land and machinery at his disposal having their reward in the protection of their farms from soil erosion. The students went up and down the country, operating bulldozers and graders, cutting contour furrows and sealing off dongas on the farms. There were about a hundred and twenty of these men who, after a three or four year course graduated with the degree of B.Sc. in Soil Conservation. They are now dispersed to all parts of Africa and abroad.

But in 1948 the Smuts Government which had so generously subsidized the project was replaced by a Nationalist Government which did not approve a permanent agricultural faculty at the University of the Witwatersrand. Subsidies were withdrawn and the Conservation course ended.

Before this happened, in 1947, Phillips had been asked to give his full-time assistance to the ill-fated groundnut scheme in Tanganyika, a project initiated by the British Government with the aim of bringing food to the starving regions of the world. This large-scale project had been too hastily undertaken, insufficient preparatory investigation had been carried out and in the event the venture suffered every setback. Phillips when first approached refused to leave his beloved Frankenwald but on being urged again by Field-Marshal Smuts, he finally went to Tanganyika. His help and sound practical approach came too late to save the enterprise which was probably doomed in any case. He reported the difficulties and disasters and in 1950 advised that the whole venture be reduced to a pilot experiment.

Frankenwald had now lost the leader and guardian angel who had inspired and directed its research and teaching for nearly twenty years. It had lost also Jean Phillips whose wisdom and gentle sympathy had meant so much to the community of students.

The University too had lost its botany professor and for two years no new appointment was made. During that period the affairs of Frankenwald and of the Botany Department were managed first by H.B. Gilliland and later by Roux who became acting head of the Department until the coming of the new professor. Research at Frankenwald was under the direction of R.L. Davidson, an ecologist trained and inspired by Phillips, who carried on in the Phillips tradition.*

In the Botany Department however, and in spite of Roux's special interest in these matters, the centre of interest was no longer Frankenwald and research in grassland ecology. The new professor was N.P. Badenhuizen, world-renowned expert in starch-grain structure, and under his leadership a sub-department of bio-chemistry grew and flourished. Roux continued as senior lecturer in plant physiology and handled also most of the lecturing to medical students in first year botany. In this he placed emphasis on physiology, knowledge of how

---

*Those who are interested to learn more of the story of Frankenwald are referred to the book *Grass—a Story of Frankenwald* by Edward Roux, Oxford University Press, 1969.

the plant lives, rather than on systematics. He had in full measure the power of inspiring enthusiasm in the young and the gift of imparting information in a vivid and interesting manner. His lectures illustrated by the beautiful chart diagrams he made were appreciated and remembered by generations of students. Always he himself found delight and inspiration, a sufficient reward, in these generations of students. It was his good fortune, as indeed it has been mine, to be paid for doing work which he enjoyed so much that he would gladly have done it for nothing. And always he continued with his own researches, in plant respiration, on the genetics of hybrids, on antibiotics, on glassiness in potatoes, on nitrogen sensitivity in veld grasses, on photosynthesis. His work which was his joy was never-ending.

When in 1960 Professor Badenhuizen left to accept a professorship at Toronto, Roux found himself once more acting head of the Department. With a full-time programme of lectures and lab sessions, carrying on his own researches, supervision of honours students in their research, coping with the heavy load of administrative work, his days were filled with exacting labour not all so rewarding as his contacts with students. An acting head of a department has the anomaly of all the troubles of a professor without full authority to make decisions. Among the staff certain enthusiasts for their own special branches would put forward claims for costly apparatus, demands which were exorbitant in view of the money available to the Department. Wits was not a wealthy university. These and other troubles made Roux's days arduous and often when I called to bring him home I could see that he was grey with fatigue.

But I should tell of my home coming from England. It was in the English autumn of 1947 that I returned. To welcome me, Eddie, his mother and Alison had spaced themselves along the sad subterranean platform of Johannesburg station. As the train drew in it was Alison that I saw first and to me she seemed incredibly beautiful with her dark eyebrows and vivid face alight with recognition. And the train passed her and she began to run. And then I saw Gran and Eddie and all was a sharp-sweet ecstasy of being home again. I could not cease from looking at Alison. But her dress was too short. She was thirteen and had grown astonishingly in my absence.

And then we were home, together at last in the house that Eddie had bought in Malvern. This was a little house, well-built and pleasant enough but too near the shunting yards at Tooronga. Harsh sounds wrenched us from sleep in the small hours. Indeed at first it seemed that sleep between midnight and four a.m. would not be possible. But humans have great powers of adaptation and presently we slept through the din and only the most outrageous bangs and clanks would rouse us. In the minute garden we grew honeysuckle, bougainvillea and a grenadilla vine.

Near us was an ancient mine dump on which ashes had been spread so that it was now covered with coarse grass, for Eddie an interesting example of what could be done to cover mine dumps and allay dust, for all of us a wonderful open space where we could go to fly kites. Eddie made remarkable kites, large and splendid. When Alison was home she would compete with him to see whose kite would fly highest. Once, disaster, the string broke and Eddie's kite, a winged box device of brilliant red, soared briefly and swooped down in some little backyard more than a mile away. Marking the spot we set off in pursuit. We found a little house and a little boy who at first denied knowledge of the kite. In the end Eddie persuaded him to return it though the five shillings he was given as consolation did not seem to him so glorious as that splendid kite.

On Sundays we visited Alison at school. Often she entertained us with some new absurd word-play. She had a new definition of boarding school: Boarding school is a place which when the bell goes you're supposed to be somewhere else. She would bring out a rug and we sat on the lovely Roedean koppie facing across the valley to the slope we remembered where the sundew wasn't and where Eddie and I had met while he was in hiding. With us we took fruit, apples, grapes, dried apricots. 'Hunger is an occupational disease of schoolgirls,' said Alison. 'I have it badly. So I tend to fill up with bread.' Sometimes she brought her chessmen and then Eddie would give her a bishop and they would play a slow careful game while the shadows lengthened and the air grew suddenly cool. A clumsy move by Eddie upset the board. 'You needn't have done that,' cried Alison, 'You weren't losing!' We shook and folded the rug and left her to another week of Roedean.

At times some friend or acquaintance would ask whether Roedean was not rather a snob sort of school. Were we wise to send our daughter there. I had previously taught at Roedean and though I had encountered a few social snobs, and indeed I could say the same of most schools I knew, yet it seemed to me that Roedean was a school where values were esteemed. Looking up snob in a dictionary, I find 'one who makes himself ridiculous by the value he sets on social standing and by his different behaviour to persons of different classes'. This is not quite my own definition. I feel that snobs are those who are given to accepting prevailing standards without considering their value. One must wear a hat when going to town; one must wear or carry gloves to a garden party; one must leave something on the plate for manners; finger-nails must be cut to long points as a sign of useless fingers. These and other trivia seemed to me to constitute social snobbery. We felt that our daughter was not endangered. And indeed in her final year she told us how one girl, speaking affectedly, said, 'I'm not sure where we are going for our holidays. Probably we shall go to one of our farms.' Alison asked her, 'How many farms have you got?' 'Well, at the moment two. But Daddy is considering buying an estate in Natal.' 'What, only two farms!' Alison was unimpressed. 'I take a poor view of that!' Indeed she seemed naturally immune to social or wealth snobbery. She did not covet possessions.

Another objection raised against Roedean was that of religion. How could freethinkers send a child into that hotbed of Anglicanism? There was perhaps more substance to this. Roedean was not a church school; its foundation was entirely secular. But schools change and under the control of Ella leMaitre then principal an atmosphere of Anglo-catholic religiosity had developed. She was on any view a most brilliant headmistress and an accomplished scholar and during the twenty-five years of her control Roedean grew to be the most important girls' school in South Africa. But there were periods of prayer during Holy Week, also much emphasis on chapel attendance; religious plays by Dorothy Sayers were performed at Easter time. I found all this more than a little nauseating. Reflecting on some things I knew of the founders of Roedean I considered that plays by Dorothy Sayers would have distressed

Harriet Martineau. But in matters of culture Roedean was still the best school I knew with its diverse staff, partly recruited from England, and the lively discussions which went on in the common room. Other staff common rooms that I remembered were dull with conventionality and carefulness, also afflicted with some snobbery, by contrast with the freedom of the views expressed among the staff at Roedean. We left Alison a free choice in matters of religion. She had not been baptized and she now decided not to be confirmed. Perhaps this nonconformism did some harm to her school career. She was never made a prefect. Anyway, there it was, she was already beginning to prefer intransigence to conformity. When a Sayers play was toward no one wanted to take the part of Judas Iscariot. Alison, whose clear voice made her an obvious choice for a leading part, offered to play Judas. We did not go to see this play nor did we ever attend the annual carol service at Roedean. Apart from such abstentions we did not attempt to persuade Alison either way in religious matters. We had not asked to have her excused from the normal religious exercises of a school. When inevitably discussions arose we spoke to her as to an adult and did not conceal our views. We were agnostic in these matters. It seems that our attitude must have influenced her. How hard it is even with the best intentions and the most careful practice to avoid influencing and indoctrinating the young. All that Eddie was in his life must have influenced her. And she had been born to an inheritance of revolt.

One incident of our life at Malvern is perhaps worthy of recall. This was at a time when we had a servant, Lena, fat and jolly, who lived in our yard with her small child, Maria, and her three-month-old baby. Her husband, Joseph, worked for a nearby bakery and was the holder of a pass-exemption certificate. He had worked for this firm for twelve years and was supposed to sleep in their dormitory for male employees. Not unnaturally Joseph preferred to sleep occasionally with Lena in her room. Each time the police raided and caught him he had to pay a fine. So presently I wrote a letter to the Native Affairs Department requesting permission for my maid to have her husband spend the night with her, on occasion and with our knowledge and approval. The reply came that our premises must be inspected and passed as suitable. Duly the inspectors came and found the servant's room was clean, sufficiently large and well-ventilated. Nevertheless I now received a communication saying that I must not 'harbour Natives in the yard.'

Now I believed that the official in charge was a reasonable and humane person who would not administer regulations with undue harshness. So I wrote again explaining that I did not wish to harbour Natives in our yard but wanted permission for Joseph to visit his wife sometimes. The reply to this was a visitation by two municipal police who threatened me with court proceedings. 'We see that your girl has a child with her who is over ten months old. This is illegal. You can be prosecuted for this. We'll bring you to court on this charge.'

I now became furiously angry and said, 'Do that! Bring me to court. I shall be most happy to explain the case.'

However for some time nothing more happened except increasingly frequent night raids by the police. Though shunting trains did not wake us we would wake at once when a raid began. Ours was the last house in the street, on the corner of the road that ran by the railway. We would hear the approaching tumult, police whistles, angry shouts, the ugliness of bullying voices, advancing slowly down the street as the police gathered up their victims and forced them into the pick-up van. Spies were set at the end of the street so that there could be no escape for Joseph if he was with Lena. Jingle of handcuffs, the shouts drew nearer. Here they were in our yard. Loud knocking. 'Open up! Police!' If Joseph was found there the police would ring our doorbell and get us up to inform us that they had arrested a Native found trespassing on our premises. Nothing that we could say of permission given could save Joseph. He was carted off and next day the fine had to be paid. This was usually at about two or three a.m. and when the pick-up van drove away with its load of misery it left behind a street that simmered with resentment. Being thus roused from sleep did not please the white artisan householders any better than the black women in their servants' rooms. The frequent raids wore Lena down and Joseph would not stay away. In the end she wept angry tears and went back to her country home taking the children. How Joseph consoled himself we could only guess. We did not see him again.

This tale of Lena is here told because it was the rule and not the exception. It was the way things were done. It seemed that the police regarded the nightly harvest of fines as regular income. Eddie and I are not given to religion. As agnostics we felt frequent shocked astonishment at these things which were done by professed Christians who would certainly protest their belief in the sacredness of the family and their abhorrence of prostitution and sodomy. I wanted to write once more to M., the official who had turned down my request, a decent kindly man who had a wife and young family, to ask him how he would like to be compelled to live away from his wife. But Eddie wisely restrained me. It could do no good.

In fact harsher usage of Africans lay ahead. In May 1948 we listened to the election results and late at night learned of the defeat of Smuts at Standerton. This was the landslide election in which the United Party suffered defeat and the Nationalists came into power. D. F. Malan became Prime Minister and Smuts went into opposition.

The official policy of the Government was now apartheid. There had always been racial discrimination in South Africa and segregation had been the practice but hitherto, in spite of police raids and the pick-up, this had been almost casual, incidental to the swift progress of the country. Mission schools had flourished and had given a liberal education to Non-Europeans. Suburbs such as Sophiatown existed, places where black men could and did own their houses and where they could feel they were citizens of Johannesburg. In those houses were sewing machines, linoleum, an aspidistra at the window, lace-edged cloths on sideboards, all the trappings of an emerging black bourgeoisie. Apartheid was to change all this. In this new concept segregation was raised to a philosophy and there was much talk of the rights of all people to separate development on their own lines, also of education in the mother tongue, of separate university colleges for each language group, of a special kind of Bantu education devised to give knowledge suited to the needs and abilities of the black man. And presently came the plan for Bantustans where different racial groups should govern themselves. With all this noble-sounding theory which did not stand up to analysis came in practice a good deal of petty apartheid which was the negative aspect of apartheid.

This meant many insulting practices, as separate entrances for European and Non-European to post offices and other buildings, separate coaches on trains, separate buses, separate ambulances, hospital services, blood banks and so on.*

In its first year of office the new government rejected the United Nations Declaration of Human Rights which was rejected by the Soviet Union also. However this story is not the place for description and analysis of apartheid with its doublethink and fantastic cruelties. Of these things Roux has written elsewhere.† We did not in May 1948 foresee all these developments though some were easy to discern. At the end of that year on our holiday in Cape Town we were shocked to see apartheid in action on the suburban trains. This seemed to us a disfigurement of the casual civilized tolerance that had characterized the 400-year-old city. And each year we went we found changes for the worse in human relations: apartheid on buses then on beaches and even in the sea.

One bit of bus apartheid is especially odd. Riding from Wynberg to Sea Point for the first part of the journey we all sit happily mixed-up on any seats. In Cape Town the conductor puts up a notice which says: Non-Europeans in back seats only, and we all rearrange ourselves. The Coloured people with their lively sense of the ridiculous call the back region 'die kombuis' (kitchen) and the front 'the louns' (lounge). If one of them remains in a front seat they say loudly 'Look at her sitting in the louns! She doesn't know she has to come into die kombuis!' And of course on any bus one often sees people straphanging because the available seats are, so to speak, of the wrong colour.

As for the beaches we may start out neatly sorted as to colour but once we are in the water the ocean will have none of such nonsense. The waves buffet us, the flying spray bewilders us, currents sweep us hither and thither, so that soon we are all mixed up again. I fancy I hear Homeric laughter: old Neptune has not seen anything sillier. Indeed such gusts of uproarious

---

*Yet as I write Professor Christopher Barnard of Cape Town has gained world fame by his successful transplant of a human heart. The donor was a Coloured youth the recipient a white man which circumstance occasioned mocking comment in the overseas press.

†In *Time Longer Than Rope*, second ed. University of Wisconsin Press. 1964.

laughter may be what is needed to make us sane for surely we could be purged by laughter. Oh for a Gilbert and Sullivan opera to our need! Yet even as the purest laughter is near tears so this apartheid silliness cuts close to the bone.

And now Alison was nearing matriculation and the end of her schooldays. She planned to go on to the University and study Fine Arts. 'Why not medicine?' we suggested.

'No, no! Make me do medicine and you'll see what will happen!'

We agreed that we would not make her do anything: the choice must be hers. She wanted to paint. But successful artists are few; she would always be poor. We had an idiotic family game of mixed-up proverbs and idioms that we played. I now said, 'When you've buttered your bread you'll have to lie on it!'

'All right! I shall be poor but I shall be painting. That's what I want. There won't be any butter!'

And so painting became what we too wanted for her.

It was partly because of Alison's plan to study at the University that we moved to Melville, near the University and a more comely suburb than Malvern. It seems that in Melville no one ever leaves except through death. We had to wait for some time to get the house at 72 Third Avenue. We moved there on April first of 1950. With us went our two Siamese cats, Nicolette and Koko, and presently we brought Henry also, the half-Persian that had been a kitten at Euglena. Henry had grown fat, being petted and a little over-fed while living at the house in Bez Valley.

Number 72 was an old house with large rooms, well built, facing north and standing high on the koppie. The garden was lovely, though it had little depth of soil, and it seemed at first enormous. Both house and garden were much larger than we had had at Euglena. This house became the love of our old age. Of course when we went there we were not old by modern standards but we knew then that this was to be our last home. Even before we unpacked I found a glass jar and gathered an armful of end of season dahlias from the garden. 'A lovely splash of colour,' said Eddie as I set them on a table. We opened a window of our bedroom to be a way in and out for our cats and this window was not closed again for seventeen years.

For Alison there was a large front room which became her studio-bed-sitter. Here she established herself with a narrow divan bed, a large working table and her easel. She said, 'I am so tired of being away. I want to live at home.' And for some years until the end of her university days we were a happy family.

And soon I was once more teaching at Roedean. Each morning we left together in the little car and at the University Eddie and Alison would leave to walk together up the hill. In the evenings at about 5-30 I called for them at the University where Alison aglow with the joy of a studio session and Eddie tired from taking a lab but never bored joined me as we made for home where all of peace, spacious rooms and a lovely brilliant garden awaited us.

This garden in summer was a riot of colour, a glory of dahlias, sunflowers, gaillardias, nasturtiums. In winter we grew bright Namaqua daisies, lupins, sweet peas and there was the wealth of pink-and-white flowers on our camellia. Always we went all out for colour and toughness in our flowers, preferring sunflowers which our neighbours considered coarse and not worth growing, perhaps because they grew so exuberantly. I liked growing what wanted to grow. I cut sunflowers and put them in vases, no arrangement needed, so that we had a van Gogh picture in every room. Alison and Eddie approved. As a housekeeper I was quite good at organizing flowers.

Our pleasure in having Alison at home with us was matched by her delight in life and in her work. I remember that one afternoon, by chance, I met her in town and she was carrying a new and quite beautiful T-square which she had bought and which was almost as tall as she was. Since she had more shopping to do I suggested that she put the T-square in the car for me to take home. 'Oh no, no! I want to keep it with me.' And she walked her ways bearing the T-square as proudly as many a girl would have carried a new tennis racquet. Oh, Alison, the darling girl!

Once more the river of Eddie's life flowed calmly. Once more the busy days slipped by and made the years. And for Eddie was the special delight of having this lovely lively daughter a student on the campus. Here he might happily encounter her at any time of the day. And once, looking together from a window of the Botany Department, we saw her walking in sunshine, with a tall fair boy who pleased her then, towards their next lecture.

But she did not always walk in sunshine. Her university days were not calm. Inevitably she became mixed up in student demonstrations. On one occasion she and other girls were holding a banner when a group of reactionary students attacked. Alison fought wildly to save the banner only to have it wrenched from her. Demonstrators and attackers ended up in the magistrate's court and there for the first time Alison heard a great crowd of Africans sing Nkosi sikelele. As a result of the banner incident Alison became more aware of student issues and even thought of standing for S.R.C. But she was warned not to do this, even if she could secure nomination, as she was considered politically unreliable at least partly because her father had been expelled from the movement on the charge of right wing deviations. She was indignant at being called unreliable and passionately resentful of the slur on her father. Even worse, we reflected, than having a father who was a haberdasher. She had read *S.P. Bunting, a Political Biography*, and we now had some talk about the past. We told her more of the manner of the expulsions and of the cruel campaign waged against Bunting and others, also of the isolation technique used against us. She listened, asked puzzled questions, clearly began to understand. Presently she said: 'I suppose they are right. I am politically naïve. I once said an idiotic thing about the Transkei. I blush to remember. Anyway I'd be no use and I do hate being on committees. What I want to do is paint.' And that was that.

However her flair for making posters made her much in demand. She made a design of grave beauty in support of a NUSAS fund for needy students and near the end of her university days was asked to paint a long strip banner. This she did at home in secrecy The paint went through the cotton material and the words DEFEND ACADEMIC FREEDOM could for long be seen faintly on the granolithic floor of our stoep. Koko, that ever curious cat, stepped in the paint and his little black painty footmarks were everywhere. The banner, by unthinkable effort, was duly stretched above the classical pillars, high across the façade of the centre block of the University where it remained for some days since to get it down was a problem.

There was a competition for a design for a mural for the library of the Non-European students hostel. Alison's design was chosen and she climbed about on ladders and trestle planks to paint it. It showed in nine panels scenes of Johannesburg life, the mine dumps, the cooling towers, Africans queueing for a bus, street vendors in Diagonal Street with their piles of oranges. It was a beautiful lively work with a wisp of blue smoke linking the vignettes. Alas, the Douglas Smit hostel is no more. There are no longer more than a dozen Non-European students. The Bernard Price Institute now uses the building and the mural has been destroyed.

I have said the days slipped by and made the years. But this was not without sorrow. Oupa Roux died early in 1951. Eddie now head of the family, spoke movingly at the rationalist funeral service. Philip Roux, that angry young man who had been so passionate in revolt and had so bitterly disputed with his children, had grown quieter with the years. He remained fixed in his political views but never lost his love of reading books on science and prehistory. He pursued also a search for a perpetual motion device. Each time a trick failed he would start off again on some new idea. I have forgotten most of the ingenious pieces of machinery he constructed. One I recall was a large cylinder of water on a turntable and having radiating exit tubes at the top. As the cylinder was turned the water rose and flowed out. We tried to make him see that to turn the mass required effort; the energy equation involved the conversion of a moment of inertia. But no failure daunted him. Always he went on trying to steal a march on nature, to catch the laws of physics napping, to get something for nothing in the energy line. Even in his last years his restless enquiring mind and his busy clever fingers made many useful gadgets. Once we were sitting on the thick grass in the back garden of the house in Bez Valley. Gran was sewing and I was darning socks. Oh dear, I had dropped my needle. Oupa hastened into the house and returned with an outsize magnet which he moved over the grass until the errant needle leaped to join it. Saturday afternoons we usually spent in Bez Valley. But after Oupa died we would drive over to bring Gran and Arthur to lunch with us and spend the sleepy afternoons in our sweet garden at Melville.

Philip Roux was seventy-six when death came suddenly.

Eddie raised a fund and with this bought books which were donated to the Johannesburg Municipal Library in memory of P. R. Roux. These were chiefly the science books he had loved so well, among them two by J. B. S. Haldane. To me this seemed a good way of remembering a life.

At the service Eddie spoke of Philip's passion of revolt and of the consistency of his life. To bear the coffin there were four sons and one son-in-law and one friend. So passed Philip Roux's rebellion, leaving his inheritance of Eddie Roux's revolt now held in leash and Alison Roux's still passionate intransigence.

Gran had presently four grandchildren and it seemed that there would be no more. First was Alison Roux whose paintings were not greatly to her taste, then Derek and Gail Roux, then Ian Robertson. Phil had married pretty Phyllis Rowan of a famous sporting family. Her brothers, Eric and Athol, were internationally known cricketers. Phyllis herself, petite and dainty, had muscles of iron and was an outstanding tennis player. Phil, having served in the North African campaign had returned to buy a house in the young ex-service men's suburb of Sandringham. Here his son Derek was in the top class at the primary school. Claud, second in the Roux family, had married a widow, Vera Cochran-Murray, but of this marriage there were no children. Enid had married Arthur Brownlee, a doctor, a member of the famous Cape liberal family. On his death she went back to nursing once more and was overseas during the War years. Back in South Africa she married Fred Robertson, a childhood companion. This was in 1948. Fred was a bearer of the coffin of Philip Roux. Their son, Ian, was born in 1953.

And now came for us the end of a chapter. Alison achieved her honours degree with distinction and was awarded a scholarship to give her two years' study in Europe. This was a tremendous distinction. At the time we rejoiced and thought it a Good Thing. Later we were less certain.

CHAPTER XVI

Persecution of the Left

Now since Roux had been expelled from the Communist Party in 1936 and from that time had played no part in politics, it may appear somewhat odd that I turn again to the political arena and record what happened to the C.P. in 1950. Of himself Roux would say apologetically that he had degenerated into a sort of radical liberal of no commitments and had served other interests. Former comrades spoke sneeringly of him and said: 'Roux keeps quiet and grows cabbages.' But what presently came about was to have the most terrible consequences in his life as still more so for others. So I tell briefly of the events of 1950 onwards.

The C.P., which in 1936 after the mass expulsions had seemed moribund, presently rallied and in time became once more an effective force. By 1947 it had trained an efficient cadre of African, Indian, Coloured and European leaders and had considerable influence in the African National Congress and in the South African Indian Congress. And in that year it achieved at last a voice in parliament. At the election of Native Representatives when D.B. Molteno did not seek re-election for Cape Western his place was taken by the Communist Sam Kahn who was elected by a large majority. Kahn's career in the House of Assembly was not easy. Although strictly representing only the interests of Africans of Cape Western, Kahn considered that since all Africans outside the Cape were not represented by anyone it was his duty at least to be in touch with some of them. This was a view that the Government did not share: they held that all Africans everywhere should have no voice in government. Kahn visited the Rand in 1949 with the intention of holding meetings. At once a magisterial order was issued which forbade him to address meetings in locations. Kahn managed to hold one meeting and then the Minister of Justice issued a general ban forbidding him to attend any meeting on the Witwatersrand.

Another device the Government developed to harass their critics and opponents was the arbitrary withholding of passports and the seizing of passports already issued. This was used against Kahn and also against E. S. Sachs, Solly Sachs, the veteran and still militant secretary of the Garment Workers Union. Sachs, when his passport was confiscated, had planned to attend a clothing and textile conference in France. Dr Yusef Dadoo, the Indian leader, was also a victim. Some appeals to the courts were successful and this led to further reactionary legislation in the form of the Departure from the Union Regulation Act of 1955, which made it a crime for a South African to leave the country without a passport or exit permit.

Meanwhile May Day of 1950 was announced by the Communists as Freedom Day: demonstrations were to be held throughout the country. The Minister of Justice, C.R. Swart, now banned all meetings. On the Rand at Benoni, Sophiatown and Orlando, the ban was defied and at these meetings thirteen were killed and twenty-four wounded by the action of the police in suppressing rioting. Margaret Ballinger moved in Parliament for a debate on the Rand riots as a matter of urgent public importance. But the debate was not held. Only the three Native Representatives and the six Labour members voted for the motion. Swart announced that he would forthwith seek wide powers against communism.

The Suppression of Communism Bill passed its first reading. A communist was defined as 'a person who professes to be a communist or who, after having been given a reasonable opportunity of making such representations as he considers necessary, is deemed by the Governor-General to be a communist on the ground that he is advocating any of the objects of communism.' The objects of communism were widely defined. The C.P. did not wait for this Bill to be passed but dissolved itself in voluntary death. Sam Kahn announced this in the House of Assembly before the completion of the third reading. The Bill was opposed by the United Party in both Houses, chiefly on the ground that persons charged with communist activities should have the right of appeal to the courts. But in June 1950 it became law and there was to be no appeal to the courts. And in August, J. deVilliers Louw, assistant magistrate of Johannesburg, was appointed Liquidator in terms of the Act, his first charge being to compile a list of former supporters of the C.P.S.A.

Among the first to be thus named was Solly Sachs. The fact that he had been expelled from the Party nineteen years earlier did not save him. In May 1952, as a named person, he was ordered to resign from the Garment Workers Union and also forbidden to attend all gatherings save those of a religious, recreational or social nature. The G.W.U. now called a meeting of protest on the City Hall steps. This was on a Saturday morning. The meeting was indignant but orderly and was well-served by a loud-speaker system. Eddie and I, forsaking the care of cabbages, stood across the road in President Street and saw all that happened. We could hear Sachs clearly. He was speaking, explaining the ministerial order on him and why he must now resign, when a small group of police advanced to arrest him. A sort of muttered growl of anger now rose from the densely packed crowd and scattered indignant shouts could be heard. Sachs, still at the microphone, urged the meeting to be quiet, to offer no resistance. I thought of Johannes Nkosi. But the relay service was now cut off and Sachs could no longer be heard. He was led away by the police. And then it happened. Out from the City Hall poured large numbers of police armed officially with riot staves and some, unofficially, with City Hall chairs. Seen from our view point there was a great whirling of staves and lifting of chairs raised and brought down with violence. The women and girls now fled in all directions, small groups of them pursued by police, and the square was soon empty save for the stunned and injured who lay still or began to crawl away helped by friends. There was a litter of smashed chairs and banners and a number of pathetically shabby high-heeled shoes.

All this we saw and all was as I have told it, but officially it was denied. It had not happened. The Minister of Justice said that no enquiry was necessary as he preferred to believe the report rendered by his trusted police who denied that they had used chairs to stun people and claimed that they had acted solely in self-defence when attacked by the girls.

Sachs was presently found guilty of addressing meetings and sentenced to six months' imprisonment. In December his appeal was dismissed but the sentence was suspended conditionally for three years. But his work in the trade union movement, in effect the meaning of his life, was destroyed. Forced to leave the G.W.U. which he had founded and served for twenty-four years, he left for England.

Of special interest to us in view of our liberal belief in freedom of speech and of the press, a belief which we knew was by no means shared by all our former communist associates who indeed would have found in this yet another right wing deviation, was the action begun in May of 1952 against *The Guardian*. This weekly newspaper, published in Cape Town, though not controlled by the C.P. always took a line strongly in favour of communists and their fellow-travellers. It was in the hands of a team of courageous people and they did not let it perish without a struggle. When *The Guardian* was suppressed it rose like a phoenix under a new name, *The Clarion*. 'I call it the Carry-on!' said Sam Kahn cheerfully as he sold a copy to the Minister of Justice near the entrance to Parliament. Presently this was suppressed and rose again as *The People's World*, to be succeeded by *Advance* which was banned in October 1954. A new company than produced *New Age* which survived till 1962. Even then the indomitable editor, young Brian Bunting, a son of Sidney Bunting, managed to raise yet one more phoenix, *The Spark*. This final flare of defiance was expertly dealt with by forbidding all concerned on pain of imprisonment, to take any part in editing, writing or publishing any journal whatsoever. Thus *The Guardian* made a brave end.

The third event of May 1952 was Kahn's expulsion from Parliament and in July he was ordered to give up his seat on the Cape Town City Council. In the parliamentary by-election which followed, Brian Bunting then editing *Advance* was elected. 'He will not be an M.P. for long!' said the Minister of Justice grimly. Soon he was expelled as Kahn had been. In 1954 in the general election of Native Representatives, Ray Alexander, a named ex-communist, was elected only to be barred by the police when she tried to enter the House. She threatened legal action and the police paid damages. Later she too was expelled.

In January 1955 Lee Warden was elected. He was not an ex-communist but a fearless printer and publisher who had dared to print matter that most printers would carefully refuse to touch. He was able to keep his seat until in 1960 all the Native Representatives were removed. Then Margaret Ballinger, the brilliant parliamentarian, that sharp thorn of clear thought and eloquent speech in the side of the Nats, also left the House for the last time. She had represented Cape Eastern for twenty-four years.

It was in September of 1950 that Roux received the first intimation that he was 'named.' This was a printed slip informing him that a registered letter addressed to him awaited collection at the G.P.O. I should explain that our maid Winnie Selemela, mission-trained, was both intelligent and literate and thus perfectly capable of receiving and signing for communications on our behalf. Indeed we had left with her a written authorization to do this. But no African could be thus trusted: the postman would not give her the letter. Roux must go to the G.P.O. where he was informed that the letter had now been returned to the Department of Justice in Pretoria. It had, by some odd mischance, been marked 'gone away.'

We had some talk about this and felt convinced that this letter must be a notification of Roux's naming as an ex-communist. Roux now wrote to the Principal of the University, Dr H.R. Raikes, to ask his advice. As to communism he stated his position in these words:

> With regard to communism as such I have long ago publicly expressed my disapproval and dislike of the totalitarian regime which has developed in Russia and particularly of the way thought is regimented and scientists persecuted there. In spite of this I have some sympathy with the communists in this country. They have consistently championed the cause of the Non-European and they were the only political party to admit all races on a basis of absolute equality.

Raikes replied at once advising Roux to write to the Secretary for Justice and ask for the letter to be sent again, as if he did not do so it might be held by the Liquidator that due time had been allowed for reply and that he had chosen not to answer. In his letter Raikes, most sincere of humanists, wrote:

> Believe me, I shall do everything in my power to help you if

help is needed. I still hope however that this silly persecution of people whose contacts with the C.P. expired years ago will be dropped. I don't like communism myself because, however sound the fundamentals of communism, Communist parties do seem to specialize in police states quite as much as Nazis. I believe there are other and better methods of benefiting the under-privileged. But I shall do my best to help you.

So Roux wrote to the Secretary for Justice and after many months received reply as follows:

Sir,
    Having been directed by the Honourable the Minister of Justice in terms of Section 4 (10) of Act 44 of 1950, you are hereby afforded a reasonable opportunity in terms of the proviso of the abovementioned section, to show why your name should not be included in a list of persons who are or have been office-bearers, officers, members or active supporters of the Communist Party of South Africa ...

In spite of the floating participial clause this seemed clear enough and a reply was required within fourteen days.
    Within fourteen days Roux replied:

2 January 1952

The Liquidator: Act 44 of 1950
Sir,
    In reply to your undated letter, number 2/50/130:
    The obvious reason I can submit for my name not being included in the list mentioned in your letter is that once my name is on that list the Minister will have the power, by arbitrary action on his part and without reference to the courts of law, to take against me any or all of a number of steps depriving me of liberties I have hitherto enjoyed as a South African citizen. This would seem to me the more iniquitous in view of the fact that my alleged membership of the Communist Party of South Africa could only have occurred at some time long prior to the passage of the Act

and when such membership was no infringement of the law.

Can you suggest any other sort of reason against my name being included in your list?

Yours faithfully,
E.R. Roux

A further letter from the Liquidator, dated 30.1.1952, very properly ignoring the moral issue and the ironic query, for morality was not his affair and the argument was probably way above his head in any case, said in part:

> I wish to grant you an opportunity of making representations to me on the merits of the allegations against you and I am, therefore, furnishing herewith the following particulars in regard to the evidence which has been placed before me:
> (1) You attended meetings of the Communist Party of South Africa which were held on the Johannesburg City Hall steps on 12 January 1936, 16 February 1936, 22 March 1936 and 3 May 1936.
> (2) You attended a Communist Party Conference held at Johannesburg on the 5 and 6 April 1936.
> (3) A letter written by you was published in the 'Nonsebenzi' of the 8 August 1936, in which you expressed your views in regard to a resolution of the Political Bureau.
> (4) You were a speaker at a Communist Party meeting held in the Trades Hall, Johannesburg, on the 16 August 1936.
> (5) An interview which you had with a correspondent of the 'Star' was published in that paper on the 30 July 1929, and clearly indicated your association with the Communist Party.

The Liquidator in apparent generosity seemed to make every concession; in fact no concession had been made and there was no generosity. What emerges from a glance at the listed evidence is that no item later than 1936 is mentioned. Nor could it be. How ironic seemed the word Justice in the letterhead! What was this justice that now punished people for acts which had not been illegal at the time they were committed?

Roux replied:

11 February 1952

The Liquidator: Act 44 of 1950
Sir,
    I have no desire to deny my former membership of the Communist Party of South Africa. I left the Party in October, 1936, and did not subsequently rejoin it.
    The facts stated in your letter of 30 January are, as far as I remember, correct, though with regard to (3) I would point out that I have never been connected with any paper known as the 'Nonsebenzi'.
                    Yours faithfully,
                        E.R. Roux

A final communication from the Liquidator informed Roux that as he had now been afforded a reasonable opportunity of showing why his name should not be on the list, his name was now included as having been a member and active supporter of the Communist Party.

Roux was often asked by well-wishers why he had not put forward argument to show that since 1936 he had not taken part in any political activity. He would reply that the sole issue in question was whether he had or not been a member of the C.P.S.A. He had no wish to deny this, nor would denial have been possible, and his subsequent abstention from politics was not relevant to this issue. He accepted the fact that he was named while protesting the essential immorality of the making of such a list. I said that he had not in fact made this protest clear in any of his letters. He held that to persons having such an odd concept of justice any protest would be words wasted. I said that some words should be spoken even if they would be wasted. But he would not even point out that he had been in disgrace when he left the Party.

The named received the distinction in their various ways. Some wore their naming with pride. Louis Joffe, that once exuberant little Mr Pickwick who had been so happy in his work with 'the boys' was proud to be named. I truly believe that if he had not been he would have written to ask why not. We were not in touch with him, had not seen him since the wretched hullabaloo of 1936, but we had heard he had suffered injury in a street accident and was now lame. We saw him one day as our car paused at a stop in Braamfontein. He limped across the road leaning heavily on a stick. We called a greeting to our former comrade. He came close and, peering at us, said: 'I don't remember who you are exactly but I know you are good kind people. I knew you once. I wish you well.' Tears came to my eyes: not only for all the persecution suffered but for the loss of not remembering. A few months later we heard of his death. With his one-track mind and perfect devotion he had also outstanding courage: many men have deserved a worse epitaph.

A named one who suffered greatly was Willy Kalk who so long ago in the Y.C.L. study group had seen, as he claimed, the genesis of the heresy that was to lead to Roux's expulsion from the Party. Like Sachs, Kalk was ordered to resign his position as secretary of the Leather Workers' Union. Thus was the meaning and pattern of his life destroyed. He found it difficult to get any work. He had married Margaret Thomas, also named, a girl from Wales who became a teacher and later a lecturer in zoology at the University. For many years these two had played no part in politics; indeed they had most carefully minded their own business. Yet in the 'emergency' of 1960 both were imprisoned for a period of about five months.

In all more than 400 persons suffered this strange retrospective penalty of being named and hence freely to be ill-used in various ways.

Many brave things happened in these turbulent years but all to no purpose. It was on an evening in May of 1951 that we stood in Plein Street waiting to see the protest march of the Torch Commando go by. This movement was led by 'Sailor' Malan, ace-pilot hero of the War, who said: 'We, ex-servicemen, see South Africa threatened by all the things we fought against and losing the freedom for which many of our comrades died.' Brave words and sad. Such words have echoed down the corridors of human history. And here they came marching six abreast bearing aloft their sticks with tins containing paraffin-soaked rags which flared and smouldered like the dip-flares at some old country fair. The faces in the light of the flickering torches were those of men in the prime of life, men who had not known defeat. These were the desert rats and those who believed in their cause. They had fought for freedom from tyranny and believed that they had won and that none could overthrow them. There was compulsion in those marching feet. Beside me Eddie Roux stirred and was restive as the war horse that crieth Aha. Among them were many of our former comrades. Some saw us and called to us to join them. Eddie shook his head. 'I wish we could march with them.' But he held to his resolve made fifteen years earlier to keep out of politics. The Torch Commando was not a political party but in South Africa everything is political. I too was remembering the days of toil and hope and faith in future freedom. But now we were middle-aged and the flame had burned low. Our resistance muscles were out of practice. I said: 'Their turn now. Theirs the battle.' So the march swept by some thousands strong, heads up and faces proud in resolve. Our hearts were lifted with hope renewed.

But the torches smouldered and died. There was no clear aim, no unity of purpose and in a few years the Torch Commando passed away.

In September of 1955 two detectives of the Special Branch came to search our house. They were not very clever young men and plainly, though they could read, had not much use for books. They were astonished to find that we had bookshelves in every room. What could a man want with all those hundreds of books? Fumbling they started on their task. They used, it seemed, certain words for clues, such as freedom, Negro, race, colour, Bantu, workers, communist, Soviet, Marx, Lenin. Even so their choice was odd. They took Hogben's *Retreat from Reason*, Sidney Hook's philosophical study *From Hegel to Marx*, Russell's *Colour, Race and Empire*, *The Communist Manifesto*, Cope's *Comrade Bill*, Padmore's *Life and Struggles of Negro Toilers*, *In Face of Fear* by Michael Scott, *The Workers' Song Book*, and Bishop Brown's naïve essay *Communism and Christianism*, also a pamphlet by Olive Schreiner. They worked hard. At some stage the maid Winnie brought them a tray with tea and biscuits. They toiled on, taking files of old newspapers, pamphlets, manuscript notes, copies of the *New Statesman*. Two heavy cases of booty they packed and carried to their car and wrote a list and left a copy with us. What they hoped to find we could not imagine. Eddie restrained them from taking any of Alison's books on art though in her room they found *Black Beauty* and eyed it with suspicion. And what else they took I forget. Rather more than a year later we got most of the books back the police still keeping a few items which we supposed they had grown fond of. We heard later that some 400 houses had been searched at this time.

The suppression of the C.P. had created a political vacuum on the left. The still all-white Labour Party which on occasion showed some concern for the interests of the black workers had still a few seats in Parliament until the election of 1958. The United Party, the official opposition, had no clear policy to offer as an alternative to apartheid. In 1957 Harry Oppenheimer put forward his New Economic Policy which envisaged a measure of industrial integration of Africans in the interests of efficiency, with total abolition of the migrant labour system and in its place settlement of African workers with their families on and near the mines and factories. As a business man Oppenheimer was concerned with the waste and inefficiency caused by apartheid and the migrant labour system. But the U.P. rejected his policy and continued merely to oppose Nationalist measures without offering any clear alternative.

In 1953 two new political parties were formed. One was the Congress of Democrats, a white organization pledged to work for equal rights for Non-Europeans. The C.O.D. and the South African Coloured People's Organization in Cape Town worked with the African National Congress and the South African Indian Congress, the four being known together as the Congress Alliance. In June 1955 the Alliance held a meeting at Kliptown near Johannesburg at which a Freedom Charter was adopted. This was based largely on the United Nations charter of human rights and contained the words:

> All shall have equal rights before the law. All shall enjoy equal human rights. There shall be work and security. The doors of learning and culture shall be opened. There shall be houses, security and comfort. There shall be peace and friendship . . . These freedoms we shall fight for side by side, throughout our lives, until we have won our liberty.

Still on the sidelines we did not join the C.O.D. We did not attend the Kliptown meeting. Alison wanted to go but we restrained her as she had just obtained a passport to enable her to study in Europe. She was just twenty-one. Did she want to jeopardize her whole future by having her passport confiscated? Some of her friends went and late that night came to tell us how the police had thrown a cordon round the meeting and had held some three thousand people who were required to give their names and addresses. With them they brought some copies of the Freedom Charter. Alison took one, framed it and hung it in her room where it stayed, more than half-forgotten, until some nine years later when the police found it.

The other organization that emerged was the Liberal Party. This was formed by individuals who held various degrees of radical thought, such as Alan Paton, D.B. Molteno, Margaret and William Ballinger, Dr Edgar Brookes. The Party gained members of all races including some leading Africans, for example Jordan Ngubane a well-known journalist. Though they lacked resources, especially money, the Liberal Party began to put up candidates in various elections. None was elected and many forfeited their deposits.

It was in 1957 that Roux was approached and asked to join the Liberal Party. To do so meant giving up his resolve to play no further part in politics. He was influenced by the decision of the Liberals to adopt the principle of universal adult suffrage rejecting any qualification for the franchise. L. who came one Sunday morning to ask Roux to join said he would be one of the Party candidates in the forthcoming municipal elections. 'And I can promise you you won't be elected!'

When L. had gone we debated the matter. I said tentatively, not facing the moral issue, 'You know you are already working much too hard. And you are never willing to do things by halves. Ought you to take on anything more?'

'That's not the point. One can always do more.'

'It is one point surely: one has only so much vitality. But then the thing is that you have steered clear of politics since you left the C.P., that's more than twenty years. Why change now?'

'This is the first time since then that a political party has granted absolute equality of membership to all races. Not a qualified franchise but one man one vote. I believe in democracy. I remember Bunting. If you believe in any aim you have to do something about it.'

PERSECUTION OF THE LEFT

I could not gainsay any of this. I had hardly known Bunting but in my early years I had been a member of a Unitarian congregation where that same categorical imperative prevailed: one must live one's ideas. I saw what Eddie's decision would be.

In a qualified franchise there was danger. It might be argued that some kind of test of comprehension should be applied to all voters. But such qualification could be so easily manipulated to the disadvantage of some section of voters. The black men had seen this sort of thing happen in the Cape and they had seen too how in 1910 their interests had been jettisoned even by their best friends in the cause of white unity. The qualification to vote could continually be raised and at the same time educational opportunity could be withheld, thus keeping the majority of South African citizens permanently in a voting minority. It all comes to the crucial question: do you believe in democracy?

Our U.P. friends would object: 'But are you prepared to be ruled by a black majority?'

'Of course not! Not by any racial group majority or minority. Not on racial lines at all. Black men are men and will vote on economic issues and not on colour.' So we believed and held that the emerging black nationalism which these people so much feared was but a reflection and reaction to the challenge and provocation of white nationalism which had caused it. 'The point is we must not talk of what colour a man's skin is but of what he is. He is a man and his colour is irrelevant. Not a multiracial pattern but a nonracial society is our aim.'

'Ah,' they said wisely, 'but you can't go against human nature.'

This was plain nonsense. Going against human nature is what we are doing all the time. Colour prejudice itself is not natural and must be inculcated afresh in each generation, a fact which is not noticed since the whole social frame-work, the human biome, in this country operates to that end. Colour prejudice has been found useful in promoting white unity, in maintaining a reactionary government in power, and therefore it has been called human nature, stimulated and fostered in every way even to the extent of making a philosophy, a political faith of apartheid. The trouble about reversing all this and learning to treat human beings as persons without reference to their colour is that it is easier to create prejudice than to eliminate it. But the attempt, said Bunting—was it in 1923?—must be made. This too is a snobbery, a form of racial snobbery. It is no ingrained quirk of human nature.

And as freethinkers Eddie and I had often been astonished at the attitude of some of our Christian friends. There is a verse in Acts which reads: 'And hath made of one blood all nations of men for to dwell on the face of the earth.'* On Sunday they might hear these words but seemed to forget them from Monday to Saturday. There was no consistency, no living their ideas.

'If God had meant people to mix he would not have made them of different colours,' argued a pious acquaintance.

I replied: 'If God had not meant people to mix he would not have made the races interfertile.'

Anyway it was plain which way the decision was to go. We both joined the young Liberal Party.

At once we were plunged into the activities of an election campaign. The Party had not many helpers and few who could write legible election cards. We spent hours writing cards and canvassing voters. In the ward where Roux was a candidate were the blocks of flats of Killarney. Here in each building we went to the top then separated taking alternate floors, working downwards and meeting now and again to report and to encourage one another. The going was heavy. In one flat Mrs Wertheim, a youngish woman, plump and obviously well-to-do, harangued me saying that as an old woman I ought to keep out of politics and leave such matters to the young. Should the old then be idle, their experience wasted? Mr Wertheim, my old friend who had shared my passion for Torquemada crosswords, was ill in bed and I could not speak with him. This was the wife of his old age. The first Mrs Wertheim whom I had loved had been cultured and sensitive. I was not now invited to sit down. Till that day I had not thought of myself as old. Only as the plump rich lady talked on did I begin to feel old age creep in my bones.

In most of the flats with their display cabinets of assorted silver and china ornaments there was a sort of rampage of bad taste. Perhaps I mean of other people's taste. The ladies were quite flat-proud. In between urging Liberal policies I wondered

*Omitted in the Revised Version, however.

who dusted all these distressing objects. One young lady, Mrs X., said: 'I'll ask my husband. He always decides how we vote.' I said, 'But aren't you interested in your city? Don't you have ideas about . .' 'Oh no! I'm not interested. I leave ideas to my husband.' She spoke in sweet innocence as though ideas were a strictly male preserve, perhaps like four-letter Anglo-Saxon words, unsuitable for females. I said I would call again.

But on top of our day's work this canvass was exhausting and it was abundantly clear that we were not getting anywhere. The Johannesburg City Council was dominated by the United Party and most of those we talked to were more or less languid supporters of this party. We urged that the U.P. was not playing a sufficiently vigorous role in city affairs and that the threat of a little Liberal opposition would stimulate them to more meaningful activity. One we tried to speak to was the novelist, Sarah Gertrude Millin, author of *God's Stepchildren*. Roux sent a special note to her asking her to see him. But she would not. Another whom Roux encountered was a man who took him to task and said: 'You are a university lecturer. You have a heavy load of work. How can you be a city councillor? Your candidature is bogus. I shall not vote for you.' This was a substantial rebuff. Roux replied that he was in fact deeply serious in the cause of Liberalism. He knew he had no hope of being elected but wanted to make people think a little and help to put Liberal thought on the map. If he were elected he would endeavour to perform his duties as city councillor at least adequately. But the fact that he did not expect to be elected did not mean that he was not serious. Nor would votes given to him be votes wasted for they would have effect in increasing the efficiency of the United Party. However this man would not vote for him.

And sometimes, astonishingly, we encountered cheerful supporters who needed no persuading. They would engage us in lively talk, urge us to stay and have a sociable session with the family. By then, invariably tired and discouraged, we found it difficult not to yield to this temptation. If we once sat down in easy chairs we knew that canvassing was over for the evening. Ah, what the hell! We sat and relaxed among friends.

In the poll as we had anticipated all six Liberal Party candidates suffered defeat, Jack Lewson by a narrow margin but some forfeiting their deposits. The attempt had proved costly in effort and money: resources had been strained. But the Party made slow but steady progress and they hoped that the continual challenge of Liberalism would bring about some kind of split in the United Party, where many were dissatisfied with the lack of any policy offering a clear alternative to apartheid.

However the split when it came in August 1959 did not help the Liberal Party. What happened was that eleven members of parliament resigned from the United Party and formed the Progressive Party. At their first national congress in November the Progressives declared themselves in favour of a non-racial qualified franchise. They were presently joined by Harry Oppenheimer and their resources in men and money greatly exceeded anything that the Liberal Party could command. In the general election of 1961 one Progressive was returned, Helen Suzman for Houghton, Johannesburg. John Cope in Parktown was defeated by only eighty-five votes. Thus the voice of non-racialism in parliament was reduced to that of one woman. Helen Suzman replaced Margaret Ballinger.

The Progressives thus stole the thunder of the Liberals many of whom left to join the new party, among them D.B. Molteno.

Roux remained an active member of the Liberal Party using what of his abundant energy could be spared from his exacting work at the University. It was not until December 1962 that he was forced to resign by reason of a Government decree that no named person could be a member of any organization where government policy was opposed or even discussed.

Meanwhile the members of the Special Branch had been getting on with their homework, sorting and investigating the masses of material seized in the house raids of September, 1955. This was no simple task and it was more than a year later in December of 1956 that 156 persons were arrested and brought to Johannesburg to be charged en masse with high treason. They were from all over the country and of all races. Some were our friends, some bore names we knew, most were unknown to us. Thus began the notorious Treason Trial which was to drag on for four years and to produce many volumes of recorded testimony. On the first morning of the preparatory examination Eddie managed to get into the Drill Hall. Coming later I could not get in but peering from sunshine into darkness saw dimly the ranks of the accused. In the front row I saw Helen Joseph, composed, bright-eyed, attentive. In the street outside an enormous crowd had gathered and was presently ordered to disperse. There were some resentful mutters and the people were slow to move. To hurry them the police now marched to stand in two files back to back across the street. On command they raised rifles and fired north and south over the heads of the fleeing people. In the drill hall all were startled and appalled to hear the shots.

The story of this grotesque Treason Trial has been told* and is in any case too long to be recorded here. The shots fired in Twist Street echoed round the world. Observers came from overseas to study the trial. The acoustic properties of the Drill Hall were poor and most of the accused were quite unable to hear what was going on. Several told us that the most terrible thing was the boredom of having to sit for hours day after day listening to vague mutters. One incident set us chuckling. This concerned Professor Andrew Murray of Cape Town who was called by the prosecution to give evidence on the nature of communism. He said, correctly enough, that many of the seized documents used the phraseology typical of communist writings. This was true: the language of the African liberatory movement was permeated by Marxist words and phrases for it was of course Marxists who had introduced the black man to political theory. Such words as proletariat, comrades, oppressed colonial masses, formed the language of African politics. We remembered the early uncouth political articles in *Umsebenzi*. But the defence had able lawyers and they had no difficulty in making Murray look foolish. Producing some written passages they asked him if these showed typical communist phraseology. Murray studied the scripts and pronounced that they did. Whereupon the defence revealed that these were extracts from Murray's own writings.

Helen Joseph, as many others of the accused, had somehow to go on earning her living during the trial. She went early to the office where she worked, then to court, then to the office

---

*In *The South African Treason Trial* by L. Forman and E.S. Sachs, publ. John Calder, and in *If This Be Treason* by Helen Joseph, published by André Deutsch, 1963.

again, to court, finally work once more. In the emergency of 1960 she was one of the detained. Each day she was brought to court by the police and taken back to gaol as the session ended.

The trial dragged on, volumes of evidence piled up, and it was not until March 1961 that all the accused were finally acquitted. Orlando, the Native township near Johannesburg, rejoiced and sang Nkosi sikelele Afrika as the released trialists were welcomed to their homes.

But for many acquittal did not mean an end to their troubles. Of these was Helen Joseph who in 1962 gained the unhappy distinction of being the first person to be placed under house arrest. This was a new persecution trick provided for in the General Law Amendment (Sabotage) Act of June 1962. Any banned person might be house-arrested by the Minister of Justice and at that time a list of 102 banned persons had been gazetted. House arrest was a kind of imprisonment in which the detained person had to bear his own cost of living expenses. In her case this was twelve-hour house arrest which meant that she must be in her little house in Norwood from 6 p.m. to 6 a.m. and also during weekends and on public holidays. She had also to report to the police at midday on weekdays. On one occasion with much pressure of office work she forgot to do this and though she went later to explain she was charged with the omission and sentenced to one year's imprisonment all but five days suspended. Seven years later as I write these words she is still under house arrest. She may not receive visitors but is allowed to have her African maid and also the companionship of Siti her Siamese cat. Recently special permission has been accorded her to attend communion service on Sundays and at Christmas. She was our friend. She is my friend but I may not visit her. We are allowed to exchange letters.

How had Helen Joseph offended authority? She had been a member of the C.O.D., now declared an unlawful organization. But her chief offence was probably that with Lilian Ngoyi she had organized African women in the Federation of South African Women. She bears her isolation well and in her lonely evenings studies and writes, though nothing she writes may be published.*

*Her second book *Tomorrow's Sun* was published by Hutchinson in 1966. American edition publ. John Day.

PERSECUTION OF THE LEFT

Lilian Nogyi was for five years restricted to the district of Orlando and at present she is prohibited from attending gatherings of any kind. It seems that Lilian and Helen will never meet again. There was a day when they led a demonstration of 2,000 women to stand before the Union Building in Pretoria in protest against passes for women. This was probably the greatest crime for which they now suffer loneliness and lack of freedom.

The state of emergency to which some reference has been made was proclaimed in March 1960. It was perhaps events at Cato Manor near Durban earlier in the year which led to the massacre at Sharpeville. During a beer raid in the location the people had turned on the police and killed nine of them including four Europeans.

But even more than beer raids passes were hated. The Pan-African Congress, led by Robert Sobukwe then lecturer in Bantu languages at the University of the Witwatersrand, was a breakaway movement from the A.N.C. They pledged themselves to the principles of the United Nations Charter but held that Africans must work out their own liberation without interference or help from Europeans. Sobukwe initiated an anti-pass campaign. The Sharpeville meeting was called for the 21st of March. The plan was that all Africans should leave their passes at home and then offer themselves for arrest. It has been estimated that some 10,000 men, women and children were gathered about the police station that morning waiting to be arrested. It was not suggested that the crowd were threatening action but their very numbers were a menace and the police, perhaps trigger-nervous with the thought of Cato Manor, opened fire with revolvers and sten guns. Volley after volley raked the densely packed crowd. Scores fell before the hail of bullets. Others fled. When the shooting at last ceased, hundreds of shoes, blankets, jackets, women's skirts, even small stools and chairs were scattered about and among the litter lay the bodies of the sixty-seven dead and the many wounded. Eleven ambulances bore the seriously wounded to hospital and the dead were piled in trucks for transport to the mortuary. So Sharpeville joined Amritsar, St Bartholomew, Peterloo, symbols of massacre, and became a name that the world will not let South Africa forget. As I write it is the ninth anniversary of that bloody deed and the Human Rights Association on Wits campus has set up an exhibition of photos taken on that day.

In the State of Emergency the police in a sudden swoop arrested and detained some hundred Europeans and about 2,000 Non-Europeans. It was a mixed bag. The gaols were full of persons of all shades of political opinion. In the case of the Europeans many of whom were known to us, the arrests seemed haphazard and no pattern could be seen. Here were the Kalks who had been quiet for decades, Helen Joseph who as a Treason Trialist had been sitting in her place in the dock for months; some had been supporters of the C.O.D. Among the detained were a fair number of Liberal Party members, Jock Isacowitz, Ernest Wentzel, Peter Brown, Hans Meidner and others. The detainees were held for about five months and released in batches in August when the emergency was declared to be over.

But leaders of the Anti-Pass Campaign were sentenced to imprisonment. Sobukwe was given a three years' sentence for his leadership of the P.A.C. After serving his term he was immediately rearrested to be detained indefinitely at the pleasure of the Minister of Justice as 'likely to advocate, advise, defend or encourage any of the objects of communism'.

Sobukwe now lived in special quarters on Robben Island in Table Bay and his wife and children were recently permitted to visit him for fourteen days. He was refused an exit permit to leave the country. His quarters, a bedroom-study and another room, were not uncomfortable. He used the ablutions block. He had a radio, a record player, books and daily papers. His meals were served from the warders' kitchen and he had fresh fruit each week. Indeed he feared that he grew fat and presently cut out breakfast. Why should he complain? What more could he want? He lived richly in idleness. But idleness did not please him. 'I have no complaint of my conditions,' he said, 'but I lack my freedom. I can do nothing.' And this was, it seemed, for ever. What was to become of Sobukwe? He wrote but none may read.

And so, with many omissions for the tale of suffering is great and more than I know or can imagine, I now end this record of persecution of the Left. I suppose that the Nationalists would not call it persecution but well-deserved retribution for wrong doing. Is this naming with persecution for acts which were not illegal when committed in any way comparable to the retrospective punishment for war crimes committed by the controllers of concentration camps? I do not think that they are at all the same. As I see it the war criminals, pleading obedience to orders, sinned against the common human tenderness of flesh, while the Communists and other rebels here, Bunting, Nkosi, Sobukwe, Roux and all the many nameless who are forgotten were trying to serve the cause of recognition of universal humanity.

CHAPTER XVII

Rationalism

THERE are those who accuse Roux of inconsistency in his life in that he began by pouring forth his energies in the cause of human equality of opportunity and ended by growing cabbages. But it is not inconsistent to change one's way of life as circumstances change. What would be inconsistent is to hold mutually irreconcilable views or to profess one belief and act another. Roux never did either. Nor did he in my judgment ever change his mind. At all times he lived in service of human needs and this remained true even when he came to disillusion with the bureaucratic power policies of the U.S.S.R. Disillusion was pain but Roux never became cynical or bitter.

I remember that once at a party we played a game in which each person had to state his deepest desire in life. Some said happiness, some chose security; one was for adventure, another wanted to live 'by doing work I love'; I said 'not to be afraid' for I know myself a coward; Eddie said 'to see life steadily and see it whole'. I think that he achieved this for in his life there was vision and steadiness: he did not change. Once rejected by the movement he had served with all the strength and vitality of his youth, he did not repine but turned to other ways of using his life.

He believed in the power of rational thought and held that by this means only could human welfare be advanced. This is not to say that he imagined that ultimate meaning could be established by thought but that the journey towards sure knowledge must always be by way of rational analysis of tested experience followed by a synthesis of suggested explanation. Pascal said: 'I look on all sides and everywhere I see nothing but darkness'; Roux had his own version of this saying: 'I look on all sides and everywhere I see growing light.' He was profoundly aware that ultimate certainty is not attainable. He strove towards increase of probability and was content to live in the knowledge that he would never know how the universe originated, why we are here, how life itself began and how it will end. Indeed he did not believe in asking 'why', that question with its load of teleology, but only 'how'. There can be no 'why'. And in this he was consistent to the end.

He held that the best defence against vain desires and idle imaginings, as expressed in the ancient religions and in modern pseudo-faiths such as spiritualism, scientology, parapsychology, lay in the disciplines of the exact sciences and in particular of biology. He never read the words of the ethologist, Konrad Lorenz: 'Expert teaching of biology is the one and only foundation on which really sound opinions about mankind and its relation to the universe can be built'.* This was exactly Roux's deep belief and, since he considered that he was not himself a brilliant pioneer in advancing knowledge, his own more humble role must be to spread existing knowledge in understandable form among those who were not biologists.

He recognized the value of discussion, of rational, informed debate on all human problems. He liked to quote Thucydides who wrote in the words of Pericles of Athens; 'We do not regard discussion as a hindrance to action: the greatest hindrance is to rush into action without adequate knowledge. When we take risks we take them with open eyes. And the bravest man, surely, is he who can see quite clearly what is painful, what pleasant, in life, yet who does not on that account shrink from danger'. Discussion was to Roux not only the best way, the only way of dealing with questions but it was greatly his delight. It was in pursuit of this considered aim that he joined the Rationalist Association.

At some time in 1953 the Rationalist Press Association wrote to certain of their supporters in Johannesburg suggesting that there were now enough of them to found a local group of freethinkers. Some of these responded with enthusiasm and presently decided to insert an advertisement in the press. In response to this advertisement a small group of enthusiasts came together in October in a room at the Carlton Hotel. They were not disconcerted to find that they numbered thirteen though disappointed that this number was so small. Under the

*In *On Aggression*. Methuen and Co., London, 1966.

chairmanship of Ittamar Romm and with Betty Lurie as secretary the group was founded, held meetings, grew slowly but steadily and presently it came about that they invited Roux to lecture to them. In 1955 at about the time when Roux was elected chairman, the society changed its name from Humanist Association to Rationalist Association for the reason that in the prevailing political climate of this country a truly humanist association could not play any part.

Roux now threw himself into the activities of the Association with characteristic enthusiasm, arranging debates, study groups, symposiums, lectures on all conceivable subjects. The Association grew and flourished and a small branch was started in Cape Town. With the import ban on Bertrand Russell's book *Why I am Not a Christian* Roux saw an opportunity for rationalist propaganda. In January 1960 with the permission of Bertrand Russell and his publishers, the Rationalist Association published in English and in Afrikaans translation the essay which gave the title to the book. About 3,000 copies were printed and sold at 2s. 6d. each. The whole issue was sold out save some two dozen copies which were kept as possible future Africana. Supporters had contributed to the cost and the venture showed a final profit of £51 8s. 6d. This seemed a splendid sum and, since Bertrand Russell did not claim any part of it, Roux now proposed to change the monthly duplicated newsletter into a small printed journal, *The Rationalist*, organ of the Rationalist Association of South Africa. The first issue of the new paper appeared in October 1960.

The Rationalist has survived to the present time though from December 1962, owing to the gazetting of further restrictions on the activities of 'named' persons, Roux was no longer able to edit the journal or to contribute articles. These had been chiefly on biological topics and on critical study of the Bible. The policy of the Association and of the journal was always strictly non-political. In the first printed issue Roux wrote:

> We are interested in the spread of rational and critical thinking and are mainly concerned with philosophical, religious and moral problems. If some of our members apply rational thought in the sphere of politics this is something to be welcomed. We have in fact members in the four main

political parties in this country, the Nationalist, United, Liberal and Progressive parties. The bulk of our members, as far as we know, are not particularly interested in politics and are unattached.

We have taken action and made pronouncements from time to time on matters that might be deemed political. But this was only because the Government of the day has done things which in our opinion interfered with freedom of conscience or liberty of thought and expression. Last year for instance we organized a protest against the import ban on Bertrand Russell's book *Why I am Not a Christian*. As an organization we are definitely opposed to Christian National Education or any other form of religious indoctrination in schools. We shall continue to propagate these views no matter what political party is in power.

It was probably in consequence of the publication of the Bertrand Russell essay that Roux received a strange sad rebuke from the past. This was a letter.

Dear Dr Roux,

I do not know you and have never seen you, but I do know you are a descendant of a family who suffered and died for their religion.

You may even be a grandson of a dear God-fearing old gentleman, Oom Eduard Roux, whom I knew more than fifty years ago in Aliwal North.

When I read about that leaflet encouraging young students to be atheists and agnostics it really grieved me.

According to the Bible an atheist is a fool. 'The fool hath said in his heart there is no God.' An agnostic is only another word for an ignoramus, isn't it?

In later life you may regret having misled these young people.

Onthou tog, Dr Roux, wat 'n mens saai moet jy later maai.

That God may open your eyes is the prayer of
          A Grieved Granny.

Roux was much moved by this artless sincerity and simple

faith. He would have liked to meet the writer, talk to her, assure her that in his fight for freedom of thought his actions were in line with the deeds of his ancestors who had sought freedom of conscience in this country. Agnostic is a humble word: it means there are things we do not know. We might, perhaps we should, have advertised to try to find the writer; but it seemed unlikely that Grieved Granny would respond. We spoke of this but in the end we let it go, one more lost opportunity of a human encounter.

And from Alison Roux now studying in Paris somewhat earlier had come the voice of an eighth generation protestant descendant of Paul Roux. She had, in pursuit of social research, made one of a pilgrimage to Chartres. A pen and ink sketch showed the procession of pilgrims winding over the plain with the towers of Chartres Cathedral in the distance. The pilgrims walked in small groups and each evening as they halted their group-leader would give a suitable talk followed by discussion of their personal problems. To promote debate Alison helpfully mentioned a few difficulties she had and the leader, a devout and pleasantly ingenuous young man, rebuked her doubts and explained with careful courtesy. 'Now it is more clear?' Alison replied with some truth: 'Not perfectly, but always there is the language difficulty. I cannot as yet express the ideas adequately in French.' A second sketch showed a pause of pilgrims, Alison with horns half-hidden by her hair and a devil's tail just glimpsed below her skirt.

The Rationalist Association flourished and under Roux's leadership its doings acquired a biological flavour with lectures on such subjects as Virgin Births, the Dionne Quins, the Origin of Life, evolution, over-population, creation, as well as on flying saucers, censorship, religious instruction in schools, life after death, religions of India and so on, until in December 1964 the ban imposed on Roux forbade membership of any organization.

The Association convened a special general meeting of local members and sent a letter to all members in other parts of South Africa asking a vote upon an appeal to the Minister of Justice. With one dissentient the proposed letter was approved and duly sent, requesting permission for Roux to continue as chairman of this strictly non-political association. With this went a list of past lecture topics during the last two years and of meetings planned for 1965. The committee respectfully pointed out that as chairman Roux had been scrupulous to maintain the non-political character of all discussion. However, some months later, came the inevitable flat refusal. Commenting in the June number of *The Rationalist* the committee stated their firm conviction that ban and refusal could not possibly have been decided on the basis of anything said or done by Roux as chairman of the Rationalist Association. Roux was elected honorary president for life and chairman in absentia.

The damage done to the Association by the ban was considerable and more than that caused by the loss of a resourceful and lively leader. Many members now resigned and others quietly allowed their subscriptions to lapse. Such is the climate of fear and cautious behaviour in South Africa under a government which is so timidly intolerant of all independence of mind. As for *The Rationalist*, I had been editing and publishing since March of 1963 and I continued to do so. The little journal suffered the loss of Roux's stimulating biological articles and thoughts on Bible polemics and on such topics as E.S.P.; it became narrower in scope, more strictly philosophical in content. It still precariously survives.

Roux had developed a special interest in this matter of extra-sensory perception, a set of phenomena which includes telepathy or thought transfer, clairvoyance or knowledge of events, pre-cognition or knowledge of events before they happen, and psycho-kinesis or the power to influence events, all these without the use of sense-perception. Such phenomena appear to violate the known laws of scientific knowledge: they do not fit in, they form no part of a coherent system of thought. They present a challenge to all that is known of the natural universe. Can they be interpreted in terms of sensory clues?

In these fields much early experimental work had been done by J.B. Rhine at Harvard.* Many experiments were devised, using Zener cards, a pack of twenty-five cards bearing five different symbols, cross, star, circle, square and wavy lines. In guessing cards in such a pack the chance score would be five hits in twenty-five tries. Many subjects of Rhine's experiments

---

*See *Extra-Sensory Perception* by J.B. Rhine, publ. by Bruce Humphries, Boston, 1964.

scored results which were consistently higher with high odds against their achievement. It seemed to Rhine that certain persons had indeed some special unexplained paranormal power of perception. But critical investigation revealed flaws in the experimental procedure. There was a possibility of concerted fraud between Subject and Agent, Subject and Experimenter or Agent and Experimenter. It was found too that designs on Zener cards could be detected by scrutiny of the backs of the cards. For any careful scientist the claim for ESP could not be acceptable until all possibility of fraud had been eliminated.

There is a sense in which the search for ESP is strictly comparable to the pursuit of the philosopher's stone, to attempts to devise a perpetual motion machine, to acceptance of miracles: it is one more attempt to catch nature breaking the known rules and thus belief in paranormal phenomena is a kind of wild faith with a large component of the will to believe. Since ESP cannot be positively defined but is held to be communication by means of unknown powers enjoyed by certain individuals only, its virtue dwells in a mystery, in the impossibility of explanation. Thus every suggested explanation of the phenomena must constitute a set-back for the claim of ESP. Nevertheless, the hunger for the marvellous, the inexplicable, the sly breach of physical laws, is so strong among many human beings that there are always those who, willing to believe, remember the marvellous scores achieved against astronomical odds and forget or disregard the humdrum and unwelcome explanations of how, without mystery, those scores might have been achieved. Investigation of experimental procedures is a thankless task ending in the suggested possibility of fraud at some point, and, since the experimenters are persons who have at least a willingness if not a will to believe that something inexplicable is happening, they are never happy to learn of suggested rational explanations.

In England S. G. Soal, at first sceptical, attempted to repeat the Rhine experiments. He had for some years no success but presently found, in Shackleton and in Gloria Stewart, subjects who seemed to have strong paranormal powers. Shackleton achieved good results in telepathy but his score in pre-cognition, in naming the card to be turned up in future, was impressive. With three agents he achieved scores of high improbability though with ten others his score fell to chance level. Here was a case in which the law of cause and effect seemed to be negated for Shackleton was aware of the effect before the event had happened, i.e. before the agent had turned up the card. However, after the series of experiments had ended Shackleton's powers waned or were said to have waned, the fact being that he was now no longer able to score above chance expectation. A similar fate befell Mrs Stewart. Indeed the waning of paranormal powers seems inevitable in all subjects who display such powers.

Now while it may be conceded that, if telepathy exists, subjects may be expected to obtain good results with some agents with whom they are said to be en rapport whereas with others they would not be successful, and further that such powers may be temporary, it is nevertheless discouraging that the waning of paranormal powers seems to occur always when critics bring forward suggestions as to how fraud might have been perpetrated. Statistical analysis applied to score patterns recorded has been able to show that certain patterns achieved are precisely those that would be expected if some particular method of fraud had been used.

C. E. M. Hansell,[*] lecturer in psychology at Manchester University, later Professor at the University College of Swansea, devoted much time to study of the experiments carried out by Rhine and Soal. For some years Roux corresponded with Hansell and discussed these matters. It seemed on economy of hypothesis that so long as any possibility of fraud could be shown to exist, no sure evidence for ESP could be claimed, particularly in view of the long history of exposed and self-confessed fraud in psychic phenomena. Roux suggested that expert illusionists and card-tricksters would be the kind of observers who could best spot the manner in which fraud had possibly occurred.

In any event Soal was being driven into the position where he must declare that though some agents and some subjects may have cheated on some occasions yet at other times they exhibit genuine extraordinary powers of telepathy, clairvoyance or precognition.

[*]Author of *E.S.P.—A Scientific Evaluation*, publ. MacGibbon and Kee Ltd., London, 1966.

In the meantime Professor A.E.H. Bleksley of the University of the Witwatersrand became interested in the investigation of psychic phenomena and in public argument took up the cause against Hansell and Roux, accusing them of attacks upon the integrity of the ESP experimenters. In particular he accused Roux of flinging accusations of dishonesty in all directions. But this Roux had been scrupulous to avoid.

In an essay written in May 1959, which was duplicated for limited circulation, Roux wrote:

> In civilized society it is usually held that men speak the truth, unless there are good reasons for assuming otherwise. Science would be impossible unless scientists had regard for truth, and this goes without saying. This has not prevented occasional attempts by scientists to deceive the scientific public, nor has it prevented scientists themselves being deceived by others. In the study of so-called paranormal phenomena, the problem of the elimination of fraud has always bulked largely, as the records of the Society for Psychic Research clearly show. One reason for this lies in the nature of the experimental material with which the psychic researcher works. The experimental biologist does not usually have to consider the possibility that his experimental animals will set out to deceive him. But this does not hold for the parapsychologist whose experimental animals are human beings fully aware of the fact that they are being experimented upon. In these circumstances one of the principal concerns of the experimenter is to ensure that those tested, whether percipients or agents, shall be given no opportunity to cheat.
>
> When critics point out that a particular experimental set-up does give opportunity for cheating, however slight this may be, the experimenter should say: Very well, I shall repeat the experiment eliminating that particular possible source of error. This is what the biochemist, the physiologist, the botanist and all other scientists do when shortcomings are pointed out in their experiments. And that is in fact why scientific knowledge steadily grows. But our local defenders of parapsychology do not appear to accept this. They respond by standing on their dignity and exclaiming: How can you

question the integrity of such and such an experimenter or of such and such persons upon whom he was experimenting?

But it is not to impugn the experimenter's honesty to suggest that he might have been and probably was deceived. It is merely to cast doubt on the adequacy of his experimental procedures and consequently to question the validity of his conclusions. In the cut and thrust of scientific controversy every experimenter who comes forward with published work must be prepared to face such criticism. As for the feelings of the experimental guinea pigs, it is just too bad.

All that we have in the case of a parapsychological experiment is a written report and a set of figures. That is true of many other scientific experiments. But in these cases we can follow the description and set up a similar experiment for ourselves and draw our own conclusions. Paranormals, unfortunately, have the strange faculty of losing their ability as soon as hostile critics get busy with them.

. . .

My reaction to the Shackleton story is that if we accept these results as being genuine we have to believe that Shackleton had the power not merely of knowing what was in the agent's mind—a difficult enough thing to believe—but that he was able to know what would be in the agent's mind in the future.

If a mathematical physicist writes down a formula and says that time runs backwards as well as forwards I stare in amazement. He is telling of a kind of world which I cannot comprehend. The suggestion is that psi-phenomena occur in that sort of world. This is all very well for the writers of science fiction and it may be great fun. But as for Shackleton's performance I prefer to seek some more mundane explanation.

For a time I sought an explanation in some peculiar properties of random numbers. With two packs of Zener cards I played snap with myself for hours on end. In many hundreds of runs I once scored 15 and only twice scored 0. I graphed the results and obtained smooth curves with the mean close to 5. I concluded that if a guesser scored an average of 7 or more on a large number of runs with Zener cards then he must have something. Because of my ideas as to the nature of the world I assumed that this something must be a trick.

A point elaborated by Hansell is that many of the patterns

shown in the Shackleton results can be explained on the assumption of some particular trick. What was needed was that the experiments should be repeated after altering the procedures in terms of the criticisms made. This was not done because both Shackleton and Stewart had completely lost the faculties they had previously shown to such a high degree. Sceptics are entitled to draw their own conclusions.

This approach to the problem does not seem to me to be unscientific. It conforms to the general principle of economy of hypothesis. This is particularly clear in the Shackleton experiments. It is much easier to assume that there was a trick than to attempt, on the basis of these controversial experiments, to revise our ideas of time and causation which fit in with so many millions of other observations.

It seems clear that it was not Soal's honesty but his perspicacity which was questioned. However the argument remained unresolved. Bleksley accused Roux of an adamantine scepticism bordering on fanatic prejudice which made him willing to shout 'fraud.' He considered that Roux opposed parapsychology for emotional and philosophic reasons, not on scientific grounds.

In 1963 Bleksley made known the results of his alarm clock experiment. What happened was that Mr W. van Vuurde of Cape Town wrote to Bleksley suggesting an experiment. He claimed that he could wake during the night at times indicated on a certain clock which he sent to Bleksley. He suggested that Bleksley should set this clock to some particular time each night and that he, van Vuurde, would record the times at which he first woke and send the record periodically. Bleksley chose the times at which he set the clock by a random number technique. A shot was counted as on target if it came within a minute either way. This odd experiment ran for many months during which time the Subject journeyed to Europe and returned to Cape Town. It is the results obtained while S. was in Cape Town that are claimed as evidence of ESP.*

Now this seemed a fraud-proof experiment and no one could question the integrity of a careful scientist such as Professor Bleksley. The results were astonishing. In a series of 74 shots,

*An experiment on long distance ESP during sleep. *Journal of Parapsychology*, vol. 27, no. 1, March 1963.

RATIONALISM

S achieved 8 successes, a score only 1 in 12×10^7 probable by chance. In a control series of 75 shots when the clock was not used no successes were scored. Bleksley kindly supplied a copy of his records and Roux spent some months studying these. He made scatter diagrams of the shots and tried to see some way in which their pattern might be attributed to chance. In this he had little success.

W. Gerke, with whom he discussed the results, now gave a new twist to the argument. Gerke held that statistical analysis could not apply to ESP phenomena. Consider two marksmen shooting at a target. A's score card reveals no bull's eyes but all shots closely clustered about the centre. B's card shows a wild distribution with most shots wide of the mark yet, say, three bull's eyes. Which is the better shot? Common sense says that A is the marksman yet statistical analysis might judge B the winner. Statistics do not apply.

Now Eddie Roux and I had had much earlier a rather similar argument. In an early lesson in a course in statistics we were asked to consider the case of a lady who claims that in a cup of tea she can detect whether the tea or milk is poured first. She is given a test of eight prepared cups of tea and she is right five times. Does this prove that she has the power she claims? Statistically, since the chance of this score is only seven in thirty-two, the answer is that it does. But I argued that if she is wrong at all she has not the power. However I conceded that if she scored five successes followed by three failures she might have the power for anyone's sense of taste would be impaired by tasting five cups of tea in succession. We ruled out this irrelevance since we did not know in what order successes had been achieved. I still argued that in the case of twenty-five Zener cards if a subject scored, say, nine hits, he had still been wrong sixteen times and his success rating should be only five. But Eddie held that in many cases statistical analysis did suggest that something was happening that needed explanation.

At this stage we began ourselves upon a series of experiments in telepathy in which we took in turn the roles of Subject and Agent, A acting also as recorder. These experiments were carried out in the evenings using a pack of twenty-five cards. Of course there was no Observer. We simply trusted each other not to cheat. Usually we managed several runs of fifty guesses on each occasion. What emerged was that Eddie in 500 guesses scored approximately chance expectation, while I in as many scored significantly below this. It seemed I had negative ESP. Unfortunately I cannot now trace the records we made.

Again Roux argued with Gerke and presently after months of toil over various statistics he became convinced. In the case of the alarm clock clearly there had been no fraud. Had S, as he asserted, some kind of mysterious sympathy with the clock? This hardly seemed credible, even more fantastic than claims of thought transference. Was there perhaps telepathy between Bleksley and S, for Bleksley, though he did not consciously think about the times set on the clock yet was at least briefly each evening aware of them? Again Gerke rejected the statistical evidence. If one accepts this ruling it becomes difficult to see in what way ESP experiments can be judged. One merely asserts that scores against astronomical odds are not relevant.*

The whole subject is evidently beset with difficulties, not least the general human tendency to crave the off-beat, the marvellous. What had any subjects to gain by organizing deception? In some cases subjects are paid for sessions but this seems trivial. In all cases of apparently successful demonstrations of paranormal powers the subjects do enjoy considerable prestige. And in the web of experiment a certain amount of self-deception may occur for to this too human beings are prone.

Roux died before this argument was resolved, before he conceded Gerke's point. Yet in the end he was almost convinced.

One has the feeling that Bleksley would comment that this rejection of statistical application to evidence is a last ditch defence on the part of Roux, still the product of prejudice and an utter unwillingness to accept the possibility of as yet unknown forces of ESP. Yet prejudice was no part of Roux's attitude to knowledge: he was always open to conviction. We might still ask why do paranormal powers fail when further investigated and why do subjects make so many errors? To this of course there is a come-back: the powers being investigated are naturally intermittent and transitory, a precarious ability.

But the new theories of ESP provide speculation which does

---

*A paper discussing the Bleksley experiment, by W.J.C. Gerke, A.M.T. Meyer and E.R. Roux is to be published soon.

not cohere with the general body of scientific knowledge, which in fact is a breakaway and contradiction. Is it more likely that known laws of the physical universe are flouted or that in fact there is explanation within the framework of these laws? Is the clock experiment evidence of ESP or is it a set of strange coincidences?

CHAPTER XVIII

Of Cabbages and Things

On an evening when we were playing chess Eddie said casually: 'Let's buy a piece of land!'

This was a serious proposition. I put the chessmen away. I wanted to know why. I felt often that the small garden at Melville required more than all our time and energy to maintain its beauty. The grass grew so swiftly in the rainy season and at all times weeds grew apace. Each year trees must be pruned and sprayed, dahlias reset, seedlings grown and planted out. We seemed always to be mowing, weeding, watering, spraying.

But Eddie said now, 'We'll build a house and live there in our old age, we'll keep a cow and have fresh milk and live simply and breathe pure air.' How lovely this sounded! But who would milk the cow?

'And grow cabbages?' I suggested, remembering the taunts of some former comrades.

'Mixed farming. Grow some vegetables, of course, but I thought of breeding rabbits.'

'I hear they breed easily. But don't they burrow under fences and escape and get stolen?' I felt we were deeply ignorant of the naughty habits of rabbits.

But Eddie was resolved to remedy this and while we went on expeditions to see various plots he bought and studied a large assortment of books on rabbits. We learned of Angora, of Flemish Giant, of Australian Red, of feeding and breeding, of diseases and of the rhythms of their lives.

The plot that Eddie chose lay some twenty miles north-west of the city. From the land he took many random samples of soil. It was a lovely piece of grassland, more than twenty acres on a north facing slope, plot 27 on division 82 of the old estate of Swartkop. Across the valley was Swartkop itself, a dark koppie with two humps, a saddleback hill which made me remember Blencathra. It was there at Swartkop Picnic Paradise

OF CABBAGES AND THINGS 233

that we had camped one Christmas when Alison was eight months old. The land sloped gently, about one in fifty. Eddie's tests showed the soil had low fertility but was still better than the average highveld soil and much better than the hilltop soils on which proteas flourished.

The tall grasses stirred in the breeze and their ripples caught the late afternoon sun. Here and there we saw sakabula, the long-tailed widow bird, rising and swooping in brief flight over the grasses which hid the females on their nests. It was a little Frankenwald. There was even a river, the Klein Krokodil, tributary of the Krokodil River which flowed to the Limpopo. And on a calm reach two small boys were paddling their homemade canoe. Our land lay on both sides of the river and at the ford was an old willow tree. Along the banks a coppice of poplars showed the silver undersides of their leaves as the wind moved them. In the midst of the main slope grew a solitary syringa tree, misshapen and mutilated by Natives who had broken branches for firewood. It was a lonely place and only a few houses could be seen in the distance with here and there a scatter of Native huts. Access was from a dirt road, the Beau Valley Road, by a rough track of loose stones which crossed the stream in a U-shaped dip needing careful driving. The first time we crossed that causeway as owners of plot 27, the mileage of our little Anglia changed from a row of nines to ten thousand and at the same time we saw the brilliant blue of a kingfisher as it flashed upstream. Our hearts overflowed with delight in the beauty of the place. Our land. But we never saw the kingfisher again.

Eddie at once set about fencing our land to keep out scrub cattle and human intruders. And here came Moffat, an African originally from Malawi, no longer young. He wanted work and stated his case in ugly words that he had learned from white bosses. 'A young man no blerry good,' he said, 'You want a man like me.' I was not so sure of this. I mistrusted Moffat but Eddie said, 'First come, first served.' So Moffat was taken on.

At the height of our land were two ancient huts, earth-floored and built of piled stones roughly held with mud. On these we fixed corrugated roofing and in one we slept on camp beds at weekends when we came to work there. The nights were bitterly cold. In the other were presently Moffat and Rozina. She too was old but a much more useful worker than Moffat. It was Rozina who discovered a spring of pure water which Eddie made into a well, some three feet deep, lined with stones and having a low stone wall. He fixed a fitted cover of wood, to keep out the frogs, and this little well supplied our drinking water which we did not boil.

Now came a time in which the Melville garden became much neglected. In large numbers of tins I was busily growing privet from seed and also pyrocantha. Presently, while Eddie and the men wrestled with barbed wire which seemed as I watched to have a malignant life of its own, I planted out the privet along our western boundary, and later the firebush along the top fence to make a thorny defence against invading cattle. All these young plants had to be watered carefully and this task we gave to Moffat who performed it indifferently. Some plants died and had to be replaced. At that time all water had to be brought up from the river and Eddie made a tank on wheels for this tiring job.

Our nearest neighbours were the Moltenos, Charles and Runica, who lived at Krugersdorp and came out at week-ends. Their plot had got off to a good start and they had already a small house and buildings for their workers. Charles was a cousin of our friends Donald and Peter Molteno and this seemed a good portent. Like all Moltenos he was a great talker and filled with boundless enthusiasm. He was delighted to find in Eddie a well-known grass expert, author of *The Veld and the Future* and of *Harvest and Health in Africa*. He would stop talking occasionally to go bird watching and had become knowledgeable about the local birds. He had, rarely, seen our blue kingfisher. The two Molteno boys we had already seen pottering on the river. Runica, also a bonny talker, made good running in competition with Charles. Indeed, since neither could hope to get a word in edgewise, they usually talked both at once. Listening was a problem but the Moltenos were delightful neighbours. I looked forward to living near them. With Runica I planned a signaling system. 'A green flag,' said I, 'means the scones have risen nicely. Come over for tea.' 'A red flag,' said Runica, 'means a warning. We need help and sympathy.' And I said, 'A sick yellow signal means we have mumps and cholera. Keep away!' And for once the men had been listening to our nonsense. But we were all working hard and did not have many such interludes.

Runica, with a few Africans, was making the Molteno plot the little green paradise it presently became. She came out often during the week to hasten the work. This we could not do since both of us were working on week days. Besides managing their own plot she would at times organize a team of African workers and set them to repairing the tracks which became rutted and eroded in heavy rains. We came at week-ends, and we subscribed to the *Farmer's Weekly* and our hearts were filled with hope and zeal and pride. We read much about rabbits.

Presently Eddie bought a Fry mould and using our clean white river sand made cement blocks, which he trained Moffat and Marumé also to do during the week. These blocks once set were refractory and heavy and they had to be transported from the river up to the building site. Wheelbarrows wore out at an astonishing speed. We fixed a luggage rack on top of the Anglia and each time we came to Plot 27 we brought a load: camp beds, wire, sheets of corrugated iron, timber, ladders, a new wheelbarrow, a table. Picks, spades, saws, trowels and the like could travel in the boot.

Marumé, younger than Moffat and of a quite different personality, proved a good worker. Moffat, complaining that he could not work alone, had persuaded Eddie to take on another man. We were lucky in Marumé. He was full of energy, bright ideas and initiative. It was Marumé who now worked with Eddie on building the garage and workroom, also on erecting the windmill which Eddie set up by the river to pump water from a sump up the land to a large reservoir at the top. Pipes were laid on the eastern boundary. While Eddie and Marumé toiled building garage, windmill and reservoir, Moffat would stand by, helpfully going errands, handing tools and lengths of piping or timber as required. This he would do with much display of slow lifting and heaving and to the accompaniment of suitable heavy grunts as of one performing prodigies of toil. Eddie noticed that gestures and grunts were much in evidence whenever I was there observing the work. Poor Moffat, clever old fraud, had little taste for work. But our hearts were tender to him for we supposed that being old was a thing that would some day, but not for a long time, happen to us.

In August of that first year, when the foundations of the garage had been laid, we bought and planted one hundred little trees, peach, apricot and nectarine, in the main orchard, also a few others, apple, pear, plum and citrus in a smaller home orchard as we grandly called it. These latter were partly Eddie's concession to my sentimentality. I said I must have apple trees. It was on a grim cold day in August that we planted the little trees and there was a spit of icy rain. I remember that as one hole was dug I seized what I took for a giant earthworm. In fact it was a little snake, probably harmless; it did not stay to be investigated but slid from my stiff muddy fingers and vanished. Then we were planting shoots of *Populus deltoides*, the matchwood poplar, near the river which murmured sweetly as we worked. And next year we put in one hundred and sixty young almond trees. When spring came these little trees made a foam of blossom, the loveliest thing we had ever seen.

Slowly, block piled on block, the garage walls rose and the cement binding was poured, and presently the walls had roof, doors and a window. Eddie bought a 500-gallon water tank to catch run-off from the roof. This huge empty cylinder was lying on its side when a gust of wind caught it, gave it a twist and set it rolling down the slope. Eddie saw this happen and rushed headlong to hurl himself into its path and hold it. He managed to stop it but then he was unable to move. He shouted for Marumé and both men came running. Together the three managed to push the unwieldy tank uphill again and wedge it in place with stones. This was only one of many incidents and disasters that befell but I think that it was now that Plot 27 became known to us privately as The Gremlins. This was a sort of sick joke.

Or it may have been a little later, when I lost my ring. When the garage was finished I made curtains for the work-room where we slept and found it warmer and cleaner than the old stone hut. It seemed a good plan to paint all doors and window frames and this we did on a Sunday. Perched on a packing case I wielded a fine brush on the wood of the window. Presently I noticed green paint on my ring. This was a diamond ring which had been my mother's and I valued it greatly. So I took it off and slipped it into a pocket of my overall. Presently we stopped for lunch, cleaned our hands approximately with paraffin and walked a short distance through tall grass to sit in the shade of the syringa tree. There we ate our sandwiches and gazed fondly upon the wind-rippled grasses on our land. Our land! It was then that I missed the ring. Eddie, instead of scolding me for carelessness, spoke comfortingly. The ring would soon be found. We walked up and down parting the grasses and peering down and then all round the garage where we had worked, but we had no success. Still Eddie was confident that the ring would be recovered since we knew so nearly where it must be. The grass was still dry and he now burnt this small area of the veld Thereafter each time we came we would sweep a portion of the ground and then sift the soil carefully. I would take some of the sweepings back to Melville where I found that all the little trees flourished on this transferred fertility. But still the ring was lost. In shame and sorrow I did not tell my sister. It was nearly two years later that Eddie, returning from a day at the plot, said happily, 'Guess what! Good news!' But I had given up hope and could not guess. What had happened was that, breaking off work for lunch, Eddie and the two Africans had stacked spade and forks in a tall pyramid near the garage. Of course it was Marumé, always quick off the mark, who later came to take the tools for more work, and it was Marumé's alert eyes that saw the diamonds sparkling in a thick tuft of grass. We gave him two pounds and I had my ring once more.

Another incident was also, at least partly, my own fault. One day as I drove after school to bring Eddie home from a three-day stay at Gremlins, I was late and carelessly drove too fast down the loose scree of the narrow hump-backed track. The car without warning shot off to the left. I pulled it back centre again but now it swung off to the right where was a dangerous narrow ditch. Again I managed to get on to the hump only to feel the car careen once more to the left. I had switched off the ignition but dared not brake and I now knew that I was headed for disaster. I felt the Anglia was helpless like one of those miniature cars which have such violent smashes on the nursery floor. At the foot of the steep slope was a place where a donga crossed the road. Hugh pipes had been placed to lead rushing water under the track but erosion had eaten in from the left leaving the track a bare car's width. We were now charging headlong straight for this donga which was about eight feet deep and alarmingly wide. I was stiff with terror as I clutched the wheel until the crash came. The Anglia turned over, fell on its left side and lay still, by a seeming miracle neatly across the donga. I was flung down against the left side and lay there a moment, half-stunned, and heard the ominous drip of oil. I scrambled up and out of the right side window and walked back along the car and so down to the ground. Oddly no one was in sight. There was a sleepy late afternoon silence all about me. No curious piccanins came running. No one had seen the accident. My shoulder was bruised, my neck twisted, and I had some small cuts but was not much hurt. I looked sadly at the car I had used so ill. There was something pathetic, almost obscene, in the exposure of its underparts. I was horrified at what I had done. I set off to walk over rough ground across four plots to reach our land.

When I came where Eddie and the men were working, I said miserably, 'Eddie, I'm so terribly sorry. I've ditched the car.'

'Gremlins! How did you manage that?' said Eddie, 'I don't believe you.' But then he saw a little blood on my blouse and the general dirt and disarray that I was in.

We set off in a rescue party, Eddie, three Africans and I. On the way we picked up two more men. I felt suddenly a terrible fatigue.

'We must hurry,' said Eddie, lengthening his stride and tugging me along as I showed a tendency to linger and the Africans drew ahead. 'We must get there before Marumé starts something on his own!'

My nerves were crying for delay, for rest, but I pulled myself together and we hurried. Marumé had not taken any precipitate action before we got there. All the men were staring in amazement at the position of the car. I was shocked again at the sight. There she was on her side, straddling the donga precariously. I supposed that it was only speed that had saved her from diving into the eroded donga, perhaps also the fact of the down slope which made the further edge a little lower than the other. But the position still looked incredible, and clearly the car was still in danger of falling in. The first thing that Eddie did was to take our strong tow rope from the boot and hitch the rear axle securely to a fence post up the hill. Then the men, five strong men and with them Moffat puffing and blowing and grunting, standing in various awkward positions managed to lift and push until up she came and was righted on her wheels. The car was now nearer the track but still astride the donga though here the donga narrowed as it neared the road. I said, 'Now we bounce her on to the road.' It was impertinence to say 'we' for in fact I did nothing but admire the men. So now, first at the rear, then in front, then rear again, the men heaved while Eddie carefully slackened the rope and the car bounced inches at a time until there she stood fairly on the narrow track, beautiful as ever and no longer in jeopardy.

'Now you get in and drive,' said Eddie as he untied the tow rope and coiled it into the boot.

'But,' I objected, 'there is no oil in this car.' And indeed we could see the oil a pool in the donga.

'In the meantime, madam,' said Resnik's man, 'I have some oil.'

So we waited while he went to bring a gallon can of oil. This was a light oil used for a petrol motor pump on a borehole, too light for the car, but we filled up with this, took the can with us, and hoped for the best. I started up nervously, but all seemed well. I drove on up a slight rise, then down into the U-shaped dip and up steeply to the height of the land where there was room to turn to go home.

Homewards I drove, Eddie insisting on this, carefully and slowly with a reek of hot oil assailing our noses. Eddie said no word of reproach to me, though I blamed myself exceedingly for having so ill-used our beloved car. In the end it seemed that all was well and little harm done beyond scratches. Our garage expert said that some connection had gone from under the front axle and this would make the car tend to leave the road. The hump-backed scree accounted for the rest of it and my rash speed. And, of course, we felt the gremlins were amused. I am rather stupid but I can learn: never again did I take that scree in top gear.

In December Eddie began to build the two joined cottages for the Africans. Abandoning the Fry mould blocks which were so heavy to handle he now experimented with pisé de terre, and of a mixture of earth and cement rammed down between barriers of wooden shuttering he made solid walls. The cottages, beautiful and strong, were a splendid achievement. About them we planted pepper trees. The Africans lived there and children and chickens played in the shade. Marumé had a succession of wives and Moffat had grandchildren who came visiting.

Rabbits were out of favour. Eddie now planned to grow grenadillas which would be easy to harvest owing to the firm rind of the fruit. We would sell the crop in bulk to a fruit drink factory. But the grenadilla vines we grew in Melville presently developed a diseased condition: the fruit rinds were thick and hard and the contents dry and without juice. The disease spread and we found no cure. So our next plan was to grow onions and potatoes.

In the third year came abnormal violent rains which drenched the land. Many peach trees died, root-drowned, and we lost all the almonds. Of the matchwood poplars some were washed away and with them willows I had planted here and there. The river banks caved in as the Klein Krokodil raged in flood and tore on its way scouring its course down to bedrock. Choked with mud the windmill broke. We grieved for the lost trees and remembered the delicate grace of the almond blossoms which we had seen only once.

Eddie now built a dam across the river in an attempt to restore that reach of calm water from which the windmill sump was filled. He bought oil drums, filled them with stones and cement, stacked them in layers held in place by packing of a mixture of cement, earth and stones. It was a well-made dam and endured for many years.

The reservoir had been completed. The wind blew, the vanes turned, the mill pumped steadily forcing water up the pipes to the height of our land. The gremlins were quiet while the water level rose and with it our hopes for Plot 27. Eddie laid pipes down to the house site and began to build, again using pisé de terre. He made a beautiful little house with a large living room with windows facing north, a kitchen that ran across the house with windows to north and south, two bedrooms, a bathroom, a pantry. The walls were painted with a cream-coloured cement paint. Before building Eddie had planned this house many times over and he had built it himself. He looked at it with an endearing modest pride. My share had been nothing: I had helped with plans, fixed pelmets and curtains and had planted some nectarines in a new orchard. About the house I had started a garden with dahlias, shasta daisies and a few rose bushes.

And now the loads the Anglia carried were beds, mattresses, tables, chairs and other furniture. Sometimes we spent weekends in the house and Eddie during his vacations would stay a few days at a time. From dawn to sundown there was always work to be done.

He planted a vineyard, about an acre of catawba vines, the tough vines which bear small dark grapes, honey sweet and good for making wine.

But now came the drought years. The Klein Krokodil dwindled and vanished. There was no more river. Along our eastern boundary we had planted wattle, eucalyptus and pine. These had grown from their nine-inch height in jam tins and some were now over thirty feet tall. But now the lovely trees were suffering: their leaves hung dry and brittle and some of them died. Along the curving drive down to the house the jacarandas were failing and the *Acacia elata*. In the orchards fruit trees withered. It was heartache to see. I no longer cared to visit Gremlins to note the stages of this slow death.

In the season of 1965, after some rain had fallen, the vines bore a heavy crop and we harvested and sold the grapes and gave them away. This was, I think, the last great pleasure that the plot gave Eddie and by then, being restricted by the ban so that even going to the plot was difficult, he had need of comfort. It was due to the ban restrictions that a large part of the crop was stolen. In 1966, after more drought, there were no grapes at all and later when I came alone to prune I found that no growth had been made, many vines had died and wherever I cut I found dead wood at the heart of the stems.

When now, alone, I think over the story of Gremlins, I realize that we made several big mistakes. One was that we did not expect the little river to fail as in prolonged drought it did. A borehole would have served us better than the windmill by the river. Our greatest error was that we did not at all understand what growing old would be like. Nor did we really face this idea at all. Of course old age must come, but not yet, not today nor tomorrow, not next year. And until the weariness of age comes it is not to be imagined. When it does come it is a shock, astonishing, incredible. It was only towards the end that we faced the fact that we were not going to be strong enough ever to live at Gremlins. The simple life is not easy nor for that matter is it simple, and we had too long been used to the shop round the corner, to clean water that gushed from the taps, to meat, milk and newspapers delivered at our door. We were city-dwellers by the pattern of all our days and would not long have survived roughing it on the plot. But this we had not understood: it had taken us by surprise. To the end Eddie resisted knowledge of the failing of his magnificent energy.

But one day he said sadly, 'He sows and he shall not reap.' This seemed a true account of all the toil he had lavished on the plot.

I remembered R.L. Stevenson and said, 'To travel hopefully is better than to arrive and the true success is to labour. Surely you have had lots of that success.'

'But what of ceasing to travel and knowing one has not arrived?'

'That has not happened exactly to you. You have arrived at many places but each time you chose to treat them just as stages and to go on and on.'

Still there was sadness in the words we said then and more in so much that we did not ever put into words. Now Plot 27 is sold and strangers, young, strong, and full of hope, live in the house that Eddie built and gaze their fill on the waving grasses. The solitary syringa has grown in beauty and the little pine we found hidden among tall grass is now a sturdy tree. Along the eastern boundary the eucalyptus trees are tall. And in this year, 1968, the catawba harvest has again been good, for the rain pattern has helped vines and trees to recover, but the harvesting has been for others.

It was in 1961 that Alison at last came home, bringing with her an Italian boy. In the years she had been away she had studied in Paris and Florence and had lived happily in Rome's Trastevere where she painted and earned a precarious living by giving tuition in English. I had spent one month with her when we had wandered in Venice, Florence, Siena, and there I had come to understand the love she had for Italy. At Fiesole we explored the Roman bath remains and the open amphitheatre.

On the stage I looked up and saw Alison in the back row high on the rim of the theatre. I remarked conversationally, 'I come to bury Caesar not to praise him.' Alison heard me clearly and replied, 'Oh, do you? But have you leave to speak at Caesar's funeral?' But the acoustics which lifted my words to her did not work in reverse: I could not hear what she said. As we ate our picnic lunch under flowering lime trees in Florence I told her how the heady scent recalled to me a garden I had loved in England long ago. I said she should come home soon. Before we parted and I went my ways to Denmark and England, she had told me of Luigi who lived in Rome. Still uncertain of her own feelings and of his, she did not wish me to come to Rome; but this I ought to have done. Later she wrote that she would come home bringing Luigi.

It was our hope that they would marry and live in South Africa. But Luigi who had little English did not like the country. His stay was a most unhappy one for him and for us all. He found our buildings ugly and lacking in character. He thought the girls and women insipid and dull. He did not like the food, the houses or the political set-up. He did not like us and my cooking disgusted him. With Alison he went out to the plot and there they planted a lawn about the house. But he remained unhappy. And in December, still sulking, he returned to Italy. Alison, unhappy, stayed to put on an exhibition of her paintings in February at the Adler-Fielding Gallery.

February is not considered a good month for art shows, but Alison was in no mood to wait. Some of the paintings we thought of high standard, others less so. Preparing for this show filled her days and she tried to forget Luigi. Lawrence Adler was helpful and kind; Major Fielding, found it distressing that we had ordered wine from a bottle store in Braamfontein which he considered a déclassé neighbourhood. 'Quite suitable,' said Alison cheerfully, 'considering that I lived so long in Trastevere.'

Professor John Fassler opened the exhibition and gave a most delightful talk praising the feeling of light and freedom in paintings of the roofs of Rome. Alison had made a study of a cat, her beloved Grubbins, a tabby of immense personality and charm, so named because he was so keen on his food, and this painting too Fassler praised. A great crowd heard his talk, so many that the pictures were hardly to be seen. In the event it was clear that Adler-Fielding had over-priced them and few were sold. Alison was greatly pleased that H. E. Winder, art critic of the *Rand Daily Mail*, bought one, a delightful study of a line of washing. On the whole the critics wrote favourably but few sales resulted. After the show we gathered up the remains and took them over to Pretoria to a smaller show opened by Dr S. deMoor. This too showed no profit. Alison shrugged away her disappointment. 'Prices too high! A rolling stone butters no parsnips.'

She now decided to go to London, to work there and be with a group of her artist friends. We wanted her to stay but it was her life: we did not urge her. She left at the end of March and at once Luigi joined her in London and she wrote that they had decided to marry. In mid-April she spoke to me from London, a trunk call put through from their wedding party, and though I could not hear her words clearly I received the feeling of her great happiness. Eddie was then away, at Kariba I think. She told me they would return at once to Rome.

In these years Eddie's mother was suffering the ravages of Parkinson's disease, the palsy of the New Testament. She had no pain but the trembling symptoms increased so that in the end she became helpless. We found a nursing home for the aged where she could be looked after and where she could sit in the sunshine in her wheel chair. As her condition grew worse she was confined to bed where she lay all her days in great misery, unable to read, to turn in bed, to ring the bell they tied to her stronger hand. Her mind was clear at all times but she had no pleasure in her days. We all visited her often and came away grieving. Gran would implore us to do something to help her. Enid wept. Eddie and I knew that euthanasia was the only help. Keeping her thus unhappily alive was a refinement of cruelty that humans would not inflict on any non-human creature. We did not act on our belief: not in fear of consequences but in ignorance of what to do. The moral issue seemed clear: we ought to bring release from this burden of life-in-death. But we could not find a way to do it. She was our beloved Gran and still we failed her. We celebrated her ninety-fourth birthday with flowers and a cake which she tasted. Soon after when she passed into a coma from which she did not rally we felt that death came as a mercy that had been too long delayed.

At the rationalist funeral Eddie quoted from Lucretius:

Rest assured that we have nothing to fear in death. One who no longer is cannot suffer, or differ in any way from one who has never been born, when once this mortal life has been usurped by death the immortal.
  The old is always thrust aside to make way for the new, and one thing must be built out of the wreck of another . . . Bygone generations have taken your road and those to come will take it no less. So one thing will never cease to spring from another. To none is life given in freehold; to all on lease . . . This is a mirror that Nature holds up to us, in which we may see the time that shall be after we are dead. Is there anything in the sight that is not more restful than the soundest sleep?

Eddie spoke of the long hard-working life that his mother had lived. He said:

For such an active person these last three years were a great trial. She would say, 'I am now like a baby to be taken up and washed and fed.' And then as her speech failed though it seemed that she still understood all that we said, life became still more unhappy for her. She wanted to ask questions: how was Arthur, how was Enid? To the end she was concerned about us all.
  I think we can say of Mother that she was one of the most unselfish and yet the sanest of persons. She had to be both sane and unselfish to manage a wayward husband and a wayward family. She tried to keep peace among us and between us and Dad, and in this she succeeded. She loved us all and I am certain that she loved us all equally. Hers was not a narrow or possessive love. When we were obstinate and rebellious she let us go our ways. But sooner or later we all returned to the house in Bez Valley.
  Mother was a woman of simple tastes and pleasures. We remember her fondness for puzzles and the clever verses she

wrote for competitions, verses which were often awarded prizes. This pleased her greatly.

She was fond of quoting a verse of Swinburne:

> From too much love of living,
>   From hope and fear set free,
> We thank with brief thanksgiving
>   Whatever gods may be
> That no life lives for ever;
>   That dead men rise up never;
> That even the weariest river
>   Winds somewhere safe to sea.

She has gone on, released at last from suffering, to her long rest but we will remember her.

. . . . .

When I retired from teaching I enrolled at the University as a part time student of Italian and philosophy. I had always been attracted to Italian and I felt I had great need to be less ignorant of philosophy. I thus found at Wits an opportunity to return to work in an African night school. There I went on Thursday evenings from seven to nine and taught algebra to a matriculation class while Eddie stayed on working in his office. My pupils were men who worked hard all their days and had to get permission from their employers to attend evening classes where often they had to struggle against their need of sleep. This school was well run by the students and had then some hundred and fifty pupils at all stages up to matriculation. It was held on week nights except Fridays for on Friday the men with pay in their pockets feared attack if they were out late.

I mention this activity of mine because I want to tell of a most revealing incident. It happened one evening that an African, well-dressed and carrying a neat satchel of books, came into the room as our lesson was beginning. He wanted, he said, to join the school. I told him that the secretary was not present that evening and also that we were not permitted to enrol students this late in the year. I invited him to join the class for an evening's algebra but he was not interested in algebra. He sat down at a desk, got out books and began on an assignment.

I had been impressed by his personality and by the standard of his speech and I noted his industry. When the lesson ended I came to look at what he was doing and saw he had worked through several exercises in English comprehension. I found he had the teaching manuals of a correspondence college.

I said, 'You know this work you are doing is good. You will not get better teaching in this school than you have already in these books.'

He explained now, 'Madam, I know these teaching books are good but I am all alone. I want to talk to some teachers. I need to hear their words.'

For a while we sat on in the cold empty room and I talked to him and got him to talk of the set books and of writing essays. Then it was late, the room must be locked. He left and I did not see him again. But over our late dinner at a Hillbrow restaurant I told Eddie about this man. I felt he had put his need so clearly and it was a need so universal that the value of the whole night school movement was now shining afresh in my mind. Indeed he had expressed the virtue of live teaching, a value not to be achieved by correspondence courses or by expert TV instruction.

This was a matter on which Eddie and I had thought much and discussed often. It is a simple fact known to all teachers that two sets of students, even considered of equal ability, will never take a lesson at the same pace. Incidental questions promote discussion and lead to rewarding by-paths; the pace of the lesson must continually be adjusted to the comprehension the teacher is aware of in the pupils. But in a canned lesson which imparts information this live argument is lost; there can be no give and take during the lesson. I have heard it argued that the pupils can save their questions and ask them of their own teacher, if they have one, at the end of the lesson. But such saved questions are seldom asked: in the end they are forgotten or no longer seem relevant and thus educational opportunity has been lost. This is, we considered, the essential difference between live education and canned instruction. There are other differences, especially the fact that in certain subjects it is desirable for students to find things out for themselves. A lesson should thus be a voyage of discovery with rewards for eager minds. Always any lesson should be rather a community of discourse than a lecture. However, in certain subjects, films, correspondence tuition and TV lessons may fill a need.

The whole of Bantu education is ill-planned in South Africa though our government is able to boast that more Africans now attend school than ever before. But Government annual expenditure is R12 per head on African children in school as compared with more than R120 for each European child. African parents, the poorest section of our community, must pay while European education is free. This results in a shocking rate of drop-out, so that of the school population in 1967, 45 per cent. were in the sub-standards, 27 per cent. in standards I and II, 25 per cent. in standards III - VI, only 4 per cent. in post-primary classes. Only ·3 per cent. were in standards IX and X. The pupil to teacher ratio was 49 to 1. Teachers are over-worked, sometimes in double sessions. Classrooms are crowded; there are often not enough desks and chairs so that children must squat on the floor doing sums on slates.

In the Bantu tribal colleges as compared with the European universities the pattern of Government expenditure is reversed. The cost of one Bantu student is more than R1400 annually, roughly three times the cost of a student at the University of the Witwatersrand. The African has no choice of college for these are strictly tribal. Turfloop in north Transvaal is for the Sotho, Ngoya in Zululand for the Zulu, Fort Hare in Eastern Cape for the Xhosa. The Coloured must go to Bellville in the Cape and Indians to a college near Durban. In 1961 numbers at these tribal colleges were stated as eighty-six at Turfloop, forty-six at Ngoya, 390 at Fort Hare.* This last college had once about 500 students. In any year fewer than 500 Africans achieve a university-level matriculation and most of these cannot afford to go on to college. In 1968 the Minister of Bantu Education, M.C. Botha, has stated that the total enrolment in the the three colleges is 1,431. Their education is in the hands of fifty-seven professors and 191 lecturers. This gives a ratio of 5·8 students to one lecturer.

We did not consider these minute colleges with their narrow range of thought as affording anything like a university education and we held that most Africans do not get even school education in any real sense. The need for African adult night

---

*Figures stated by the Hon. Leslie Blackwell, Q.C., in an article in the *Rand Daily Mail*.

schools was plain. Moreover there was evidence of this in the great numbers of would-be entrants who had, each year, to be refused since a school could take only so many.

Yet in pursuit of the ignis fatuus of apartheid the Government has now suppressed such schools. The once flourishing night school at Wits is closed down. This is a grief that Eddie was not to know.

At the end of 1966 the Department of Bantu Education sent a circular to all night schools in Johannesburg. There were eleven of these at the time. Wits night school had been running for twenty-five years and another school, Lutheran, had been founded in 1906. These schools were informed that they had official sanction to continue for one year more but that at the end of 1967 they must close down.

At Wits the students were troubled and resentful and resolved to make the attempt to continue their work in a tutorial system with one university student teaching one African pupil at a time. Two more such tutorial schemes were planned, one by the Wits branch of the South African Voluntary Service, the other by a group of Young Progressives. Of these only the S.A.V.S. scheme is working, the plan at Wits being frustrated by trouble over classroom space.

The record of the Wits Students African Night School was good. In 1965 it gained twenty-five per cent. of all Transvaal African matriculation passes and scored a higher proportion in the two following years. The suppression of such a school is matter for shame and regret.

The whole furnishes one more instance of the double-talk at which our Government is so expert. For export is a flaunting of the numbers of African children in school, no matter how and no matter what they learn or if they learn anything in this stunted education which begins and continues for two years in their mother tongues, also much display of the fine photogenic tribal colleges; while for home use, in the name of education according to the black man's needs and abilities, there is virtually complete suppression of any meaningful education of the African.

What is being given to the African? It is not education in spite of all this lavish spending on tribal colleges which is so much window-dressing to impress the world.

We believed that to deny education to a man is as wicked as to deny him food.

But this final blow to the night school movement which Roux had once promoted so devotedly was not ever known to him. He died before this government action extinguished these schools.

CHAPTER XIX
Clothed With Derision

It was in September of 1962 when Roux had been acting head of the Botany Department for two years that he was appointed Professor of Botany. In the Department he was welcomed by a party with amiable speeches and the presentation of a book. Dr H. Swart plied his clever pen and made a sketch of the empty professorial chair festooned with cobwebs and before it a two-year stop sign. Roux was then near retirement but the University asked him to stay on for another five years. All this was ironical enough for the term of his professorship was to be only two years.

In June of 1963 for his inaugural lecture Roux took as his theme the Veld and the Future, the cause which had claimed his lifelong enthusiasm.* Deliberately he chose to give at non-technical level a talk which could be understood by laymen. He spoke of his distinguished predecessors: Charles Edward Moss, taxonomist who founded the invaluable Moss Herbarium; John Vicars Phillips who established the Grassland Research Station at Frankenwald, Nicholaas Badenhuizen whose interests lay chiefly in cell physiology and plant genetics and who initiated the bio-chemistry section in the Department.

Roux turned then to his own wide range of interests, using the English phrase Jack of all trades and master of none and the more poignant Afrikaans 'n man van twaalf ambagte and dertien ongelukke, 'a man of twelve trades and thirteen disasters.' He spoke of his interest in ecology, his hopes for the preservation of the veld and his enthusiasm for the grassland succession studies at Frankenwald. Using diagrams he described the results of a nitrogen tolerance experiment, results which in reversal of earlier views suggested that fertility decreased as succession advanced. He told also of experiments in intensive grazing and in fertilization of the veld. He ended:

In any case the veld as we know it must increasingly be

*The Veld and the Future, Wits University Press, 1963.

changed to suit man's nutritional needs. Though the botanist is aiding in this process he may not be entirely happy with the outcome. Climax veld and tree scrub is to the biologist more interesting than primary grassland. It contains a wealth of plants with their associated wild animals. Even on the thousand acres of Frankenwald we have little climax grassland left and what we have we preserve jealously. What goes for Frankenwald goes for the earth as a whole. Man destroys the variety of nature to feed growing millions of hungry mouths. Unrestricted human multiplication will not only cause famine and war but will inevitably destroy those wild animals and plants which the aesthete likes to observe and the biologist wishes to study.

This was a happy year and Roux found rewarding work with his third year and honours students and with other postgraduate research workers. At the end of the year he gave a Christmas dinner party to senior students, staff and demonstrators. Some sixty in all we sat at two long tables and afterwards played a slightly literary botanical game followed by charades. In view of what was to come it was good that Roux had this satisfying year and the happiness of that evening.

The first hint of trouble came in September of 1964 in an interview given by B. J. Vorster, Minister of Justice, who stated that all persons named as ex-communists would in terms of the Act be banned from all educational institutions. He said: 'I have given these people ample opportunity. Those who have refrained from applying for the removal of their names from the new list must now expect that action will be taken against them.' The news item added that of 433 persons still listed, six were university lecturers; these included Professor H.J. Simons of the University of Cape Town and Professor E. R. Roux of Wits. Lawyers too were threatened and among those listed were V. C. Berrangé, H. S. Bloom, G. S. Findlay, Bram Fischer, Joe Slovo and others.

In the next few days the press carried comment and protest. Advocate George Findlay, who had previously protested the immorality of the naming, now said:

When the Suppression of Communism Act was passed it

was not retrospective. It listed persons who at the time of the Act were members of the Party. In the following year by deliberate amendment it was made restrospective. Anyone who had ever been a member had to be listed whatever had happened since. It is in my view neither honourable nor competent to remove names of those listed, because they were in fact once members. It is highly irregular to favour people by removing their names and the more so when assurances and promises are exacted from them. In public life today people are frightened and hope to gain favour—if I may use an ungainly phrase for an ugly thing—by sucking up the authorities. It is not decent for the authorities to invite it.

Findlay's own membership had ended some years before the Party was made illegal.

A leader in the *Rand Daily Mail*, captioned Baton on the Campus, stated that there was no threat of communism in our universities, that Roux and Simons had been at their tasks for many years and had won the respect of colleagues and students. No university would tolerate lecturers who abused their positions to propagate communist doctrine. There was no need for Vorster to wield his baton.

In a letter to the press, Julius Lewin, lecturer at Wits, pointed out that Roux had left the C.P. in 1936. In his book, in the introduction to the new edition, Roux had written: 'If I were asked now if I am still a Communist or Marxist, I would say no.' He had served the University since 1946. 'Those of us who know him well believe that such men are the salt of the earth. To drive him out of the University is simply an act of persecution.'

Persecution it seemed to be. But the Minister of Justice was not impressed by such views and a few days later, addressing the Free State Nationalist Congress at Bloemfontein, he indicated that persecution was the intention. He said that people listed as Communists might find life less pleasant in future and added, 'If I were one I would pack up and go.' The malice, so unbecoming in a servant of justice, was not hidden. We were warned.

Early in November an Afrikaans paper, *Dagbreek*, announced that listed Red professors and lecturers had now made application to have their names removed from the list and that the Minister magnanimously, in spite of the fact that the time allowed for such applications had lapsed, was prepared to reconsider their cases. The names of those who had thus applied were not stated but Simons, Roux and one other were named as being threatened. In fact neither Simons nor Roux ever applied for both freely admitted former membership of the C.P.

The case of Berrangé who had somewhat earlier applied is of interest. He had at once been visited by detectives and subjected to an inquisition on his current opinions. He found it was not enough to have left the Party long ago; one must repudiate all sympathy, disown former friends and speak against them. This he would not do. Anticipation of this kind of questioning, ugly, impertinent, intolerable, would be enough to prevent most victims from applying. Neither Simons nor Roux would concede that the Government had any sort of moral right to punish people for past actions which were not illegal when committed, still less any right to require conformity of present opinion.

In December the ban was served. It was for five years and prohibited Roux from leaving the magisterial district of Johannesburg, from entering any Native location, any factory, any place where any publication was prepared, compiled, printed or distributed, any premises of a university, college, school or other educational institution. He was prohibited also from attending any gathering of whatever nature, from communicating with any named or banned person, from saying or writing anything for publication, and finally from giving any educational instruction to anyone except one of whom he was a parent. In other words, stay put and shut up!

By special permission Roux was allowed to attend to the affairs of the Botany Department until the end of January.

This document of many pages came upon us one evening when Enid had come to dinner and as we sat relaxed with shaded lights. It was served by two detectives. Eddie switched on bright light to read the many restrictions. The terms of the ban were a great shock to us. We had known that it would be unpleasant but all these prohibitions were much worse than we had expected. We had thought that Roux would be required to resign his post and all teaching connections. The confinement to one small area, the prohibition on meeting people and on writing, these seemed in vicious spite to bear out suggestions of malice on the part of the Minister. We felt it was more than likely that Vorster had been much annoyed by Roux's seeming defiance in that he had never applied to have his name removed from the Red list.

An immediate problem was our usual annual visit to Cape Town. We had planned to leave soon after Christmas and to spend more than a month with the mountains and the sea in the part of the world that to us was paradise. Roux at once wrote to ask permission for this holiday to happen as planned. And presently, the day before we were due to leave, permission was granted.

But in the meantime the Special Branch had phoned to know where we would stay in Cape Town and how travel and so forth. I told them an address in Rondebosch. Now this was a folly on my part though I did not know it and had no thought of magisterial districts but only visions of tumbling seas and sun-warmed beaches. The permit when it came was for a visit confined to the magisterial districts of Cape Town and Wynberg and Roux was to report to the police before leaving and on arrival and similarly in reverse on the return journey.

This restriction on our movements in Cape Town was vexatious and again we were astonished. It meant that we could visit only the cold ocean beaches of Sea Point and Clifton and Hout Bay. The warm waters of the Indian Ocean at Muizemberg, Fishoek and Kalk Bay were forbidden. Roux at once sent a telegram applying for permission to visit these places. And presently, to the flat where we were staying in Rondebosch, came two plain clothes men to enquire in all dead seriousness why we wanted to go to Muizemberg. I showed them our unused surfboard. We said for the surfing and swimming and to lie in the sun on the rocks at Fishoek, also to continue study of the invasion by exotic acacias in the nature reserve. They noted our replies and went away. Much later, in fact on our last day, Roux received a telegram: Regret Simonstown district not included—Magistrate. But by then we were all set for home. This holiday, our last ever, was cut short by the need for Eddie's return to try to set the affairs of the Botany Department in order before the end of January.

While in Cape Town, at Constantia Nek and at Sea Point we had glimpses of many old friends. Some came to Eddie with lively sympathy, spoke a few hasty words and passed on in order not to make a gathering; others, averting careful eyes, did not seem to see us. It was a foretaste of what was to be the isolation of Roux's last year of life. Once, reporting to the Rondebosch police, he met a stranger who shook his hand and wished him well. 'I've read about you,' said this man, 'and now I've met you. I wish you good luck.'

Back in Johannesburg Roux plunged into the difficulties of organizing the Botany Department for the coming year. All staff were on vacation and all timetable plans had already been made. He now had to eliminate himself and load his work on to others without consulting them. The final clearing of desk and office fell on a Sunday. We went early and toiled there all day. There were loads of papers, diagrams and books to transport home, books to arrange on the professorial shelves, and in the end a terrible mound of papers left on the floor. When we drove out by the familiar gates it was nearly dark and we were almost too exhausted to note that this was for the last time. Roux's life as an unperson was about to begin.

During this last week in the Botany Department Eddie had known the lively sympathy of his friends the Africans who worked there as lab assistants. He was much moved when they presented him with a clock. Lazarus Ntshingila made a sad little speech of farewell and inside the case of the clock he wrote on a paper a message 'in affection and sorrow' which they all signed. This clock has a sad gentle chime and Eddie valued it greatly.

It seemed that our absence in the Cape and the fact of the holiday season had spared Roux so far but now came a flood of telephone calls. Some were friendly, even from people we did not know, others vindictive and triumphant. One caller said: 'Is this the house of Professor Roux who said that Jews are his most intelligent students?' I agreed that Roux had once said not that exactly but something rather like that. 'Is he a Jew?' I said, 'Of course not. Hy's 'n ware Afrikaner! One does not need to be Jewish to notice that many Jews are intelligent.' 'Yah! So I tell you that he is about as intelligent as an ape.' And the caller hung up feeling he had scored. Other calls were worse, some unprintable.

Letters of sympathy came from all over the world. Also offers of posts came from England, the U.S.A., Australia. Eddie wrote thanking well-wishers and refusing these offers. He explained that he considered himself a South African and did not plan to be driven from the land of his birth. For Jack Simons in Cape Town, a younger man who had still children in school, the ban was more grievous. Eddie could retire but Simons must find another job. We were not surprised to learn presently that he had left the country to go at first to Manchester and later to Zambia.

Financially we were in fact better off than we had ever been, for the University proved generous in payment of salary in lieu of notice and of accumulated leave, also the Council paid benefit due from the Provident Fund. However, the Secretary for Social Welfare and Pensions informed the University that the customary Government contribution had not been approved.

But it is odd how hard it is in old age to change established habit. We found it difficult to grasp the idea that we need no longer practise economies. I found myself still shopping at the bazaars to get envelopes and typing paper a few pence cheaper than at the C.N.A. And it was ironical that now we had money we could not use it, as we had planned, on travel about the world.

A *Sunday Times* reporter came to interview me, since Eddie was forbidden to make any statement to the press. This was before we knew of our position as to money. Asked what we were living on I replied incautiously, 'On our savings I suppose; but we are not hard up.' Drawing on her imagination the reporter described me as Roux's frail grey-haired wife and repeated my answer without the qualification. This had an embarrassing result in the arrival of a Christmas parcel of good things sent by an anonymous donor. We never knew who had been thus generous. I hope the sender may read these words and know that though not in need we greatly valued this kindness.

It was in this report that Roux was referred to as one of South Africa's most brilliant scientists. Later press items spoke of a most distinguished botanist, an eminent botanist engaged on important work on invasion by exotic acacias, an ecologist of world repute. Eddie commented dryly, 'Since I was banned I grow ever more distinguished.'

In South Africa serious protests were made by the University principals of Cape Town and Wits. In an interview with Vorster they stated their conviction that neither Simons nor Roux had ever made use of their position as lecturers to promote ideas of communism. In Roux's case he had left the C.P. nearly thirty years ago. Other local protests were made, some in the form of signed petitions, some by mass meetings of students, others by the Lecturers' Association, the Academic Staff Association, Convocation and by individual colleagues of the two banned professors.

At Wits, *Convocation Commentary* wrote in March 1965:

> Professor E.R. Roux, distinguished graduate of the University and a leading South African scientist, can no longer enter the gates of Wits. An unprecedented series of banning orders by the Minister of Justice has stripped him of his position as head of the Department of Botany at the University.
>
> He is prohibited from entering any educational institution, from teaching anyone and from publishing any writing. The banning orders have deprived Professor Roux of his livelihood and will make it virtually impossible for him to carry out further scientific research in this country. He has in effect been cut off from the main interest of his life. To an intellectual this is as vicious a ban as has ever been imposed in any civilized country.

Among protests notable was that made by the South African Association for the Advancement of Science. They wrote to the Minister of Justice requesting permission for Roux to retain his membership and to continue to play a role in the activities of the Association. Permission was refused.

In spite of this storm of protest Vorster found himself able to state in the House of Assembly in March of 1965 that with the exception of protest from leftist students' organizations he had not received representations on Roux's behalf from any organization. This may have been true at that time if the S2A3 and the S.R.C. of Wits and other universities could be described as leftist, but protest continued and from overseas came resolutions and petitions. A petition signed by 243 members of the Senior Common Room of Birmingham University was addressed to the South African Ambassador in London. Later when Helen Suzman, Progressive, asked a question in the House of Assembly and made mention of the fact that Roux had left the C.P. in 1936, Vorster commented, 'Do you believe that?' The implication of dishonesty was ludicrous to all who knew Roux.

Among the letters came one from Hector Hawton of the Rationalist Press Association, who also published an article in *The Humanist*. He expressed the hope that Roux would be able to keep *The Rationalist* going. However, within the Rationalist Association of S.A. there was alarm and dismay at this banning of their chairman. Something of this has been recorded in a previous chapter. It is not easy to convey to those who live in lands where freedom of thought is taken for granted the terrible fear of being suspected of independent thought that is now common in South Africa where Liberalism is a swear word and free thought is anathema. Being banned carries a smear and the victim cannot defend himself. People shook their heads wisely and said, 'There's no smoke without fire. Roux is banned and there must be some good reason for this. Naturally it is not politic for the authorities to reveal all the facts.' Doubt and suspicion, fear and care to avoid involvement, these made Roux's days lonelier than they need have been. Few visitors came to the house in Melville.

The essential is that man is a social animal. The specifically human attribute is communication. In this regard the ban was only a degree less of deprivation than a sentence of solitary confinement. Roux could not speak to former colleagues, unless one at a time they sought him out; he could not discuss his work with anyone; he could not go to the chess club; he could not visit friends. He lived in isolation.

Once we went to lunch at the Zoo Lake restaurant. At a nearby table sat a former comrade, Julius Myerson. Eddie scribbled on a twist of paper, 'Are you named? E.R.' and the waiter took it to Julius who at once came to our table. We heard the tale of his release from the Red list. Eddie and Julius talked for a long time until Julius had to go. Such encounters came seldom.

Plot 27, Gremlins, lay outside the magisterial district of Johannesburg. Roux applied for leave to go out to work on the plot but the permission granted allowed him to go once a week only for a day or two, reporting to the police before and after each visit. Since we now had a tenant in the house the two-day visit was of no use. In effect Roux could go there on one day only in each week. Marumé had died and Moffat was now old and often sick. To take Moffat to a doctor or hospital in Krugersdorp or to the Bantu Affairs Department for renewal of his service contract required each time a special permit which had to be applied for in writing and granted by the magistrate. It was now as has been mentioned previously that our catawba vines bore their first abundant crop. We went there early each Thursday, worked all day harvesting, loaded the Anglia and returned to spend the evening trimming, weighing and packing the grapes in trays. Next morning we took these to various greengrocers and sold them. This was quite hard work and we had no need of money but Eddie wanted to prove to himself that these grapes could be sold. The inefficiency of this method of harvesting resulted in the loss of a good part of the crop which was stolen regularly. The conditions were vexatious as no doubt was the intention. Roux was refused permission to go out more often at harvest time.

As before when one occupation failed him Roux found other outlets for his energy. He spent his days chiefly on three things. Research was not easy for now he had no assistants, no access to a laboratory, very little ground, no opportunity to discuss problems with colleagues. One research, on colour inheritance in Cosmos, he had already begun at the University where, by accident, his experimental stand of Cosmos plants had been destroyed. I discovered this when I went on his behalf to see if the plants had begun to flower. *Cosmos bipinnatus* is the graceful wild flower that grows on recently disturbed earth by the sides of our roads. The flowers are mostly pink, less commonly white, rarely dark red. The pink are hybrid offspring of the red and white parents. We went out along permitted roads within the magisterial district of Johannesburg and made careful counts of the numbers of each colour in stands of Cosmos plants. Roux used frequency analyses to show that colour inheritance could not be explained by a simple Mendelian pattern on the basis of one factor pair of genes with the homozygous dominant red, the heterozygous pink, the homozygous recessive white. It could not be so simple for the red flowers occurred too rarely. So now Roux collected seed and sowed them in our garden. He secured cross-pollination and self-pollination by enclosing the flower heads in small polythene bags. The offspring proportions repeated the challenge of the wayside stands.

While Roux puzzled over these results a most welcome visitor came. This was Roux Wilsenach, a friend and colleague from the Botany Department. They discussed the figures. It seemed that two pairs of colour factors were involved, this being further complicated by the possibility that one pattern of crossing resulted in incompatibility and by the fact of a self-sterility condition. This discussion was the last for Wilsenach's visit was a few days before Roux's death. Later Wilsenach rescued the records of Roux's work and presented a paper to the South African Association for the Advancement of Science.* So this research was not wasted.

A second research Roux was able to pursue concerned secondary grassland succession with restoration of climax purple veld on land once denuded. Work at Frankenwald had shown stages in the succession on such lands: a ruderal stage with weeds and some annual grasses, a primary grass stage with kweek grass and certain of the lovegrasses, a secondary stage with thatch grass, the climax of purple veld. Experiment begun in 1950 had established the first three of these stages but it seemed that the final transition from Hyparrhenia to purple veld required many years. Even in experiments that had run for thirty years this change had not occurred. The difficulty was to find grassland known to have been once denuded and thereafter left undisturbed for long periods. On the Witwatersrand the archaeologist Dr Revel Mason has discovered many sites of Iron Age furnaces. These stone-walled enclosures must be of great age though there is no certain knowledge of when they were abandoned. Mason believed that it was Moselekatze's impis that in 1823 had destroyed the Iron Age culture in this

*Flower Colour inheritance in *Cosmos bipinnatus*, by R. Wilsenach, presented at the Stellenbosch Congress of the Association in July 1966. Published in the *South African Journal of Science* in August 1967.

area. In certain of these enclosures, which resemble ruins associated with the Zimbabwe culture, the stone walls are little damaged and the entrances have been blocked by stones, so that it seems that these areas may thus have been protected from grazing and from fire. On Melville koppie, right at our front door, are some of these enclosures and there Roux was able to make exhaustive study of the grasses. He prepared a paper and requested permission to present this at the Science Congress in July 1965. He submitted to the Minister an abstract of his paper.

Permission was refused.

Another gathering at which Roux ought to have been present came in February 1966 when the inaugural Congress of the Grassland Society of South Africa was held in Pietermaritzburg. As the author of popular books on grassland preservation and also by reason of his association with grassland research at Frankenwald, Roux had a strong claim to attend. But inevitably permission was refused.

As to these refusals we did not consider that they were inspired by any fear that Roux in associating with these scientists would be spreading liberal views but by the sole aim of rendering the ban vexatious to the limit, that is by vindictiveness. We still found such petty malice incredible in a Department of Justice and Roux continued to make his hopeless applications for permits.

However, in May of 1965 the University held a farewell gathering in honour of Roux and for this occasion permission to attend was granted. The Principal, Professor I.D. MacCrone, who had done all in his power to save Roux from the ban, now made a warmly generous speech which he ended by saying that he and all his colleagues would continue to regard Roux as a member of the University.

One more hurtful refusal came. We had hoped to go to Cape Town once more for our annual visit. I had suffered a coronary thrombosis and the specialist who was treating me wrote that a holiday at sea level would be beneficial. But Eddie was not to see Cape Town again.

The deprivation which Roux felt most keenly was his isolation from the students, from the world of the bright-eyed and curious. During his teaching years he had lectured to more than

4,000 students. Many of these who had gone on to make a name in the world now wrote letters of sympathy and paid tribute to the lucidity of his lectures and to the clear diagrams he had used. Present students did not at once forget Roux who had been well-known on the campus and by ones and twos they came to visit and tell him of student doings. Officially the president of the S.R.C. and the science faculty representative came to report the students' decision to found a Roux Memorial Scholarship and to discuss what form this should take. It was decided to begin at once to collect for the fund and presently to offer annually a bursary to help a graduate in biochemistry to further study in ecology.*

Roux felt there was some good fortune in the place to which he was restricted. The city of Johannesburg has excellent libraries and he was not forbidden to read, though when he needed reference books from the University library I had to go in search of them while he waited outside the gates.

The impossible prohibition was that on writing. One might as well have forbidden him to breathe. He could not cease from writing though it might be that no one would ever read what he wrote. Writing his long-planned book on grass was the comfort to which he turned each day when Cosmos and Iron Age sites had been dealt with. This book tells the story of the grassland Research Station at Frankenwald from its brave beginnings and through the research carried out on secondary succession on the veld. It reviews early theories and states the current view that this succession is not a progression of increasing fertility of the soil. In service of human needs it may become necessary to halt this development short of the purple veld climax so that we maintain earlier stages with their fodder grasses.

Everywhere man is destroying the variety of nature in order to feed growing millions of hungry mouths. This must go on if man does not succeed in limiting his numbers. If he does manage this—and the future of civilization if not of mankind depends upon it—the question will arise as to what is an optimum population. There are still untapped sources for

*The first award was made in 1968 to Roger Porter, a botany honours student majoring in ecology and physiology.

food production and these should be developed to produce adequate diets for the under-nourished two-thirds of mankind rather than to fill the earth with semi-starving people.

Attempts of ecologists to direct the course of exploitation into what they consider desirable channels may be doomed to failure. This plucking at the rein of modern man who is riding to the townland may be in vain. We may be riding to a world of sky-scrapers with hydroponic tanks on their roofs.

In this brave new world there will be no jungle, forests, savannas or veld where men may roam, and no wild life. It is a rather frightening picture of a future which we hope will not come about. Mankind may still devise ways of having the best of both worlds, the world of civilization and the world of nature.

Here Roux laid down his pen. Could this book ever be published? It happened that Mnr W. van Heerden, a member of the University Council, was also Chairman of the National Veld Trust. He undertook to obtain permission from the Minister of Justice for the book, a purely scientific essay, to be published. Roux hoped that the book would appear in 1966.*

It is on any view a most readable book and Roux planned many illustrations. The delicate drawings he made from live specimens of grasses were accurate and with his normal skill would have been beautiful. But now his hand trembled and the black lines lacked purity and firmness. I was anxious about this and suggested that we should find an artist to repeat the drawings, but Eddie said that when the sketches were reduced the lines would look well enough.

In this work he had continual help and advice from T.C. Robertson, Editor of *Veldtrust*, who also considered that the sketches would have to be redrawn.

It was Roux's fancy to place an appropriate quotation at the head of each chapter. This led to his writing to John Howland Beaumont for permission to use one of his poems as introduction to the book. Beaumont gave permission instantly and offered also to read the typescript. We discovered that he was

*Permission was given. *Grass—A Story of Frankenwald* appears this year, 1969, published by Oxford University Press.

totally deaf and the lovely poem he had written seemed a miracle.

An Obeisance to Grass

Of all that lives and grows
　Most humble is the grass.
High pride is in the rose
　And vanities that pass
　　Are clothed in arrogance.

But grass is meek. The strong
　Need pride nor arrogance.
As blood is in the heart,
As strength is in the sea,
　So grass is in the earth,
　And sings as bright a song—
　　As pure and humble mirth—
As sings in blood the heart,
　As sings in strength the sea.

For grass is sea and sun,
　Is dust of earth in song,
Is blood in vein and bone:
　Most humble and most strong.

　　　　John Howland Beaumont

Out of his experience as publisher's editor Beaumont gave much sound advice. His judgment on the book was wholly enthusiastic; as a layman he had enjoyed the reading. He came to visit Roux in Melville and though all our sayings had to be written for him, we felt the warmth and generosity of his nature and Roux felt that he was a new friend. He finally sent back the script and comments in February of 1966, a few days before Roux's death.

What other things did Roux do in these lonely days? We worked together in the garden. Often he would try to mow the grass and at short intervals have to pause to breathe while his heart laboured. I tried to stop him. He said, 'I can do it, a few feet at a time, then rest, then a few feet more.' He would not wait for Henry, our more than casual gardener, to turn up.

'The grass needs mowing now.' I was worried about him. He was so easily tired, his magnificent energy failing at last. His face looked grey and sick. I urged him to let me call a doctor but he would say that he had been recently too much indoors and this explained his pallor. I had no idea how grievously he was a sick man with little of life left to him.

What else did he do? Often in the evenings when we had written ourselves to a standstill we played chess. Everything that one does in life one does once for the last time. Our last chess contest was on a Sunday evening at the end of February. On this occasion, surprisingly, I won two games. Then Eddie, grey with fatigue, said, 'Let's stop, Win. I'm tired.' So we went to bed. On his working table lay the last drawing he ever made, a beautiful sketch of the awns of grasses. He asked what I thought of it. I thought it perfect in beauty and I said so. Here was one time his hand had been sure. It was my grief in the midst of greater, that this drawing was lost. I never saw it again.

It was the next night that Eddie suffered a feverish night and had little sleep. He was too hot, he was too cold. I got up and found a blanket but he refused it. Towards dawn he fell asleep. I called Dr Fine. The diagnosis was of extreme anaemia of unknown cause and pneumonia. Eddie was admitted to the General Hospital. That evening he seemed exhausted but cheerful. I came home and set about straightening the confusion on his work table. There I found the large envelope in which Beaumont had returned the typescript and within it a smaller envelope with a letter. Eddie had been disappointed that Beaumont had not written.

Next afternoon in visiting hours I told him of this letter and said I would bring it that evening. Eddie was sitting up, cheerfully, and said he had enjoyed fruit salad for lunch. He looked forward to reading the letter.

But that evening I found him exhausted, his breathing laboured. Suddenly he seemed to have turned away from life. He said, 'Oh Win, I'm so tired.' I could not even read Beaumont's wise comments to him for he was lost in the loneliness of death and no joy or sorrow could touch him any more. Presently I knew that he was dead.

Late that night Ruth Hayman phoned to tell me that the death would be in the morning papers. I could not credit this for I had spoken to no one. But in the morning the news was on the radio and was flashed about the world. In England my sister and brother heard it. Those who admired Roux heard and those who despised him and the indifferent.

And very early that morning came Willy Kalk, so long banned from visiting Eddie. Enid came. And our old friends Mary and Donald Livingstone came to bring comfort and help. I have never known such kindness as they showed me that day. Mary stayed by the phone and received callers while with Donald I went about sending cables to Italy and England, going again to the hospital,* to a funeral parlour. All this seemed intolerable but Donald helped me to do what had to be done.

And from Italy Alison cabled that she would be here in time for the funeral.

---

*A post mortem showed death due to aplastic anaemia. This had apparently been caused by the use of a certain insecticide spray to which Roux had developed a sensitivity. I remembered that he had sprayed our fruit trees in the previous October. Since then he had been dying slowly.

CHAPTER XX

Rationalist Tribute

A GREAT crowd attended the memorial service on the afternoon of Saturday, 5 March. Roux's academic colleagues were there, old comrades of the Left, members of the Liberal Party, many friends, and probably some members of the Special Branch noting who thus honoured the memory of Eddie Roux.

The service was organized by the Rationalist Association and conducted by Donald Livingstone, lecturer in political science at the University. The Principal of the University Professor I. D. MacCrone paid tribute to Roux's good life. He recalled that Eddie Roux was among early students of the newly-established University. He had a distinguished record as a science student and was the first student to be awarded an 1851 Exhibition Scholarship which took him to Cambridge.

> On his return to South Africa he became a member of the Communist Party of South Africa which at that time was a perfectly legal organization. I have no doubt that this political affiliation arose from his identification with the underprivileged and with all those who are economically exploited in any social system, but particularly by the social system as it exists in South Africa.
>
> The cause that Eddie espoused was not a popular cause, but his convictions left him without any other choice. For that cause he suffered but he was quite prepared to accept the consequences of his convictions.
>
> For Eddie Roux was, above all, a man of conviction and when he finally broke with the Communist Party he would have claimed that it was not he who had changed but it was the Party that had changed. And his convictions, I have no doubt were based on his deep sense of compassion for the underprivileged.
>
> When at some time in the future the history of the common

people of South Africa comes to be written, there is no doubt that Eddie Roux will figure largely in it. He has himself made a major contribution to that history by his own book *Time Longer than Rope*.

I can only vaguely recall Eddie as a student while I was still a young lecturer at the University. Our paths occasionally crossed but I really got to know him well only when he was appointed senior lecturer and later professor at the University. Although I did not share many of his convictions, that did not affect our personal relations which always remained cordial. And that was the case also with regard to his personal relations with other members of the University, however much argument and discussion there may have been in the Staff Common Room. For Eddie Roux was always tolerant of the views of others—the only thing he was intolerant of was injustice.

When his appointment at the University was terminated a year ago by ministerial decree, I know that he felt it deeply. We had long talks about it in my office. He fully realized that he might have avoided that dismissal had he been prepared to retract his convictions—but that was something that this man would never do whatever the cost to himself. He was not the kind of man who would bow his head under any yoke—whether of the Left or of the Right.

Julius Myerson, an old comrade from Y.C.L. days spoke next with simple sincerity. He said:

As an old friend I am proud to be asked to talk about Eddie. I notice everyone, at every time, uses the name Eddie, never Edward, never Professor Roux, just Eddie. I cannot clearly remember when I first met him but it must have been at Jeppe High School when we were sixteen.

He spoke of certain incidents of Y.C.L. days and continued:

I remember that for many years Eddie wore the same old sports jacket and flannels, but never looked unkempt except one day when I met him and he looked dishevelled and cold. He told me he had been sleeping out at night on the grass at the Wanderers and had not eaten for three days. I realized from certain things he said that he was suffering for his principles. He always lived what he believed and often by the sheer nobility of his behaviour made me ashamed of myself.

I have never known Eddie raise his voice in anger. He never called anyone an idiot or fool for his opinions but always used calm reasoning and discussion. I have been about the world and met many men but none were closer to being a saint than Eddie.

Jack Unterhalter of the Liberal Party spoke briefly and read out telegrams received.

The final tribute was paid by W. J. C. Gerke of the Rationalist Association.

> Rationality, as Bertrand Russell once observed, has two sides, theoretical and practical: rational opinion and rational conduct. The theoretical side to which Roux clearly and consistently subscribed is in essence the point of view which regards reason, logic and factual experience rather than metaphysical superstition, tradition and dogma, as ultimate criteria for our knowledge and beliefs. The practical and more difficult side is to base one's actions on rational principles rather than on personal desires, passions and prejudices. Philisophy is only too often associated with text book theories and esoteric arguments which look real only in the lecture room, to be immediately discarded in real life. Roux would have no part of this. It would have struck him as irrational and inconsistent to argue in one way and act in another. Rationalist, positivist principles were for him truly a way of life. He firmly believed with Russell 'that all solid progress in the world consists in an increase in rationality, both practical and theoretical.' And everything which Roux has ever said and done during all the time I knew him could be explained in terms of these few simple tenets, on which he was never prepared to compromise.
>
> He had the uncommon ability to view every facet and problem of life dispassionately, logically and objectively, and if I should have to single out one quality which made Roux conspicuous among his fellow men it would be his intellectual integrity.

This is not to say that Roux did not hold firm views about morals, religion, politics and all those other issues on which men are so strongly divided. But he had that high degree of understanding, so rare in human beings, which necessarily excludes prejudice and impatience with those who hold opposite views. He was ever ready to debate and defend his convictions on scientific and objective grounds and on a high intellectual level. His public debates with professional theologians were memorable, for he always displayed an insight into religious dogma and a knowledge of religious writings, including the Bible, which astounded his adversaries.

This background explains his interest and enthusiasm for the Rationalist Association, without which it could never have survived. His ideal was to provide a forum for free thought and rational discourse, in which a place could be found for people of all shades of political, moral and religious convictions, who were prepared to discuss and defend their views rationally and without prejudice. He was always scrupulously careful to avoid the intrusion of political issues into the affairs of the Association. There has often been the trend, particularly in this country, that free thought, agnosticism and atheism are equated with communism. Roux demonstrated convincingly that this thesis is absurd. In an early journal of the Association he wrote, 'we are a non-political association interested only in the spirit of critical thinking' and this principle was always meticulously observed. No politics have ever been discussed at functions of the Rationalist Association and members include people of all shades of political opinion.

The main activity of the Association has been in the form of public meetings, lectures and debates. Roux often gave lectures himself and he will be particularly remembered for his outstanding contribution to a number of debates which ranged from subjects such as evolution to the historicity of Jesus and the miracles at Lourdes. These lectures were an example of clear logical thinking and scientific approach and I cannot remember any occasion where an argument became angry or acrimonious.

We are all aware that Roux suffered many trials and disappointments in his life and that there were often times of great stress and sorrow. But we know that he often found happiness and satisfaction in his association with the Rationalists. One of the most important events in the life of the Association, and one that gave Roux great satisfaction, was when, after the banning in South Africa of Bertrand Russell's book *Why I am not a Christian*, Roux was instrumental in publishing the title essay in this country together with an Afrikaans translation.

Roux could have had an easier and more comfortable life, but he chose instead to be faithful to his convictions and principles as rationalist and scientist. Many thinking men will wish that they had the moral courage and intellectual power to make the same choice. Bertrand Russell's essay concludes with these words: 'A good world needs knowledge, kindliness and courage; it does not need a regretful hankering after the past, or a fettering of the free intelligence by the words uttered long ago by ignorant men. It needs a fearless outlook and a free intelligence.'

Roux contributed in no small measure to satisfy these needs. And this, in spite of his troubles, made him a happy man. In spite of a banning order and physical restraint, I think that Roux was one of the free-est men I have ever known. For his was essentially an intellectual freedom, which, as has been realized since the time of the Greeks, is perhaps the greatest gift a man can have.

The address of Livingstone had made mention of the wide range of Roux's interests and of his great compassion. He said:

> Perhaps it was difficult to see in this gentle and retiring man one who had been a leading spirit in the storm and stress of the twenties and early thirties. But however we may have met him we could not fail to come under the spell of this shy man's wholly unconscious charm and to realize that a deep human compassion was the mainspring of his being. It was a compassion indeed so deep that it gave him understanding of those whose convictions he most strongly opposed and enabled him to retain, even through the trials of the last year, his infectious faith in human nature. As the ties which bound him to the activities which had been his life were compulsorily

loosened, he showed no trace of bitterness or cynicism.

And before the committal this speaker read the words of George Eliot:

> O may I join the choir invisible
> Of those immortal dead who live again
> In minds made better by their presence; live
> In pulses stirred to generosity,
> In deeds of daring rectitude, in scorn
> For miserable aims that end with self;
> In thoughts sublime that pierce the night like stars,
> And with their mild persistence urge man's search
> To vaster issues. So to live is heaven,
> To make undying music in the world,
> Breathing as beauteous order, that controls
> With growing sway the growing life of man.
> . . . . . This is life to come,
> Which martyred men have made more glorious
> For us who strive to follow. May I reach
> That purest heaven; be to other souls
> The cup of strength in some great agony;
> Enkindle generous ardour, feed pure love;
> Beget the smiles that have no cruelty . . .
> So shall I join the choir invisible,
> Whose music is the gladness of the world.

And then we came away from that place and tried to take up the routine of ordinary life once more.

CHAPTER XXI

The Next Page

EDDIE and I had spoken of death, that last act of life which all must face. We agreed that it was not death itself we feared but the ignominy and pain and the trouble to others of biological failures before the end. Another thought we had was that when events cease for us, still, without us, events go on happening. It is like being interrupted in reading a book: one cannot turn the page to see what happens next.

Prophecy is precarious but Eddie had always a sensitive awareness of the political field and though he had not foreseen the results of the election in which the Nationalist Government came into power yet he had foretold that once in power they would use every device to ensure their continued dominance, in effect this country would have a totalitarian government. In the years since 1948 we have seen this happen and it now seems that by sundry manoeuvres and by a series of tyrannical laws suppressing opposition the Nationalist Government has ensured its rule for at least fifty years.

Roux believed also that the continual play upon the theme of Afrikaner nationalism would come in the end to be seen as a gesture of sterility and that within the ranks of the Nationalists themselves the influence of a less sectional, a more enlightened and more humanist thought would presently be felt. In this was hope for the future of the Non-European. Although I respected his judgment and in my heart agreed that this was how it would be, not soon but in the far future, I argued. We both enjoyed argument. I said, 'What of outside pressures? What of world opinion?' He replied that South Africa is rich enough to withstand such pressures. We have gold and uranium and coal, wool and citrus. What then of armed attack? Our coasts are inhospitable and for air attack on our cities the distances are great. It will not be by such means that extreme nationalism will be shaken but by reform from within. Also there will be the factor of the inevitable increasing role of the Non-European in our economy. As to this, Harry Oppenheimer, whether or not he lives to see it, will be proved right in the end. The bubble fantasy of apartheid is doomed by the plain facts of South Africa's population pattern and by the needs of industry and trade, and no fanatic avowals that it is better to have this country poor than to see the lessening of white baasskap can avert this doom. It simply is not possible for twenty per cent. of our people to supply all our needs at technical, administrative and academic level. But on Roux's view apartheid must first be seen to be unworkable: all things must get worse before they begin to get better. Clearly this is happening.

The Government, having liquidated the C.P., C.O.D., A.N.C. and other organizations of the Left, turned its guns on the Liberal Party. The Liberal slogan was: the future non-racial, the path non-violent. The concept of non-racialism is in Nationalist philosophy the ultimate horror. In the new edition of *Time Longer than Rope*, Roux wrote that freedom of speech is a luxury a government can afford so long as it does not threaten its existence. The Liberal Party was not strong but it was not silent and its non-racial aim and multi-racial membership were not to be tolerated. The Party must be destroyed.

This has been achieved, at first by persecution of leaders and finally by the Prohibition of Political Interference Act of 1968 which made all multi-racial parties illegal.

The open persecution began in 1965 with the banning of David Craighead, national vice-president of the Party and chairman of Defence and Aid, an organization which assisted in the legal defence of political accused and also gave help to dependants of prisoners. It happened that Craighead was a Catholic and so the Catholics who had not previously objected to any bannings now expressed shock and indignation. We knew David well. He was no extremist but the mildest of men and it was certain that no act or words of his could ever be inflammatory. No charge could conceivably have been brought against him, only that he was reasonable, compassionate and brave.

Then Peter Brown, national chairman, was banned, and Jordan Ngubane national vice-president, also Barney Zackon, Samuel Dick and Eric Harben in the Cape, John Aitchinson in

Natal, Adelaine and Walter Hain in Pretoria. The list of banned leaders goes on and on. Others came forward to fill their places.

In London earlier, South Africa's ambassador, Dr Carel de Wet, had stated that the Liberal Party had every opportunity as there was complete freedom for political parties in South Africa. Heavy and humourless, he is yet an impressive speaker and no doubt many believed him. But here the storm of persecution grew ever more violent. Raids, banishments, 90-day arrests, house arrests, 180-day arrests, passport seizures, became so frequent that they were hardly news. The victims were Liberals, Defence and Aid workers, lawyers, lecturers, church leaders, students, leaders of N.U.S.A.S. All were caught up into a Kafka nightmare of unreason where was no court, no accusation, no appeal, no defence. The only escape which opened for a few was into death. In 1965, before Roux's death, we read of the spectacular suicide of Saloojee. He was under 90-day arrest and while being interrogated hurled himself from a seventh floor window of the Grays, headquarters of the Special Branch. Official reaction was not an enquiry into methods of interrogation but the fixing of burglar-proof bars to the seventh floor windows. No second victim should find this way open.

During 1963-4 some 3,605 persons were held on 90-day arrest. They were kept in complete isolation without books, pencil or paper. The case of Ruth Slovo is well known and worthy of mention here, not because Ruth was our friend or that she was beautiful and proud but because her voice is clear. She has made an unemotional record.

> Daydreams replaced activity and purposeful thinking. It was partly a succumbing to the difficulty which I felt acutely of thinking systematically without the aid of pencil and paper. Ninety days. My calendar had been left at Marshall Square. Here in Pretoria my calendar was behind the lapel of my dressing gown. Here with needle and thread I stitched a stroke for each day passed. Now and then I would examine the stitching and decide that it was not neat enough and the strokes could be more deadly exact in size; I'd pull the thread out and remake the calendar from the beginning. This gave me the feeling that I was pushing time on, creating days.

While time was passing it crawled. Yet when it had passed it had flown out of remembrance. There was so little to distinguish one day from another. Feeling, experience, accumulated but without relation to days or nights or markings of time. It was not only the pain of existing in a vacuum. It was the indefiniteness of it all. As the S.B. detectives said at every possible opportunity: This is the first period of ninety days; there can be another after that and yet another.*

On the eighty-ninth day Ruth was informed that she would be released. When, leaving the prison, she hastened to a telephone to tell of her freedom she was re-arrested.

Since then she has been seen and heard on Britain's TV, clear and factual, telling of the anguish of denied communication. Let her voice speak for the sufferings of thousands. She and Joe Slovo and their children are now safe in England.

The 180-day arrest was officially supposed to protect state witnesses. In practice those arrested were isolated, interrogated, persuaded by all means to give evidence for the state. Some resisted and were penalized. Isaac Heymann was sentenced to a year's imprisonment for his refusal to testify.

Lawyers too are persecuted. Attorney Ruth Hayman, Liberal Party member, was house arrested and banned early in 1966. The conditions of ban and house arrest made it impossible for her to continue her work. Her offence was probably that she had acted on behalf of certain accused persons. She too is now in England.

The open universities are menaced. The Association for the Advancement of Science has been compelled to exclude all Non-European members. These can of course form their own scientific association. There are perhaps twenty of them.

The Press is not immune. L.O.V. Gandar, editor of the *Rand Daily Mail*, the most forthright opposition paper, has had his passport confiscated and, with reporter B. Pogrund, was charged with publishing false information concerning prison conditions. In this case which began in June 1967, the state seemed to find difficulty in framing the charges so that it was five times postponed. Judgment was finally given in July 1969, when both accused were found guilty of publishing reports

*From *117 Days* by Ruth First, Penguin Books.

about gaol conditions 'without taking reasonable steps to verify the information'. Evidence given as to the role of the press, by the editor of the London *Times* and by the writer Colonel Laurens van der Post, had not availed to save them. The sentence was a fine on the newspaper company, a fine on Gandar with the alternative of three months' gaol, and for Pogrund three months without alternative but suspended for three years. The case has not been taken to appeal. The implications of the judgment are clearly damaging to what remains of freedom of the press in this country. Overseas papers commented unfavourably.

Since the trial began a new and more restrictive measure has been enacted: the General Law Amendment Act, known as BOSS. This provides that any statement considered by the authorities to affect the Bureau of State Security may not be used in evidence in court. A storm of protest by the parliamentary opposition, by the press, by law societies and faculties, was ignored by the Nationalist Government which indeed did not care a jot what anybody thought.

It was in 1964 that Vorster, then Minister of Justice, said: 'As soon as the rule of law is undermined everything collapses.' But by making laws which themselves undermine the rule of law Vorster, now Prime Minister, is securing the suppression not of communism but of all liberal thought. As Roux foretold, all things grow worse before they can change for the better.

Sobukwe has at last been released from his living death on Robben Island where he had spent six years, serving nine years in all for his leadership of the P.A.C. in the Anti-Pass Campaign of 1960. His release is a strange one into a limited life. He is to live in a house in Kimberley, under twelve-hour house arrest, with daily report to the police and all the usual restrictions on banned persons. He is allowed to go to church. His family may live with him but, since he is forbidden to lecture, teach, talk or write, the things he does well, it is not clear just how he is supposed to make a living.

Helen Joseph is held under a second period of house arrest. Brian and Sonia Bunting have escaped to England where so many of our political exiles now live. Others who have not escaped live here in silence earning a livelihood with difficulty. It is a scene of devastation, of the destruction of human dignity and the collapse of independent thought which in broad outline Roux foresaw but which if he had seen it in detail would have greatly increased his pain.

In *Time Longer than Rope* he wrote:

Ideas are difficult to suppress. The Liberatory movement has been long at work: its message has penetrated deep into the minds of hundreds of thousands, perhaps millions, of people. While racial discrimination remains the movement cannot die. There can be no going back to the old system of slavery and rural serfdom.

In the words of William Morris, 'not one but thousands must they slay'. For the present there is suffering and fear: the rope scourges and binds fast but time is longer than rope.

APPENDIX I   Books by Edward Roux

1. General and Scientific
S. P. Bunting—A Political Biography, Roux, 1944. Reissued in Library of African Studies, Frank Cass & Co., London, 1970
Time Longer Than Rope—A History of the Black Man's Struggle for Freedom in South Africa, Gollancz, 1948. Second edition with added chapters, University of Wisconsin Press, 1964
Why Not Easy English? Unpublished, 1945
Botany for Medical Students, Juta & Co., 1951
A First-Year Plant Physiology—for medical, agricultural and science students, Juta & Co., 1961
Grass—A Story of Frankenwald, Oxford University Press, 1969

2. In Basic English
The Mayibuye Reader, The African Defender, 1938

3. In Easy English
Harvest and Health in Africa, Thos. Nelson & Sons, 1942
The Cattle of Kumalo, 1943
The Easy English Handbook, 1944
The A B Adult Readers, E. R. Roux and L. D. Lerner, 1945
The How and Why of Science, in the Sixpenny Library, 1945
The Veld and the Future, 1946
   The above published by The African Bookman, Cape Town
James Mabeta Goes to Sea, Sir Isaac Pitman & Sons, 1949

APPENDIX II   Scientific papers by E. R. Roux

Observations on *Marsilea macrocarpa* Presl. *South African Journal of Science*, Dec. 1929
A Combustible Soil from the Witwatersrand. *S.A.J.S.*, Mar 1937
A Form of Low-temperature Injury in Detached Leaves. *The New Phytologist*, vol. XXXIX no. 3, 1940
The Role of Sorbitol in the C-metabolism of the Kelsey Plum, Izak Donen and Edward R. Roux. *Biochemical Journal*, vol. XXXIII no. 12, 1939
Respiration and Maturity in Peaches and Plums. *Annals of Botany*, vol. IV no. 14, Apr. 1940
South African Fish Products: the Liver Oils of some Elasmo-branch Fishes of South African Waters. C. J. Molteno, W. S. Rapson,

E. R. Roux, (Miss) H. M. Schwartz and N. J. van Rensburg. *Journal of the Society of Chemical Industry*, June 1945

South African Fish Products: Variations in the Oil and Vitamin A Contents of Livers of the Cape Hake. E. R. Roux and C. J. Molteno. *Journal of the Society of Chemical Industry*, Oct. 1946

Growth Rate of the Cape Hake or Stockfish. *South African Science*, Sept. 1947

Hake Catch Data from the West Ground. *South African Science*, Feb. 1949

Migrations of the Cape Hake or Stockfish on the West Coast of South Africa. *Transactions of the Royal Society of South Africa*, vol. XXXII, part II, 1949

Effect of Benzene Hexachloride and Inositol on the Growth and Respiration of Baker's Yeast. J. Paterson and E. R. Roux. *South African Industrial Chemist*, Aug. 1949

Interspecific Plant Hybrids. *S.A.J.S.*, vol. 47 no. 3, Oct. 1950

Selective Herbicides. *The South African Industrial Chemist*, Aug. 1951

Effect of Antibiotics produced by *Trachypogon plumosus* on the Germination of Seeds of Kakiebos. *S.A.J.S.*, June 1953

Preliminary account of Glassy End in Potatoes. *Farming in South Africa*, Oct. 1953

Nitrogen Sensitivity in *Eragrostic curvula* and *Trachypogon plumosus* in Relation to Grassland Succession. *S.A.J.S.*, Feb. 1954

Further Investigation of the Nitrogen Sensitivity of Veld Grasses. K. Jong and E. R. Roux. *S.A.J.S.*, Aug. 1955

Photosynthesis. *S.A.J.S.*, May 1956

Plant Succession on Abandoned Fields in Central Oklahoma and in the Transvaal Highveld. E. R. Roux and Margaret Warren. *Ecology*, vol. 44, no. 3, 1963

History of the Introduction of Australian acacias in the Cape Flats. *S.A.J.S.*, Apr. 1961.

Studies in the Autecology of the Australian Acacias in South Africa:

1. Occurrence and Distribution of *Acacia cyanophylla* and *A. cyclops* in the Cape Province. E. R. Roux and E. Middlemiss

2. Symbiotic Nitrogen Fixation in *Acacia cyclops*, A. Cunn. E. R. Roux and Jennifer L. Warren

3. Production of Toxic Substances by *Acacia cyclops* and *A. cyanophylla* and their possible Ecological Significance. R. M. Jones, E. R. Roux and Jennifer L. Warren. *S.A.J.S.*, June 1963

The Australian Acacias in South Africa. *Ecological Studies in Southern Africa*, vol. XIV, 1963

The Veld and the Future, inaugural lecture by E. R. Roux, Professor of Botany in the University of the Witwatersrand. *Witwatersrand University Press*, 1963

Rhizobial Nitrogen Fixation in some South African acacias. E. R. Roux and C. C. G. Marais. *S.A.J.S.*, July 1964

Salt Tolerance in four Invasive Exotic acacias of the Cape Peninsula. *S.A.J.S.*, Dec. 1965

also, unpublished:—

Plant Succession on Iron Age I Sites in the Neighbourhood of Johannesburg. June, 1965

Index

AB Adult Readers 179
Abantu-Batho 35
ABC of Communism 67
Abdurahman, Dr A. 80
Abdurahman, Waradea 80
Academic Staff Association (Wits) 258
Act of Union (1910) 170
Adler, A. 50
Adler-Fielding Gallery 243
Adler, Lawrence 243, 244
Advance 200
Africana 85n., 167, 220
African Bakers Union 59
African Bookman 178
African Clothing workers Union 59, 105
African Defender 174
African Explosives and Chemical Industries, A.E.C.I. 181, 182
African Laundry Workers Union 59
African National Congress, A.N.C. 35, 69, 71, 73, 83–6, 90, 102, 197, 207, 215, 275
African People's Organisation 80
Afrikaans, the Taal 10
Aitchinson, John 275
alarm clock experiment 228–31
Alexander, Ray 200
Allen, Alice 165
Altona, R.E. 182
Amalgamated Engineering Union 46
Anatomy of African Misery, The 52, 172
Ancient Society 18
Andrews, W.H. (Bill) 26, 28, 38, 52, 66, 102, 145, 206
Anglo-American Secretariat (of Comintern) 60
Anglo-Boer War 2, 9
Annals of Botany 152
Anna, S. 109, 145
Anti-Fascist League 144
anti-pass campaigns 15, 90, 91, 215, 216, 278
apartheid 190, 191, 209, 249, 275

Bach, Lazar 96–8, 101, 103, 105, 109, 112, 129, 130, 131, 135, 136, 142–6, 167
Badenhuizen, Professor N.P. 184, 185, 251
Baia dos Tigres 158, 159
Baker, Charles 67
Ballinger, Margaret 148, 198, 201, 208, 212
Ballinger, William 208
bannings 214, 241, 254–66, 272, 275–8
Bantu Affairs Department 260
Bantu education 190, 248, 249
Bantu languages 20, 36, 66, 81, 84, 85, 172, 176, 215
Bantustans 190
Bantu tribal colleges 248, 249
Bantu World, The 130
Barber, Donald 50
Barnard, Professor Christopher 191n.
Basic English 173–9
Basner, H.M. 148, 149
Beattie, Sir James Carruthers 152
Beaumont, J. Howland 264, 265, 266
Bechuanaland campaign 2
beer raids 87, 215
Beit, Alfred 181
Bennet, alias Petrovsky 60, 62, 64
Benson, A.S., 45
Bernard Price Institute 195
Bero river 158
Berrangé, V.C. 252, 254
Bezuidenhout Valley 3, 8, 14, 16, 18, 40, 41, 95, 106, 114, 123, 138, 183, 192, 195, 245
Bio-chemical Journal 152
Birmingham University 259
Blackman, Dr F.F. 48, 49, 65, 152
Blackwell, Hon. Leslie, Q.C. 248n.
Bleksley, Professor A.E.H. 226, 228, 229, 230
Bloom, H.S. 252
Blumberg, Willy 28, 29, 30, 31, 40, 45, 140

INDEX

Bodmer, Frederick 77, 78, 94, 99, 113, 165, 172
Boers 1, 2, 9, 41
Böeseken, Dr Anna 172
bolshevik 14, 16, 17, 25, 54, 93, 98, 129, 144, 146, 168, 169
Bosazza 31
Bosman, Herman Charles 12, 13, 24, 25
Boswell, J. G. 182
Botany Department 182, 183, 184, 194, 251, 254, 256, 258, 261
Botha, Gideon 106, 112, 115, 124, 130
Botha, J. M. 8, 17, 53
Botha, M.C. 248
Bradlaugh, Charles 2
Branson 15
Bresler, Frank Ross 16, 28
Brookes, Dr Edgar 208
Brown, Captain (of police) 118
Brown, Peter 216, 275
Brownlee, Arthur 196
Building Workers Union 14, 102
Bukharin 63, 67
Bunting, Brian 200, 278
Bunting Memorial Scholarship 106n., 108, 169
Bunting, Rebecca 59, 62, 64, 67, 85, 92, 106, 108, 166, 167, 169
Bunting, Sidney Percival 11, 15, 18, 22, 26, 27, 34, 38, 45, 46, 48, 57, 59–65, 66, 67, 68, 72, 74, 82, 84, 91, 92, 93, 98, 100–108, 129, 130, 131, 135, 142, 143, 145, 146, 147, 148, 150, 155, 166–9, 194, 200, 208, 209, 210, 217
Bureau of State Security, BOSS 278
Burns Elinor 52
Burns Emile 52

cadet corps 10–13, 24, 107
Cambridge 48, 49–54, 57, 64, 65, 70, 71, 78, 100, 114, 151, 152, 165, 166, 268
Cambridge Labour Club 49–54
Campbell, Jock 7, 18, 32
Campbell, Professor 114
Cape Native franchise 148
Cape Town City Council 80, 200
Carnarvon Football Club 14, 21
Cartwrights Flats 91, 92, 99, 103
Cato Manor 215

cats, 155, 160, 161, 162, 183, 192, 194, 214, 243
Cattle of Kumalo, The 179
Chain Gang 33
Chamber of Mines 21, 22, 34, 116
Champion, W.G. 58, 91, 92
chauvinism 62, 101, 105, 107
Chiang Kai Shek 56
Childe, A. H. 16, 17
Christian National Education 221
Chudleigh, J., mayor of Johannesburg 7
Churchill, Winston 178, 179
City Hall steps 28, 47, 68, 112, 121, 137, 199, 203
Clare College 49
Clarion, The 200
Clothing Workers Union (African) 59
Cochran-Murray, Vera 196
Coke, Rachel 163
colour bar, 128, 131, 171
colour prejudice 209
Coloured 74, 75, 80, 86, 87, 88, 89, 104, 153, 154, 155, 165
Comintern 19, 51, 59–66, 90, 92, 93, 96, 98, 103, 111, 130, 143, 146, 147, 167, 169
commandos 22, 26
Communist Manifesto 33
Communist Party (Germany) 59
Communist Party of Great Britain 51, 52
Communist Party of South Africa, C.P.S.A. 19, 22, 26, 28, 35, 36, 38, 41, 57, 59, 60, 64, 65, 66–70, 74, 75, 90–94, 97, 100–108, 109–112, 115–120, 121, 124–6, 127–131, 135–7, 139, 142–8, 153, 166–8, 197–9, 200–205, 207, 208, 253, 254, 258, 268, 275
Congress Alliance 207
Congress of Democrats, C.O.D. 207, 214, 216
conscience clause 9, 11
Convocation Commentary (Wits) 258
Cope, John 206, 212
cosmos 260, 261n.
Council of Action 26
Craighead, David 275
Cresswell, Colonel F.H.P. 166
Criminal Investigation Department, C.I.D., see Special Branch 47

INDEX

Dadoo, Dr Yusef 198
Dagbreek 253
Darwin, Charles 2, 10, 18
Davidson, R.L. 184
Debating Society, Cambridge 49
  Jeppe High School 17, 18, 21
  Liverpool University 127
  Wits 40
Defence Act 11
Defence and Aid 275, 276
Defence Force 22, 24
deLeon, Daniel 7, 10, 26
deMoor, Dr S. 244
Department of Justice 201, 262
Departure from the Union Regulation Act (1955) 198
Descent of Man 18
deWet, Carel 276
Diamond, Issy 43, 85, 101, 102, 112, 115, 121, 124, 135, 145, 167
Dick, Samuel 275
Dimitrov 146
Dingaan's Day 71–3, 90–92, 99, 116, 137
District Six 80, 153
Dobb, Maurice 49
Donen, Izak 151, 152
Douglas, Sholto 152
Douglas Smit hostel 195
Downing College 48, 49, 151
Dream We Lost, The 53
Driberg, Tom 50
Drill Hall 212, 213
Dunjwa 35
Durban 82, 91, 92, 99, 100, 128, 129
Dutt, Clements 52, 63, 76
Dutt, Palme 52

Easy English 176–9
Economic and Wage Commission 52
Education through Reading 179
Eisenstein 64
Eliot, George 273
Eliot, T.S. 50, 161
Emergency, State of 205, 214, 215, 216
Engels 10, 33, 76, 97
Ennismore, Viscount, Mr Hare 53, 54
Ethiopia 141, 146, 171
Euglena 160, 183, 192
euthanasia 244
Extra Sensory Perception, E.S.P. 223, 224, 228n., 229, 230, 231

Fabian Society 127

Fairbairn, John 170
Farmer's Weekly 235
Fassler, Professor John 243
Federation of South African Women 214
Ferreirastown 66, 128, 130
Fielding, Major 243
Field Research Station 180, 181, 183, 251, 263
Findlay, George 252, 253
Fine, Dr Maurice 266
First, Ruth, see Slovo 277
Fischer, A. (Bram) 252
Fisher, P. 23, 26
fish liver oils 153, 155–9
Five Year Plan 63
Ford (American Negro) 62
Fordsburg Commando 22
Forman, Lionel 213n.
Fort Hare Native College 108, 131, 132, 134, 169, 248
Forward 34
Fourie, Lieut. (of police) 118
Fourth Congress of Comintern 62
Fox, Ralph 52
Fox Street, 41, 66
Frankenwald 180–84, 233, 251, 252, 261, 263
Freedom Charter 207, 208
Freedom Day 198
Friends of the Soviet Union, F.S.U. 100, 104, 105, 106, 129, 130, 139, 142, 144, 145, 147
Frota, Mario 157, 158, 159
fruit storage 151, 152, 155
Fursey brothers 6

Gandar, L.O.V. 277, 278
Gandhi 171
gaol 99, 100, 106, 115, 116, 121, 124, 135, 136, 137, 138, 277
Garment Workers Union 102, 105, 121, 198, 199, 200
General Law Amendment Act (1969), BOSS 278
General Law Amendment (Sabotage) Act (1962) 214
Gerke, W.J.C. 229, 230, 270
Germiston 116–21, 125, 126
Gilliland, H. B. 184
Ginsberg, Mrs 31
Glass, C.P. 60
God's Stepchildren 211

God that Failed, The 51
Gollancz, Victor 172
Gomas, John 75, 88, 89, 90, 99, 136, 146, 153
Gool, Cissie 60, 82, 83, 94, 99, 165
Gool, Dr A. H. 80, 82, 83, 94, 99, 165
Gorki 64
Grant, Professor W.F. 160
Grass—A Survey of Frankenwald 184n., 264n.
Grassland Research Station, see Field Research Station
Grassland Society of South Africa 262
grassland succession 251, 261, 263
Grays, The (Specialist Branch headquarters) 276
Gremlins 238–42, 260
Griffiths 71
groundnut scheme 184
Guardian, The 200

Haden-Guest, Angela 89
Haeckel, Ernest 2, 18
Haile Selassie 141
Hain, Adelaine 276
Hain, Walter 276
Haldane, J. B. S. 196
Hall, Elsie 165
Hall, Major 37
Hall, T. D. 182
Handbook of Easy English 178
Hansell, C.E.M. 225, 226, 227
Harben, Eric 275
Harvest and Health in Africa 179, 234
Hawton, Hector 259
Hayman, Ruth 266, 277
Haynes, Harry 32–4
Heffer, Barney 165
Hemming, G.K. 149
Heretics, the 49
Herschel School 163
Hertzog, J.B.M. 53, 71, 73, 104, 148
Heymann, Isaac 277
Hilda S. 109, 110, 118, 124, 144, 145
Hitler 60
Hofmeyr, J.H. 170
Hogarth Press 52, 58
Hogben, Enid (née Charles) 77, 78, 88, 89
Hogben, Lancelot 75–8, 80, 81, 83, 88, 94, 109, 113, 114, 160, 165, 177, 206
Hogwood 154
Holism 181

Hook, Sidney 206
hooligans 26, 42–8, 137
Hornby and Palmer's Thousand-word English 176
hostility clause 72
house arrest 214, 276, 277, 278
House of Assembly (Parliament) 34, 99, 198, 200, 201, 207, 258, 259
Huerta 8
Huguenot 1, 10, 158
Hull, H. 23
Humanist, The 259
Human Rights Association (at Wits) 216
Hutchinson 156
Huxley, T. H. 2, 10, 18

Ikaka labaSebenzi 103, 104, 141
Imprecor 96, 97, 98, 100, 110, 111, 112, 129, 130, 142, 143, 172
Imvo Zabantsundu 170
Inchcape Hall 35, 103
Independent Labour Party (British) I.L.P. 58
Indela Yenkululeko 131, 134, 139
Industrial and Commercial Workers Union, I.C.U. 35, 37, 39, 40, 57, 59, 65, 69, 75, 90, 91, 92, 99, 102, 171
Industrial Conciliation Act 135
Interglossa 177
Interim Report on Vocabulary Selection 176
International Federation of Trade Unions 57
International Socialist League 19, 25, 62, 66, 106, 107, 130
International, The 22, 26, 166
Iron Age sites 261, 263
Irvin and Johnson 155, 156
Isacowitz, Jock 216

Jabavu, John Tengo 170
James Mabeta Goes to Sea 179
Jeppe Commando 22
Jeppe High School 10, 12, 13, 16, 18, 24, 114, 269
Jeppe Preparatory School 10, 18
Jewish Workers Club 103, 109, 112, 115, 117, 139, 145, 166
Joffe, Louis 98, 111, 124, 128, 139, 142, 144, 145, 146, 204
Johannesburg Municipality 12, 14, 211
Johannesburg Municipal Library 196

INDEX

Johns, Muriel 79, 165
Joint Council of Europeans and Africans 175
Jones, David Ivon 84
Joseph, Comrade 74, 75
Joseph, Helen 213, 214, 215, 216, 278
Joubert, Miss A. 9, 10
Journal of Parapsychology 228
Jukskei river 180, 181

Kadalie, Clements 35, 39, 57, 58, 59, 90, 91, 171
Kaffrarian Rifles 2
kafir beer 87
Kahn, Sam 197, 198, 200
Kalk, Willy 31, 34, 35, 37, 38, 43, 76, 107, 114, 121, 205, 216, 267
Kalk, Margaret 205, 216
Kamenev 63
Kapital, Das 18, 34
Kate 139
Keyworth, Rodger 6
Kirstenbosch 79
Kitchener's Horse 3
Klein Krokodil river 233, 240, 241
Kotane, Moses 68, 128, 136, 142, 143, 144, 145, 146, 153, 174, 175
Krantzkop gaol 116
Krikst 92

Labour Club, Cambridge 49, 50, 52
Labour Defence, Ikaka labaSebenzi 103
Labour Monthly 76
Labour Party (British) 53
Labriola 33
Ladysmith 2, 3
Lamont, Henry P. 42
Last Chance in Kenya, A 58
Leather Workers Union 205
Lectures Association of Wits 258
leMaitre, Ella 187
Lena and Joseph 188-90
Lenin 10, 20, 25, 26, 63, 93, 97, 143, 206
Lenin School 92
Lerner, L. D. 179
Leslie, Johnny 17, 18
Letanka 35
Lewin, Julius 253
Lewis, D. 23
Lewson, Jack 211

Leys, Norman 58, 59
Liberal Party of South Africa 208, 210, 211, 212, 216, 221, 268, 270, 275, 276, 277
Lipman, Jack 174
Liquidator 198, 202, 203, 204
Liverpool University 127
Livingstone, Donald 267, 268, 272
Livingstone, Mary 267
lodgers tax 117, 118
London, Jack 10, 13, 130
Long, S. A. (Taffy) 23
Loom of Language, The 78
Lorenz, Konrad 219
Louw, J. de Villiers 198
Lovestone 62
Low Temperature Research Laboratory 70
Lucas, F.A.W. 166
Lucretius 245
Lunt, Winifred (Belinda), see Roux 75, 76, 79, 83, 89, 94, 104, 109, 110, 111, 112–115, 121, 122, 123, 124, 127-9, 131-5
Lurie, Betty 220

MacCrone, Professor I.D. 262, 268
Maduna 58
Mafeking Road 12
Makabeni, Gana 68, 99, 103, 104, 105, 107
Makana 170
Malan, D.F. 190
Malan, 'Sailor' 205
Malkinson 98, 100
Manduel, M.D. 11, 13, 17
Mann, Tom 8
Marais, Nettie 154, 162, 163
Marais, Peter 162, 163
Marks, John B. 69, 112, 116, 119, 125, 128
marriage 132
Marshall Square 47, 48, 276
Martineau, Harriet 188
Martyrdom of Man 18
Marumé 235, 236, 237, 238, 240, 260
Marxist, -m 7, 34, 61, 76, 85, 213, 253
Marx, Karl 10, 18, 20, 33, 34, 50, 85, 97, 206
Mason, Dr J. Revel 261
Matthews, Tom 46
Mau-Mau 59
Maurice, Mary 165

INDEX

Max, Comrade 81, 83
May Day 59, 101, 102, 115, 198
Mayibuye 69, 86, 90
Mayibuye Reader 174
Mbeki, Thomas 35, 39, 55
McCarthy 34
McGregor, Reith 24, 25
McKenzie 2
McKibbon, Ronald 16
Meidner, Hans 216
Melville 192, 195, 232, 234, 237, 240, 259, 262, 265
Meredith, Dudley 182
Merriman, J. X. 170
Meyer, A.M.T. 230n.
Millin, Sarah Gertrude 211
Mines and Works (Colour Bar) Act (1926) 37
Mine Workers Union 26
Modderfontein 182
Moffat 233, 234, 235, 239, 240, 260
Mofutsanyana, Edwin 68, 128, 129, 145, 148, 149
Mogg, A.O.D. 182
Molteno, Charles 234
Molteno, C. J. (Peter) 151, 152, 153, 155, 156, 234
Molteno, D. B. 149, 151, 197, 208, 212, 234
Molteno, Runica 234, 235
Morgan 18
Morning Post 56
Morris, William 279
Moscow 59–64, 89, 90, 92, 93, 95, 96, 97, 110, 142, 144, 146, 147
Moselekatze 261
Mossamedes 157–9
Moss Herbarium 251
Moss, Professor Charles E. 40, 48, 70, 73, 251
Movene, Jeffery 118, 119
Mpama, Josie 129
Murray, Professor Andrew 213
Mussared, Charles 166
Myerson, Julius 43, 45, 259, 269

'named' or listed 199, 200, 201, 204, 212, 220, 252, 253, 254, 259
Nationalist Congress 253
Nationalist Government 72, 116, 183, 190, 197, 200, 248, 249, 254, 257, 274, 275
Nationalist-Labour Pact 36, 37

Nationalist Party 46, 72, 116, 117, 120, 121, 190
Nationalists 26, 116, 117, 120, 121, 190, 201, 216
National Union of South African Students, N.U.S.A.S. 194, 276
National Veld Trust 264
Native Administration Act 72
Native Affairs Department of Johannesburg 188
Native Land Act (1913) 53
Native Representation Act (1936) 148
Native Representative Council 148, 149
Native Representatives 148 et seq., 197, 200, 201
Native Republic slogan 60, 61, 64, 90, 92, 143
Nayiya, Miss 40
Nazi Party 60, 168, 202
Ndabeni 75, 83
Ndobe, Bransby 71, 72, 73, 86, 87, 88
New Age 200
New Economic Policy (of Comintern) 63
New Economic Policy (H. Oppenheimer) 207
New Statesman and Nation 178, 206
Ngedlane, Josiah 75, 81, 85, 136, 145
Ngubane, Jordan 208, 275
Nicholls, Miss M.E. 8
night school 66, 67, 68, 70, 86, 92, 99, 129, 144, 173, 174, 176, 246, 247, 248, 249
90-day arrest 276, 277
Nkosi, Johannes 91, 92, 99, 144, 147, 199, 217
Nkosi Sikelele 194, 214
Noel, Conrad 54
Non-European Trade Union Federation 65, 66, 70, 102, 105
Nonqause 170
Normal College, College of Education 24, 25
Nourse, 37
Ntshingila, Lazarus 256
Nzula, Albert 68, 112, 113, 136

Oates, Comrade 28
Ocean Gold 156
Ogden, C.K. 173, 174, 178
Olivier, Lord 52, 53, 172
117 Days 277n.

INDEX

180-day arrest 276, 277
Oppenheimer, Harry 207, 212, 275
Order of Ethiopia 171
Origin of Species 18
Orthological Institute 174
Ossewa Brandwag 156
Ovenstone, Russell 156
Oxford English Course 176

Padmore, George 206
Pan-African Congress, P.A.C. 215, 216, 278
Pannigennis 47
Papst, Otto 152
parapsychology 223-31
Park of Culture and Rest 63
Pascal 218
passes 15, 16, 68, 90, 91, 92, 118, 215
pass laws 15, 90, 121
Pass Office 115
Paterson, Nellie 55
Paton, Alan 208
Payne, J.H.A. 11
People's World, The 200
Pepper 62
Philip, Dr John 170
Phillips, Jean 183, 184
Phillips, Professor J.F.V. 180, 181, 182, 183, 184, 251
Piatnisky 51
pick-up van 136, 137, 189, 190
Pineschi, Luigi 243, 244
Piper 53
Pirow, Oswald 71, 72, 73, 104, 121, 125
Pitman, Sir Isaac 179
Pogrund, B. 277, 278
Pole Evans, Dr 70
police 15, 16, 25, 44, 45, 46, 47, 68, 83, 87, 118, 119, 120, 122, 123, 125, 128, 136, 137, 155, 188, 189, 190, 199, 200, 208, 216, 255, 256, 276
police raids 87, 117, 125, 136, 188, 189, 190, 206, 212, 215, 276
political bureau of C.P.S.A. 94, 96, 98, 100, 102, 103, 104, 105, 106, 111, 131, 135, 136, 142, 143, 144, 145, 146, 203
poll tax 119, 171
Porter, Roger 263n.
Porto Alexandre 158
Potemkin 64
Prince of Wales 43, 46
Pringle, Thomas 170

Profintern 89
Progressive Party 80, 212, 221
Prohibition of Political Interference Act (1968) 275
Protter, J. 182
Pudovkin 64
Purple veld 261, 263

Quinan, K. B.

Rabb, Mrs 31
rabbits 232, 240
Raikes, Dr H.R. 201
Ramutla, Peter 129, 144, 146
Rand Club 7
Rand Daily Mail 123, 125, 244, 253, 277
Rand Revolt 20, 23
Rapson, Dr W. S. 151
rationalism 218 et seq., 270, 271
Rationalist Association of South Africa 220, 222, 223, 259, 268, 270, 271, 272
Rationalist, The 220, 223, 259
Reade, Winwood 18
Red Flag 23, 48, 50, 127
Resnik, J. 239
Rheinallt Jones 149
Rhine, J.B. 223-5
Rhodes, Cecil 71
Richter, P. 146, 147
Rider, Lady Frances 55
Ridout 75
riksha men 35
Riotous Assemblies Act 72, 135
Robben Island 170, 216, 278
Robertson, Fred 196
Robertson, Ian 196
Robertson, T.C. 264
Rochlin, S.A. 166
Roadean School 113, 123, 127, 139, 149, 153, 154, 163, 164, 183, 186, 187, 188, 193
Roman Catholic 9, 67, 275
Romm, Ittamar 220
Roos, Tielman 46
Rose-Innes, James 170
Round Table, The 57
Roux, Alison 139, 140, 149, 153, 155, 159, 160-64, 179, 183, 185, 187, 188, 192, 193, 194, 196, 206, 207, 208, 222, 233, 242-4, 267
Roux, Arthur 3, 41, 95, 123, 195, 245

INDEX

Roux, Claud 3, 4, 5, 8, 9, 11, 12, 13, 14, 18, 27, 41, 95, 196
Roux, Derek 196
Roux, Edith May (née Wilson) 4, 5, 8, 9, 10, 20, 27, 28, 29, 41, 96, 138, 163, 185, 195, 196, 244, 245
Roux, Edna 3, 9, 18, 27, 28, 29, 41, 95, 138, 139, 163
Roux, Eduard 6, 221
Roux, Enid 3, 18, 41, 95, 123, 138, 196, 244, 245, 254, 267
Roux, Gail 196
Roux Memorial Scholarship 263
Roux, Paul 1, 222
Roux, Petronella, Aunt Pietjie 28
Roux, Philip Rudolf 1-11, 13, 14, 15, 16, 19, 20, 25, 26, 27, 28, 29, 41, 95, 96, 123, 166, 195-6, 245
Roux, Philip Rudolf, junior 3, 41, 95, 139, 196
Roux, Winifred (née Lunt) 131-5, 137, 138, 141, 144, 145, 146, 147, 149, 164
Rowan, Athol 196
Rowan, Eric 196
Rowan, Phyllis 196
Rozina 233, 234
Russell 97, 110, 130
Russell, A.G. 206
Russell, Bertrand 220, 221, 270, 271
Rustenburg Junior School 155, 163

Sabel, Mrs 31
Sachs, Benny 12, 13, 31, 44, 47, 114, 169
Sachs, Emil S. (Solly) 37, 38, 85, 102, 105, 121, 125, 145, 198, 199, 205, 213
Saloojee 276
Sauer, J.W. 170
Schlosberg, Hertsel 17, 18
Scholarship, 1851 Exhibition 48, 64, 268
Schreiner, Olive 206
Schreiner, W.P. 171
Scott, Michael 206
Secretary for Justice 201, 202
Selemela, Winnie 201, 206
Sepeng 132
Settlers' Club, Cape Town 89
Seventh Congress of Comintern 146
Seward, Professor 49
Shackleton 224, 225, 227, 228
Sharpeville 215
Shaw, Harry 26

Shaw, G. Bernard 100
Shochat 109, 110, 145
Silone, Ignazio 51, 127
Silwana, Stanley 35
Simons, Professor H.J. 252, 253, 254, 257, 258
Sixpenny Library 179
Sixth Congress of Comintern 59-63, 92, 93
Slovo, Joe 252, 277
Slovo, Ruth (née First) 276, 277
Smartt Memorial Scholarship 155
Smeath Thomas, Professor 151, 152
Smuts, J.C. 8, 17, 36, 37, 116, 120, 125, 148, 181, 182, 183, 184, 190
Smuts, S.J. 182
Sneguireff, I.L. 85
Snell 1
Soal, S.G. 224, 225, 228
Sobukwe, Robert 215, 216, 217, 278
Socialist Labour Party 7
Social Welfare and Pensions 257
Society for Psychic Research 226
soil conservation 16, 180, 182, 183, 184
Soil Conservation Act 182
South African Association for the Advancement of Science, S2A3 180, 183, 258, 261, 262, 277
South African Coloured Peoples Organisation 207
South African Indian Congress 197, 207
South African Institute for Medical Research 13
South African Institute of Race Relations 149
South African Journal of Science 261n.
South African Trades and Labour Council 102
South African Labour Party 8, 19, 21, 36, 84, 103, 119, 198
South African Party 17, 37, 116, 119, 120, 125
South African Trades Union Congress, S.A.T.U.C. 38, 52
South African Voluntary Service 249
South African Worker, The 64, 66, 67, 69, 74
Spark, The 107, 200
S.P.Bunting – A Political Biography 84n., 106n., 166-9, 194
Special Branch 206, 212, 255, 268, 277
Spencer, Herbert 18

INDEX

Spendiff, H. 23, 26
Stalin, J. 63, 93, 97
Star, The 7, 203
Starke, Laetitia (Starkey) 79, 83, 94, 165
statistics 229, 230
Stephens, Edith 164
Stevenson, R.L. 242
Stewart, Gloria 224, 225, 228
Stockenstrom, Andries 170
Stohr, Dr F.O. (Fritz) 165
Strauss, J.N. 120
Strike Prisoners Release Committee 23
strikes 7, 14, 15, 16, 17, 20–26, 32, 36, 130, 135
Students Representative Council, S.R.C. (Wits) 194, 258, 263
Sunday Times 16, 257
Suppression of Communism Act 198, 252, 253
Suzman, Helen 212, 259
Swart, C.R. 198
Swart, Dr H. 251
Swartkop 139, 232
Swinburne, A.C. frontispoem, 39, 40, 67, 78, 114, 246

Taivka 109
Tantsi, J.N. 69
Teachers Training College 24, 25
Tefu, Stephen 129, 130
telepathy 223, 224, 225, 229, 230
Theron, Aunt Betty 3
Theron, Oom Hendrik 2, 3
Thibedi 66–8
Thomas, Margaret, see Kalk 205
Thorlund's Commercial College 123
Thorne, Ronnie 14
Thucydides 219
Time Longer Than Rope 53, 84n., 169–72, 191n., 269, 275, 279
Times, The (London) 57, 277
Toerien, Detective 123
Tomorrow's Sun 214n.
Tonjeni, Elliot 71, 72, 73, 86, 87, 88
Torch Commando 205, 206
tot system 87
Trades and Labour Council 102
Trades Hall 19, 28, 66, 147, 203
Trades Union Congress (British) 57
Transkei 54, 72
Treason Trial 212–14, 216
Trek 155, 169

Trigger, Major, J.P. 47, 48
Trotsky, -ist 25, 63, 107, 147
Turner, W. 50
Turton, location superintendent 126
Tyler, C.B. 102, 107, 145

Umsebenzi 81, 82, 85, 86, 90, 91, 92, 93, 94, 95, 97, 99, 101, 103, 104, 105, 106, 107, 110, 111, 112, 114, 115, 116, 121, 130, 131, 136, 137, 138, 141, 142, 145, 147, 162, 166, 172, 213
Umteteli wa Bantu 130
Umvikele Thebe—African Defender 141, 142
unemployed 32, 102, 115, 121, 129, 130
Unitarian 209
United Nations Declaration of Human Rights 191, 207, 215
United Party 190, 198, 209, 211, 212, 221
University of Cape Town 75, 77, 151, 155, 164, 252, 258
University of the Witwatersrand, Wits 18, 49, 71, 79, 114, 180–85, 192, 193, 205, 212, 215, 226, 246, 248, 249, 251, 252, 253, 257, 258, 260, 261, 263, 264, 268, 269
University Labour Federation, U.L.F. 52, 53
Unterhalter, Jack 270
Urban Areas Act 99, 117
U.S.S.R. 109, 110, 218
Utley, Freda 53

van der Kemp, Dr 170
van der Post, Laurens 278
van der Stoep, Floris 16, 22
van Heerden, W. 264
van Vuurde, W. 228
Veld and the Future, The 234, 251
Veldtrust 264
Vitamin Oils Ltd. 155, 156
Volunteer Medical Corps 5
Voortrekkers 73
Vorster, B.J. 252, 253, 255, 258, 259, 278

Wade, Colin 30, 32
Warden, Lee 200
War on War League 25
War, Wine and Women 42

Weinbren, Benny 65, 66, 70, 85, 102, 107, 145, 167
Weintroub, Dora 79, 94
Welwitchia mirabilis 158
Wentzel, Ernest 216
Wertheim, O. 210
West, Michael 172
West's Defining Vocabulary 172
Whitman, Walt 100
Why I am not a Christian 220, 221, 272
Why Not Easy English? 178, 179
Wilsenach, Roux 261
Wilson, Dr Malcolm 55
Wilson, Edith May see Roux 3, 9
Wilson family 28, 55
Winder, H.E. 244
Wits Students African Night School 246–9
Wolton, Douglas 61, 67, 68, 92–4, 95, 97, 101–7, 112, 115, 121, 128, 130, 135, 142, 167
Wolton, Molly 61, 67, 85, 92, 96–8, 101, 103, 106, 107, 112, 115, 121, 128, 130, 135, 142, 167

Woolf, Barney 53
Woolf, Leonard 50, 52, 58
Woolf, Virginia 52, 58
Wordingham, J. 26
World War I 10, 11, 27
World War II 152, 155, 182, 196
Woudberg 34

Young Communist International, Y.C.I. 24, 38
Young Communist League 19, 20, 23, 24, 27, 28, 29, 31, 33, 34, 35, 37, 38, 46, 76, 107, 147, 166, 205, 269
Young Communist, The 34

Zackon, Barney 275
Zelikowitz, Molly, see Wolton 67, 96
Zener cards 223, 227, 229
Zimbabwe 262
Zinoviev 63
Zonnebloem College 153–5
Zoond, Alec 78
Zwarenstein, H. 78,